★ Highlights ★ of this Study Guide

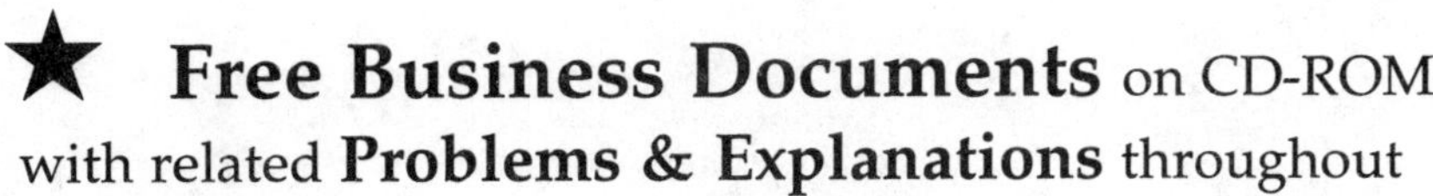

★ **Free Business Documents** on CD-ROM with related **Problems & Explanations** throughout

Each Chapter of this **Study Guide** includes—

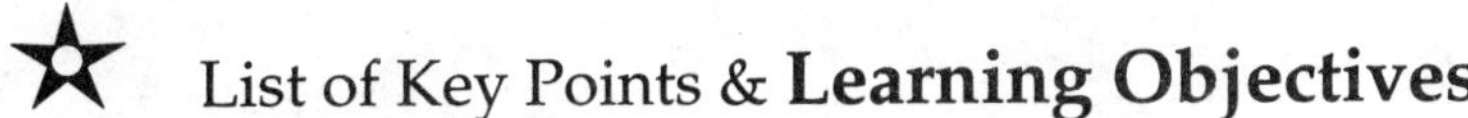

- ☆ List of Key Points & **Learning Objectives**
- ☆ Chapter **Introduction**
- ☆ Easy to Read & Understand, Comprehensive **Outline**
- ☆ **True-False** Questions
- ☆ **Fill-In** Questions
- ☆ **Multiple-Choice** Questions
- ☆ **Short Essay** Questions
- ☆ **Issue Spotters**—hypothetical fact problems & black letter law questions on key issues

Study Guide
and
Test Preparation
with
Quicken® *Business Law Partner* ® *3.0* CD–ROM
to Accompany
Fundamentals of Business Law
Fourth Edition

ROGER LeROY MILLER
Institute for University Studies
Arlington, Texas

GAYLORD A. JENTZ
Herbert D. Kelleher
Professor in Business Law
Department of MSIS
University of Texas at Austin

Prepared by

William Eric Hollowell
Member of
U.S. Supreme Court Bar
Minnesota State Bar
Florida State Bar

Roger LeRoy Miller
Institute for University Studies
Arlington, Texas

WEST
WEST EDUCATIONAL PUBLISHING COMPANY
An International Thomson Publishing Company

Publisher/Team Director: Jack Calhoun
Senior Acquisitions Editor: Rob Dewey
Acquisitions Editor: Scott Person
Developmental Editor: Jan Lamar
Production Editor: Bill Stryker
Marketing Manager: Michael Worls

ISBN: 0–324–00088–X

2 3 4 5 6 7 PH 3 2 1 0 9 8

Printed in the United States of America

I(T)P®

International Thomson Publishing
West Educational Publishing is an ITP Company.
The ITP trademark is used under license.

Table of Contents

Preface

To the Student

This **study guide** is designed to help you read and understand ***Fundamentals of Business Law,*** **Fourth Edition**.

How this Study Guide Can Help You

This study guide can help you maximize your learning, subject to the constraints and the amount of time you can allot to this course. There are at least six specific ways in which you can benefit from using this guide.

1. This study guide can help you concentrate on the *crucial topics* in each chapter.

2. If you are forced to miss a class, you can use this study guide to help you learn the material discussed in your absence.

3. There is a possibility that the questions that you are required to answer in this study guide are representative of the types of questions that you will be asked during examinations.

4. You can use this study guide to help you review for examinations.

5. This study guide can help you decide whether you really understand the material. Don't wait until examination time to find out!

6. Finally, the questions in this study guide will help you develop critical thinking skills that you can use in other classes and throughout your career.

The Contents of the Study Guide

Business law sometimes is considered a difficult subject because it uses a specialized vocabulary and also takes most people much time and effort to learn. Those who work with and teach business law believe that the subject matter is exciting and definitely worthy of your efforts. Your text, ***Fundamentals of Business Law,*** **Fourth Edition**, and this study guide have been written for the precise purpose of helping you learn the most important aspects of business law. We always try to keep you, the student, in mind.

Every chapter includes the following sections:

1. Learning Objectives: Five "learning objectives" are presented to you. By the time you finish studying each chapter you should be able to "pass" each checkpoint.

2. What this Chapter Is About: You are introduced to the main subject matter of each chapter in this section titled: What this Chapter Is About.

3. **Chapter Outline:** Using an outline and paragraph format, the salient points in each chapter are presented.

4. **True-False Questions:** True-false questions are included for each chapter. Generally, these questions test knowledge of terminology and principles.

5. **Fill-in Questions:** Here you are asked to choose between two alternatives for each space that needs to be filled in.

6. **Multiple-Choice Questions:** Multiple-choice questions are given for each chapter.

7. **Short Essay Questions:** Two essay questions are presented for each chapter.

8. **Issue Spotters:** These questions alert you to certain principles within the chapter.

9. **Quicken CD-ROM *Business Law Partner* Application:** These questions relate to certain documents on the Quicken CD-ROM Business Law Partner.

10. **Quicken *Business Law Partner* Enhancement—Exploring the Guide to Personal Law:** These are references to related topics in the *Personal Law Handbook*.

How to Use This Study Guide

What follows is a recommended strategy for improving your grade in your business law class. It may seem like a lot of work, but the payoffs will be high. Try the entire program for the first three or four chapters. If you then feel you can skip some steps safely, try doing so and see what happens.

For each chapter we recommend you follow the sequence of steps below:

1. Read the Learning Objectives, What This Chapter Is About, and Chapter Outline.

2. Read about half the textbook chapter (unless it is very long), being sure to underline only the most important topics (which you should be able to recognize after having read no more than two chapter outlines in this study guide). Put a check mark by the material that you do not understand.

3. If you find the textbook's chapter easy to understand, you might want to finish reading it. Otherwise, rest for a sufficient period before you read the second half of the chapter. Again, be sure to underline only the most important points and to put a check mark by the material you find difficult to understand.

4. After you have completed the entire textbook chapter, take a break. Then read only what you have underlined throughout the entire chapter.

5. Now concentrate on the difficult material, for which you have left check marks. Reread this material and *think about it*; you will find that it is very exciting to figure out difficult material on your own.

6. Now reread the Issue Spoters and answer them in the book. Next, do the True-False Questions, Fill-In Questions, and Multiple-Choice Questions. Now reread the Learning Objectives and see if you have mastered all of the points.

7. If you still have time, do one or both of the essay questions.

8. Before your examination, study your class notes. Then review the chapter outline in the text and write out your answers to the Issue Spotters in the study guide again. Reread the Learning Objectives and Chapter Outline in this study guide, then redo all of the questions within each chapter. Identify your problem areas and reread the relevant pages in ***Fundamentals of Business Law,* Fourth Edition**. Think through the answers on your own.

If you have followed the strategy outlined above, you should feel sufficiently confident and be relaxed enough to do well on your exam.

Study Skills for *Fundamentals of Business Law,* Fourth Edition

Every student has a different way to study. We give several study hints below that we think will help any student to better master the textbook ***Fundamentals of Business Law,* Fourth Edition**. These skills involve outlining, marking, taking notes, and summarizing. You may not need to use all these skills. Nonetheless, if you do improve your ability to use them, you will be able to understand more easily the information in ***Fundamentals of Business Law,* Fourth Edition**.

MAKING AN OUTLINE

An outline is simply a method for organizing information. The reason an outline can be helpful is that it shows how concepts relate to each other. Outlining can be done as part of your reading or at the end of your reading, or as a rereading of each section within a chapter before you go on to the next section. Even if you do not believe that you need to outline, our experience has been that the act of *physically* writing an outline for a chapter helps most students to improve greatly their ability to retain the material in ***Fundamentals of Business Law,* Fourth Edition** and master it, thereby obtaining a higher grade in the class, with less effort.

To make an effective outline you have to be selective. Outlines that contain all the information in the text are not very useful. Your objective in outlining is to identify main concepts and to subordinate details to those main concepts. Therefore, your first goal is to *identify the main concepts in each section*. Often the large first-level headings within your textbook are sufficient as identifiers of the major concepts within each section. You may decide, however, that you want to phrase an identifier in a way that is more meaningful to you. In any event, your outline should consist of several levels written in a standard outline format. The most important concepts are assigned a roman numeral; the second most important a capital letter; the third most important, numbers; and the fourth most important, lower-case letters. Even if you make an outline that is no more than the headings in the text, you will be studying more efficiently than you would be otherwise. As we stated above, the process of physically writing the words will help you master the material.

MARKING A TEXT

From kindergarten through high school you typically did not own your own textbooks. They were made available by the school system. You were told not to mark in them. Now that you own your own text for a course, your learning can be greatly improved by marking your text. There is a trade-off here. The more you mark up your textbook, the less you will receive from your bookstore when you sell it back at the end of the semester. The benefit is a better understanding of the subject matter, and the cost is the reduction in the price you receive for the resale of the text. Additionally, if you want a text that you can mark with your own notations, you necessarily have to buy a new one or a used one that has no markings. Both carry a higher price tag than a used textbook with markings. Again there is a trade-off.

Different Ways of Marking The most commonly used form of marking is to underline important points. The second most commonly used method is to use a felt-tipped highlighter, or marker, in yellow or some other transparent color. Marking also includes circling, numbering, using arrows, brief notes, or any other method that allows you to remember things when you go back to skim the pages in your textbook prior to an exam.

Why Marking is Important Marking is important for the same reason that outlining is—it helps you to organize better the information in the text. It allows you to become an *active* participant in the mastery of the material. Researchers have shown that the physical act of marking, just like the physical act of outlining, helps you better retain the material. The better the material is organized in your mind, the more you will remember. There are two types of readers—passive and active. The active reader outlines and/or marks. Active readers typically do better on exams. Perhaps one of the reasons that active readers retain more is because the physical act of outlining and/or marking requires greater concentration. It is through greater concentration that more is remembered.

Points to Remember When Marking

1. Read one section at a time before you do any extensive marking. You can't mark a section until you know what is important and you can't know what is important until you read the whole section.

2. Don't over mark. Just as an outline cannot contain everything that is in a text (or in a lecture), marking can't be of the whole book. Don't fool yourself into thinking you've done a good job just because each page is filled up with arrows, asterisks, circles, and underlines. When you go back to review the material you won't remember what was important. The key is *selective* activity. Mark each page in a way that allows you to see the most important points at a glance. You can follow up your marking by writing out more in your subject outline.

SUMMARIZING THE MATERIAL

Even if each chapter has a chapter summary, it is still worthwhile for you to make your own summary points. The reason is that the more active you are as a reader, the better you will understand the material.

Summarization helps you in your reading comprehension. It is the final step in reviewing the book. There is probably nothing else you can do that works as well to help you remember what your textbook has to say.

The importance of summarization is that the notes you make are in your own words, not in the words of the author. Writing down a summary in your own words is the most effective use of your time. This allows you to process the information into your own memory by being required to think about it. You also have to make it part of your vocabulary. Whenever you cannot state important legal concepts in your own words, you probably haven't understood the concepts necessary to master the material. Indeed, summary notes are a good way to determine whether you have actually understood something. Don't simply make a mechanical listing of quotes taken right out of the textbook. Rather, you should make summary notes using complete sentences with correct grammar. This forces you to develop your ideas logically and clearly. Also, summary notes written in this matter can be more easily remembered.

Be Brief. Your notes should condense the information in the text into statements that summarize the concepts. It is when you force yourself to make the statements brief that you best learn the material. By making only brief summary notes, you have to think about the essence of each concept and present it in a form that is compact enough to remember. You should typically have no more than a one-paragraph summary for each important topic in the chapter.

What Format to Use? The authors find that using 5" x 8" cards is the best way to take summary notes. Don't fill up each note card. You need to leave room to make additional notes later on when you are reviewing for the final exam. That is to say, leave margins for further notes and study markings. Additionally, if you leave enough room, you can integrate the notes that you take during lectures on to these summary note cards.

Another reason to place your summary notes on 5" x 8" cards is because in so doing you have a set of flash cards that you can use in studying for a final exam.

HOW TO STUDY AND TAKE EXAMS

There is basically one reason why you have purchased this study guide—to improve your exam grade. By using this study guide assiduously, you will have the confidence to take your mid-terms and final examinations and to do well. The study guide, however, should not just be used a day before each exam. Rather, the guide is most helpful if you use it at the time that you read the chapter. That is to say, after you read a chapter in ***Fundamentals of Business Law,*** **Fourth Edition,** you should directly go to the appropriate chapter in the study guide. This systematic review technique is the most effective study technique you can use.

Besides learning the concepts in each chapter as well as possible, there are additional strategies for taking exams. You need to know in advance what type of exam you are going to take—essay or objective or both. You need to know which reading materials and lectures will be covered. For both objective and essay exams (but more importantly for the former) you need to know if there is a penalty for guessing incorrectly. If there is, your strategy will be different: you will usually only mark what you are certain of. Finally, you need to know how much time will be allowed for the exam.

FOLLOWING DIRECTIONS

Students are often in a hurry to start an exam so they take little time to read the instructions. The instructions can be critical, however. In a multiple-choice exam, for example, if there is no indication that there is a penalty for guessing, then you should never leave a question unanswered. Even if there only remains a few minutes at the end of the exam, you should guess for those questions about which you are uncertain.

Additionally, you need to know the weight given to each section of an exam. In a typical multiple-choice exam, all questions have equal weight. In some exams, particularly those involving essay questions, different parts of the exam carry different weights. You should use these weights to apportion your time accordingly. If an essay part of an exam accounts for only 20 percent of the total points on the exam, you should not spend 60 percent of your time on the essay.

You need to make sure you are answering the question correctly. Some exams require a No. 2 lead pencil to fill in the dots on a machine-graded answer sheet. Other exams require underlining or circling. In short, you have to look at the instructions carefully.

Lastly, check to make sure that you have all the pages of the examination. If you are uncertain, ask the instructor or the exam proctor. It is hard to justify not having done your exam correctly because you failed to answer all the questions. Simply stating that you did not have them will pose a problem for both you and your instructor. Don't take a chance. Double check to make sure.

TAKING OBJECTIVE EXAMINATIONS

The most important point to discover initially with any objective test is if there is a penalty for guessing. If there is none, you have nothing to lose by guessing. In contrast, if a half-point is subtracted for each incorrect answer, then you probably should not answer any question for which you are purely guessing.

Students usually commit one of two errors when they read objective-exam questions: (1) they read into the questions things that don't exist, or (2) they skip over words or phrases.

Most test questions include key words such as:

- all
- always
- never
- only

If you miss these key words you will be missing the "trick" part of the question. Also, you must look for questions that are only *partly* correct, particularly if you are answering true/false questions.

Never answer a question without reading all of the alternatives. More than one of them may be correct. If more than one of them seems correct, make sure you select the answer that seems the most correct.

Whenever the answer to an objective question is not obvious, start with the process of elimination. Throw out the answers that are clearly incorrect. Even with objective exams in which there is a penalty for guessing, if you can throw out several obviously incorrect answers, then you may wish to guess among the remaining ones because your probability of choosing the correct answer is high.

Typically, the easiest way to eliminate incorrect answers is to look for those that are meaningless, illogical, or inconsistent. Often test authors put in choices that make perfect sense and are indeed true, but they are not the answer to the question under study.

WRITING ESSAY EXAMS

To write an essay exam, you should be prepared. One way of being prepared is to practice writing timed essays. In other words, find out in advance how much time you will have for each essay question, say 15 minutes, and then practice writing an answer to a sample essay question during a 15-minute time period. This is the only way you will develop the skills needed to pace yourself for an essay exam. Do your timed essay practice without using the book, since most essay exams are closed book.

Usually you can anticipate certain essay exam questions. You do this by going over the major concept headings, either in your lecture notes or in your text; search for the themes that tie the materials together and then think about questions that your instructor might ask you. You might even list possible essay questions as a review device; then write a short outline for each of those most likely questions.

As with objective exams, you need to read the directions to the essay questions carefully. It's best to write out a brief outline *before* you start writing. The outline should present your conclusion in one or two sentences, then your supporting argument. It is important to stay on the subject. We can tell you from first hand experience that no instructor likes to read answers to unasked questions.

Finally, make a strong attempt to write legibly. Again speaking from experience, we can tell you that it's easier to be favorably inclined to a student's essay if we don't have to reread it five times to decipher the handwriting.

Acknowledgments

We wish to thank Suzanne Jasin of K & M Consulting for her expert design and composition of this guide.

We welcome comments and criticisms to help us make this guide even more useful. All errors are our sole responsibility.

William Eric Hollowell
Roger LeRoy Miller

Learning Objectives

The learning objectives in this chapter include:

1. What is generally meant by the term *law*.
2. The origins and importance of the common law tradition.
3. The four major sources of American law.
4. The difference between national law and international law.
5. How the Constitution and the Bill of Rights affect business.

Chapter 1: Sources of Business Law and the Global Legal Environment

WHAT THIS CHAPTER IS ABOUT

The chapters in Unit 1 provide the background for the entire course. Chapter 1 sets the stage. From this chapter, you must understand that (1) the law is a set of general rules, (2) in applying these general rules, a judge cannot fit a case to suit a rule, but must fit (or find) a rule to suit the case, and (3) in fitting (or finding) a rule, a judge must also supply reasons for the decision. The chapter also covers constitutional law.

CHAPTER OUTLINE

I. THE NATURE OF LAW

Law is a body of rules of conduct with legal force and effect, prescribed by the controlling authority (the government) of a society.

II. THE COMMON LAW TRADITION

A. COMMON LAW

The American legal system, based on the decisions judges make in cases, is a **common law** system, which involves the application of principles applied in earlier cases with similar facts.

B. *STARE DECISIS*

The use of precedent in a common law system is known as the doctrine of ***stare decisis***. *Stare decisis* makes the legal system more efficient, just, uniform, stable, and predictable. When there is no precedent, a court may look at other legal principles and policies, social values, or scientific data.

C. EQUITABLE REMEDIES

Courts grant an equitable remedy only when a remedy at law is inadequate.

1. **Remedies at Law**
Remedies at law include awards of land, money, and items of value. A jury trial is available only in an action at law.

2. **Remedies in Equity**
Remedies in equity include decrees of specific performance, injunctions, and rescission. Awards of the remedies are guided by equitable maxims.

III. SOURCES OF AMERICAN LAW

A. CONSTITUTIONAL LAW
The U.S. Constitution distributes power among the branches of government. It is the supreme law of the land. Any law that conflicts with it is invalid. The states also have constitutions, but the federal constitution prevails.

B. STATUTORY LAW
Statutes and ordinances are enacted by Congress and by state and local legislative bodies. Uniform laws (such as the Uniform Commercial Code) are created by panels of experts and adopted at the option of each state.

C. ADMINISTRATIVE LAW
Administrative law consists of the rules, orders, and decisions of administrative agencies. Federal agencies are created by Congress through enabling legislation, which specifies the powers of an agency. The powers may include rulemaking, investigation and enforcement, and adjudication.

D. CASE LAW
Case law includes courts' interpretations of constitutional provisions, statutes, and administrative rules. Because statutes often codify common law rules, courts often rely on the common law as a guide to the intent and purpose of a statute. Case law governs all areas not covered by statutes.

IV. CLASSIFICATIONS OF LAW

A. SUBSTANTIVE AND PROCEDURAL LAW
Substantive law includes laws that define, describe, regulate, and create rights and duties. *Procedural law* includes rules for enforcing those rights.

B. CRIMINAL AND CIVIL LAW
Criminal law regulates relationships between individuals and society. *Civil law* regulates relationships between individuals.

V. NATIONAL AND INTERNATIONAL LAW

A. NATIONAL LAW
National law is the law of a particular nation. Generally each nation has either a common law or civil law system.

1. **Common Law Systems**
Based on case law, common law systems exist in countries that were part of the British Empire (Australia, India, United States, etc.).

2. **Civil Law Systems**
Based on codified law (statutes)—courts interpret the statutes and apply the rules without being bound by precedent. Civil law systems exist in most European nations; countries that were colonies of those nations; the state of Louisiana; Puerto Rico; Quebec; and Scotland.

B. INTERNATIONAL LAW

International law consists of written and unwritten laws observed by independent nations and governing the acts of individuals and governments.

1. Treaties

A treaty is an agreement or contract between two or more nations that must be authorized and ratified by the supreme power of each nation. A bilateral agreement occurs when only two nations form an agreement; multilateral agreements are those formed by several nations.

2. International Organizations

Composed mainly of nations; usually established by treaty; such entities adopt resolutions that require particular behavior of nations.

C. CONTRACTS IN AN INTERNATIONAL SETTING

Special provisions avoid problems in international contracts.

1. Choice of Language

A choice-of-language clause designates the official language by which a contract will be interpreted in the event of disagreement. Clauses may also provide for translations and arbitration in certain languages.

2. Choice of Forum

A forum-selection clause designates the jurisdiction, including the specific court, in which a dispute will be litigated (if one arises). The forum may be anywhere—it does not have to be in the nations of the parties to the contract.

3. Choice of Law

A choice-of-law clause designates what law to apply in a dispute. There is no limit on the parties' choice. If no law is specified, the governing law is that of the seller's place of business.

VI. FINDING AND ANALYZING THE LAW

A. FINDING STATUTORY AND ADMINISTRATIVE LAW

1. Publication of Statutes

Federal statutes are arranged by date of enactment in *United States Statutes at Large*. State statutes are collected in similar state publications. Statutes are also published in codified form (the form in which they appear in the federal and state codes) in other publications.

2. Finding a Statute in a Publication

Statutes are usually referred to in their codified form. In the codes, laws are compiled by subject. For example, the *United States Code* (U.S.C.) arranges by subject most federal laws. Each subject is assigned a title number and each statute a section number within a title.

3. Publication of Administrative Rules

Rules and regulations adopted by federal administrative agencies are published initially in the *Federal Register*. They are also compiled by subject in the *Code of Federal Regulations* (C.F.R.).

4. Finding an Administrative Rule in a Publication

In the C.F.R., administrative rules are arranged by subject. Each subject is assigned a title number and each rule a section number within a title.

B. FINDING CASE LAW

1. Publication of Court Opinions
State appellate court opinions are often published by the state in consecutively numbered volumes. They may also be published in units of the *National Reporter System*, by West Publishing Company. Federal court opinions appear in other West publications.

2. Finding a Court Opinion in a Publication
After a decision is published, it can be referred to by the name of the case and the volume, name, and page number of one or more reporters. This information is called the **citation**.

C. READING AND UNDERSTANDING CASE LAW

1. Plaintiffs and Defendants
In the title of a case (*Adams v. Jones*), the *v.* means **versus** (against). Adams is the **plaintiff** (the person who filed the suit) and Jones the **defendant** (the person against whom the suit was brought). An appellate court may place the name of the appellant first (*Jones v. Adams.*).

2. Appellants and Appellees
An **appellant** (or **petitioner**) is the party who appeals a case to another court or jurisdiction from the one in which the case was brought. An **appellee** (or **respondent**) is the party against whom an appeal is taken.

3. Judges and Justices
These terms are designations given to judges in different courts.

4. Decisions and Opinions
An opinion contains a court's reasons for its decision, the rules of law that apply, and the judgment.

VII. THE CONSTITUTION AS IT AFFECTS BUSINESS

A. THE COMMERCE CLAUSE

The Constitution (Article I, Section 8) gives Congress the power to regulate commerce among the states.

1. The Breadth of the Commerce Clause
The national government can regulate every commercial enterprise in the United States. This power means that Congress can legislate in areas in which it has no explicit grant of power.

2. The Regulatory Powers of the States
States possess police powers (the right to regulate private activities to protect the public order, health, safety, morals, and general welfare).

3. When State Laws Impinge on Interstate Commerce
Courts balance the state's interest in the merit and purpose of the law against the burden on interstate commerce. State laws that *substantially* interfere with interstate commerce violate the commerce clause.

VIII. BUSINESS AND THE BILL OF RIGHTS

The first ten amendments to the Constitution protect individuals and businesses against some interference by the government.

A. FREEDOM OF SPEECH

The First Amendment guaranty of freedom of speech applies to the federal and state governments.

1. Speech That the Constitution Does Not Protect

a. Defamatory Speech

Speech that harms the good reputation of another. Such speech can take the form of libel (if it is in writing) or slander (if it is oral).

b. Lewd and Obscene Speech

States can ban child pornography. One court has banned lewd speech and pornographic pinups in the workplace.

c. "Fighting Words"

Words that are likely to incite others to violence.

2. Speech with Limited Protection

a. Commercial Speech

A state restriction on commercial speech (advertising) is valid as long as it (1) seeks to implement a substantial government interest, (2) directly advances that interest, and (3) goes no further than necessary to accomplish its objective.

b. Political Speech

States can prohibit corporations from using corporate funds for independent expressions of opinion about political candidates.

B. FREEDOM OF RELIGION

Under the First Amendment, the government may not establish a religion (the establishment clause) nor prohibit the exercise of religion (the free exercise clause). Restrictions on commerce on Sunday have been upheld on the ground it is a legitimate government function to provide a day of rest.

C. DUE PROCESS

Both the Fifth and the Fourteenth Amendments provide that no person shall be deprived "of life, liberty, or property, without due process of law."

1. Procedural Due Process

Procedural due process requires that any government decision to take away the life, liberty, or property of an individual be accompanied by procedural safeguards to ensure fairness.

2. Substantive Due Process

Substantive due process focuses on the content (substance) of legislation.

a. Compelling Interest Test

A statute can restrict an individual's fundamental right (such as all First Amendment rights) only if the statute promotes a compelling or overriding governmental interest (speed limits, for example, protect public safety).

b. Rational Basis Test

Restrictions on business activities must relate rationally to a legitimate government purpose. Most business regulations qualify.

IX. CONSTITUTIONAL LAW IN CYBERSPACE

A. ONLINE OBSCENITY

The Communications Decency Act (CDA) (part of the Telecommunications Act of 1996) regulates "indecent" online speech (defined by "community standards"). Courts have ruled the CDA is too vague and too broad.

B. CRYPTOGRAPHY

1. **Criminal Investigations**
   Under the Fourth Amendment, police can access data encrypted on hard and floppy disks if it falls within the description in a search warrant. One issue is whether, under the Fifth Amendment, the police can compel the owner of the data to provide the cryptographic code.

2. **Free Speech**
   Cryptographic code is "speech" protected by the First Amendment. But First Amendment principles that apply to government (or shopping mall) regulation of free speech do not also apply online to, for example, America Online's access system.

TRUE-FALSE QUESTIONS

___ **1.** Law is a body of rules of conduct with legal force and effect, prescribed by the controlling authority (the government) of a society.

___ **2.** *Stare decisis* refers to the practice of deciding new cases with reference to previous decisions.

___ **3.** Common law is a term that normally refers to the body of law consisting of rules of law announced in court decisions.

___ **4.** In a civil law system, statutes are the primary source of law.

___ **5.** Each state's constitution is supreme within each state's borders even if it conflicts with the U.S. Constitution.

___ **6.** The Uniform Commercial Code was enacted by Congress for adoption by the states.

___ **7.** The civil law regulates relationships between individuals.

___ **8.** In most states, the same courts can grant both legal and equitable remedies.

___ **9.** Under the commerce clause, Congress can regulate every commercial enterprise in the United States.

___ **10.** Because of the First Amendment protections, a state cannot restrict advertising.

FILL-IN QUESTIONS

The common law system, on which the American legal system is based, involves the application of principles applied in earlier cases ____(with similar facts/whether or not the facts are similar). This use of previous case law, or ______________ (precedent/preeminent), is known as the doctrine of *stare decisis*, and ______________________ ______________ (emphasizes a flexible/permits a predictable) resolution of cases.

MULTIPLE-CHOICE QUESTIONS

___ **1.** The doctrine of *stare decisis* performs many useful functions, including

a. efficiency.
b. uniformity.
c. stability.
d. all of the above.

___ **2.** In addition to case law, when making decisions, courts sometimes consider other sources of law, including

a. the U.S. Constitution.
b. state constitutions.
c. administrative agency rules and regulations.
d. all of the above.

___ **3.** Laws can be classified in various ways, including civil and criminal. Civil law concerns

a. duties that exist between persons or between citizens and their governments.
b. wrongs committed against the public as a whole.
c. both a and b.
d. none of the above.

___ **4.** Which of the following is a CORRECT statement regarding the distinction between law and equity?

a. Equity involves different remedies from those available at law.
b. Most states maintain separate courts of law and equity.
c. Damages may be awarded only in actions in equity.
d. None of the above

___ **5.** State appellate court opinions may appear in

a. consecutively numbered volumes published by the state.
b. units of the *National Reporter System.*
c. both a and b.
d. none of the above.

___ **6.** A reference to "32 F.3d 580" is a reference to

a. page 32 in volume 580 of the *Federal Reporter, Third Series.*
b. page 580 of volume 32 of the *Federal Reporter, Third Series.*
c. section 580 of Title 32 of the *Federal Reporter, Third Series.*
d. section 32 of Title 580 of the *Federal Reporter, Third Series.*

___ **7.** In the title of a case (*Abel v. Cain*, for example)

a. the names are always in alphabetical order.
b. the first name is always the name of the party who brought the suit.
c. the names are in no particular order.
d. none of the above.

____ 8. A civil law system is one in which the primary source of law is

a. case law.
b. a statutory code.
c. principles of civility.
d. principles of equity.

____ 9. A common law system is one in which the primary source of law is

a. case law.
b. a statutory code.
c. principles of civility.
d. principles of equity.

____ 10. A state law prohibits pharmacists from advertising the prices of prescription drugs. Ted, a pharmacist, challenges the law, claiming that it is unconstitutional. Under the First Amendment, advertising is

a. protected unless it concerns an unlawful activity or is misleading.
b. protected to the same extent as "fighting words."
c. protected to the same extent as defamatory words.
d. not protected.

SHORT ESSAY QUESTIONS

1. What is the primary function of law?

2. What is the commerce clause? What is its significance?

ISSUE SPOTTERS

1. The First Amendment to the U.S. Constitution protects the free exercise of religion. A state legislature enacts a law that outlaws all religions that do not derive from the Judeo-Christian tradition. Is this state law valid? Why or why not?

2. In the title of a case (*Jones v. Smith,* for example), is the name on the right (Smith) always the name of the party against whom the suit was brought?

3. If a farmer grows wheat wholly for consumption by her family on her farm, under what clause of the Constitution can Congress regulate that activity? Why?

4. Can a state, in the interest of energy conservation, ban all advertising by electric utilities if conservation could be accomplished by less restrictive means? Why or why not?

5. Would a state law imposing a fifteen-year term of imprisonment without allowing a trial on all businesspersons who appear in their own television commercials be a violation of substantive due process? Would it violate procedural due process?

★ **Learning Objectives**

The learning objectives in this chapter include:

1. The concepts of jurisdiction and venue.
2. The requirements for federal jurisdiction.
3. The basic components of the federal and state court systems.
4. The functions of trial courts and appellate courts.
5. The various ways in which disputes can be resolved outside the court system.

Chapter 2: Courts and Procedures

WHAT THIS CHAPTER IS ABOUT

This chapter explains which courts have power to hear what disputes and when and outlines what happens before, during, and after a civil trial. The chapter also covers alternative dispute resolution—alternatives to litigation.

CHAPTER OUTLINE

I. THE JUDICIARY'S ROLE IN AMERICAN GOVERNMENT

The power of **judicial review**: the courts can decide whether the laws or actions of the executive branch and the legislative branch are constitutional.

II. BASIC JUDICIAL REQUIREMENTS

A. JURISDICTION

To hear a case, a court must have jurisdiction over (1) the defendant or the property involved and (2) the subject matter.

1. **Jurisdiction over Persons or Property**
A court has *in personam* (personal) jurisdiction over state residents. Long arm statutes permit courts to exercise jurisdiction over nonresidents who have *minimum contacts* with the state (e.g., do business there). A court has *in rem* jurisdiction over property within its borders.

2. **Jurisdiction over Subject Matter**
A court of **general jurisdiction** can decide virtually any type of case. A court's jurisdiction may be **limited** by the subject of a suit, the amount of money in controversy, or whether a proceeding is a trial or appeal.

B. JURISDICTION OF THE FEDERAL COURTS

1. Federal Questions

Any suit based on the Constitution, a treaty, or a federal law can originate in a federal court.

2. Diversity of Citizenship

Federal jurisdiction covers cases involving (1) citizens of different states, (2) a foreign government and citizens of a state or of different states, or (3) citizens of a state and citizens or subjects of a foreign government. The amount in controversy must be more than $50,000.

C. EXCLUSIVE V. CONCURRENT JURISDICTION

Exclusive: when cases can be tried only in federal courts or only in state courts. Concurrent: When both federal and state courts can hear a case.

D. VENUE

Venue is concerned with the most appropriate location for a trial.

E. STANDING TO SUE

Standing is the interest (injury or threat) that a plaintiff has in a case. A plaintiff must have standing to bring a suit, and the controversy must be justiciable (real, as opposed to hypothetical or purely academic).

III. THE STATE AND FEDERAL COURT SYSTEMS

A. STATE COURT SYSTEMS

1. Trial Courts

Trial courts are courts in which trials are held and testimony is taken.

2. Courts of Appeals

Courts that hear appeals from trial courts look at *questions of law* (what law governs a dispute) but not *questions of fact* (what occurred in the dispute), unless a trial court's finding of fact is clearly contrary to the evidence. Decision of a state's highest court on state law is final.

B. THE FEDERAL COURT SYSTEM

1. U.S. District Courts

The federal equivalent of a state trial court of general jurisdiction. There is at least one federal district court in every state. Other federal trial courts include the U.S. Tax Court and the U.S. Bankruptcy Court.

2. U.S. Courts of Appeals

The U.S. (circuit) courts of appeals for twelve of the circuits hear appeals from the federal district courts located within their respective circuits. The court of appeals for the thirteenth circuit (the federal circuit) has national jurisdiction over certain cases.

3. The United States Supreme Court

The highest level of the federal court system. The Supreme Court can review any case decided by any of the federal courts of appeals, and it has authority over some cases decided in state courts.

4. How Cases Reach the Supreme Court

To appeal a case to the Supreme Court, a party asks for a writ of *certiorari*. Whether the Court issues the writ is within its discretion.

IV. FOLLOWING A CASE THROUGH THE STATE COURTS

A. THE PLEADINGS

1. The Plaintiff's Complaint

Filed by the plaintiff with the clerk of the trial court. Contains (1) a statement alleging the facts for the court to take jurisdiction, (2) a short statement of the facts necessary to show that the plaintiff is entitled to a remedy, and (3) a statement of the remedy the plaintiff is seeking.

2. The Summons

Served on the defendant, with the complaint. Notifies the defendant to answer the complaint (usually within twenty to thirty days).

3. The Defendant's Response

No response results in a default judgment for the plaintiff.

a. Motion to Dismiss

The defendant may file a motion to dismiss. If the court denies the motion, the defendant must file an answer. If the court grants the motion, the plaintiff must file an amended complaint.

b. Answer

Admits the allegations in the complaint or denies them and sets out any defenses. May include a counterclaim against the plaintiff.

B. DISMISSALS AND JUDGMENTS BEFORE TRIAL

1. Motion to Dismiss

(See above.) Either party may file a motion to dismiss if they have agreed to settle the case. A court may file such a motion on its own.

2. Motion for Judgment on the Pleadings

Any party can file this motion (after the pleadings have been filed), when no facts are disputed and only questions of law are at issue. A court may consider only those facts stated in the pleadings.

3. Motion for Summary Judgment

Any party can file this motion, if there is no disagreement about the facts and the only question is which laws apply. A court can consider evidence outside the pleadings.

C. DISCOVERY

The process of obtaining information from the opposing party or from witnesses. May include depositions; interrogatories; requests for admissions, documents, objects, entry on land, and physical or mental examinations.

D. PRETRIAL CONFERENCE

This is an informal discussion between the judge and the attorneys, after discovery, to identify the issues, consider a settlement, and plan the trial.

E. JURY SELECTION

The process by which a jury is chosen is *voir dire*—the jurors are questioned, and a party may ask that some not be sworn.

F. AT THE TRIAL

First, each side presents opening statements. Second, the plaintiff presents his or her case, offering evidence, including the testimony of witnesses. The defendant can challenge the evidence and cross-examine the witnesses.

1. **Motion for a Directed Verdict**
After the plaintiff's case, the defendant can ask the judge to direct a verdict on the ground the plaintiff presented no evidence to justify relief. If the motion is not granted, the defendant presents his case.

2. **Closing Arguments**
Each side summarizes his or her version of the facts, outlines the evidence that supports his or her case, and reveals the shortcomings of the points made by the other party. The plaintiff goes first.

3. **Jury Verdict**
In a jury trial, the jury decides the facts and the amount of damages to be paid by the losing party. This is the verdict.

G. POSTTRIAL MOTIONS

1. **Motion for Judgment *N.O.V.***
The defendant can file this motion, if he or she previously moved for a directed verdict. The standards for granting this motion are the same as those for granting a motion to dismiss or for a directed verdict.

2. **Motion for a New Trial**
This motion is granted if the judge believes that the jury erred but that it is not appropriate to grant a judgment for the other side.

H. THE APPEAL

1. **Filing the Appeal**
Appellant files a notice of appeal with the clerk of the trial court, and the record on appeal, an abstract, and a brief with the reviewing court. Appellee files an answering brief. The parties can give oral arguments.

2. **Appellate Review**
Appellate courts do not usually reverse findings of fact unless they are contradicted by the evidence presented at the trial in the lower court.

   a. **Options of an Appellate Court**
   (1) Affirm: enforce the lower court's order; (2) reverse (if an error was committed during the trial); or (3) remand: send back to the court that originally heard the case for a new trial.

   b. **Further Appeals**
   If the reviewing court is an intermediate appellate court, the case may be appealed to the state's highest court. If a federal question is involved, the case may go to the United States Supreme Court.

V. ALTERNATIVE DISPUTE RESOLUTION (ADR)

A. NEGOTIATION
Parties come together informally, with or without attorneys, to try to settle or resolve their differences without involving independent third parties.

B. MEDIATION
Parties come together informally with a mediator, who may propose solutions for the parties. A mediator is often an expert in a particular field.

C. MINI-TRIAL
A private proceeding in which attorneys briefly argue each party's case. A third party indicates how a court would likely decide the issue.

D. EARLY NEUTRAL CASE EVALUATION

Parties select a neutral third party (generally an expert) to evaluate their positions, with no hearing and no discovery. The evaluation is a basis for negotiating a settlement.

E. SUMMARY JURY TRIAL (SJT)

Like a mini-trial, but a jury renders a nonbinding verdict. Negotiations must follow. If no settlement is reached, either side can seek a full trial.

F. ARBITRATION

An arbitrator—the third party hearing the dispute—decides the dispute. The decision may be legally binding.

1. **Arbitration Clauses**
   Disputes are often arbitrated because of an arbitration clause in a contract entered into before the dispute. Courts enforce such clauses.

2. **Arbitration Statutes**
   Most states have statutes under which arbitration clauses are enforced. The Federal Arbitration Act (FAA) enforces arbitration clauses in contracts involving interstate commerce.

3. **The Arbitration Process**
   At an arbitration hearing, the parties make their arguments, present evidence, and call and examine witnesses, and the arbitrator makes a decision. The decision is called an **award,** even if no money is involved.

G. ADR AND THE COURTS

Many courts require parties to attempt to settle their differences through some form of ADR before going to trial. The arbitrator's decision is not binding—if either party rejects the award, the case goes to trial.

TRUE-FALSE QUESTIONS

___ 1. Under a long arm statute, a state court can compel someone outside the state to appear in the court.

___ 2. A court that has jurisdiction always has venue.

___ 3. The decisions of a state's highest court on all questions of state law are final.

___ 4. Federal district courts have original jurisdiction in federal matters.

___ 5. Federal courts may refuse to enforce a state or federal statute that violates the U.S. Constitution.

___ 6. Under the Constitution, Congress has the power to limit the jurisdiction of the federal courts.

___ 7. The United States Supreme Court has only original—not appellate—jurisdiction.

___ 8. To obtain documents and other materials in the hands of an opposing party, a party uses the appeals process.

___ 9. A major difference between negotiation and mediation is that mediation involves fewer procedural rules.

___ 10. In a jury trial, the parties have a right to conduct *voir dire.*

FILL-IN QUESTIONS

A motion ____________________ (to dismiss/for summary judgment) alleges that even if the facts in the complaint are true, their legal consequences are such that there is no reason to go on with the suit and no need for the defendant to present an answer. A motion ____________________ (to dismiss/for judgment on the pleadings) is properly filed after the complaint, answer, and any counterclaim and reply have been filed, when no facts are disputed and only questions of law are at issue. A motion for ____________________ (summary judgment/a new trial) is proper if there is no disagreement about the facts and the only question is which laws apply to those facts.

MULTIPLE-CHOICE QUESTIONS

___ 1. The first step in a lawsuit is the filing of pleadings, and the first pleading filed is the complaint. The complaint contains

a. a statement alleging jurisdictional facts.
b. a statement of facts entitling the complainant to relief.
c. a statement asking for a specific remedy.
d. all of the above.

___ 2. After the pleadings are filed, the next step is discovery. The purposes of discovery include

a. saving time.
b. narrowing the issues.
c. preventing surprises at trial.
d. all of the above.

___ 3. Werner Corporation was incorporated in Nebraska, has its main office in Kansas, and does business in Missouri. Able is subject to the jurisdiction of

a. Nebraska, Kansas, or Missouri.
b. Nebraska or Kansas, but not Missouri.
c. Nebraska or Missouri, but not Kansas.
d. Kansas or Missouri, but not Nebraska.

___ 4. An essential step that a court must determine before it considers a dispute is whether it has proper venue. Venue concerns

a. subject-matter jurisdiction.
b. the most appropriate location within a judicial system for bringing a case.
c. *in personam* and *in rem* jurisdiction of the parties and property involved.
d. the standing of the plaintiff.

___ 5. Abracadabra, Inc., sued Candelabra, Inc., in state court. Abracadabra lost and files an appeal with the state appeals court. The appeals court will

a. not retry the case, because the appropriate place for the retrial of a state case is a federal court.
b. not retry the case, because an appeals court examines the record of a case, looking at questions of law and procedure for errors by the trial court.
c. retry the case, because after a case is tried a party has a right to an appeal.
d. retry the case, because Abracadabra was the litigant.

___ **6.** A suit can be brought in a federal court if it involves

a. a question under the Constitution, a treaty, or a federal law.
b. citizens of different states, a foreign country and an American citizen, or a foreign citizen and an American citizen, and the amount in controversy is more than $50,000.
c. either a or b.
d. none of the above.

___ **7.** Grant serves a complaint on Lee. Lee files a motion to dismiss. Lee will also need to file an answer to the complaint if

a. the motion to dismiss is granted.
b. the motion to dismiss is denied.
c. Grant files a motion for judgment on the pleadings.
d. none of the above.

___ **8.** Jim and Bill are involved in an automobile accident. Sue is a passenger in Bill's car. Jim wants to ask Sue, as a witness, some questions concerning the accident. Sue's answers to the questions are given in

a. a deposition.
b. a response to interrogatories.
c. a response to a judge's request at a pretrial conference.
d. none of the above.

___ **9.** After a verdict, the losing party can file a motion for

a. a directed verdict.
b. summary judgment.
c. a new trial or for a judgment notwithstanding the verdict.
d. a judgment on the pleadings.

___ **10.** Arbitration is an alternative to judicial resolution of disputes. Arbitration is the settling of a dispute

a. by an impartial third party.
b. that must involve less than $50,000.
c. that arises only from a contract in writing.
d. all of the above.

SHORT ESSAY QUESTIONS

1. What is jurisdiction? How does jurisdiction over a person or property differ from subject matter jurisdiction? What does a long arm statute do?

2. What are the advantages and disadvantages of alternative dispute resolution?

ISSUE SPOTTERS

Jan contracted with Dean to deliver a quantity of computers to Jan's Computer Store. They disagree over the amount, the delivery date, the price, and the quality.

1. Their state requires that their dispute be submitted to mediation or nonbinding arbitration. If the dispute is not resolved, or if either party disagrees with the decision of the mediator or arbitrator, will a court hear the case?

2. Mediation is unsuccessful. Jan wants to sue Dean. What are the first steps?

3. As Jan prepares her suit against Dean, Jan wants to see copies of Dean's paperwork relating to the deal—Dean's copy of the original order, any notes of later telephone conversations, and so on. Jan also wants Dean to answer some questions relating to their dispute. What means should Jan use to see the papers and get Dean's answers?

4. At the trial, after Jan calls her witnesses, offers her evidence, and otherwise presents her side of the case, Dean has at least two choices between courses of actions. Dean can call his first witness. What else might Dean do?

5. After the trial, the judge issues a judgment that includes a grant of relief for Jan, but the relief is not as much as Jan wanted. Neither Jan nor Dean are satisfied with this result. Can either party—or both—appeal to a higher court?

QUICKEN CD-ROM BUSINESS LAW PARTNER APPLICATIONS

Open **Quicken Business Law Partner**. Click on the *New Documents* icon. Choose the *Small Claims Worksheet*. Respond to the *Interview* questions with actual facts or hypothetical ones. For example, imagine that Henderson and Smith live in Virginia, that Henderson breaches a contract to buy apples from Smith, costing her $1,000 in spoiled produce, and that now Smith wants to have her case heard in small claims court. After you complete the *Interview*, answer the following questions.

____ **1.** The maximum amount for which a lawsuit can be brought in a small claims court in Virginia is

a. $1,000.
b. $5,000.
c. $10,000.
d. $15,000.

____ **2.** To initiate her claim, Smith (the plaintiff) must obtain from the court clerk

a. a complaint form.
b. a service of process form.
c. both a and b.
d. none of the above.

____ **3.** If Henderson receives service of process and does *not* respond

a. Smith (the plaintiff) wins by default.
b. Henderson (the defendant) wins by default.
c. a date and time is assigned for a hearing or a trial.
d. none of the above.

____ **4.** If Henderson receives service of process and responds

a. Smith (the plaintiff) wins by default.
b. Henderson (the defendant) wins by default.
c. a date and time is assigned for a hearing or a trial.
d. none of the above.

___ **5.** If a judgment is entered on Smith's behalf and there is no appeal

a. Smith must pay the amount of the judgment.
b. Henderson must pay the amount of the judgment.
c. Henderson and Smith must pay equal amounts of the judgment.
d. none of the above.

QUICKEN BUSINESS LAW PARTNER ENHANCEMENT: EXPLORING THE PERSONAL LAW HANDBOOK

Personal Law Handbook, within Topic 3, Consumer Law, gives you a useful review, in the *Small Claims Court* section, of those courts' requirements and procedures.

Chapter 3: Ethics and Social Responsibility

Learning Objectives

The learning objectives in this chapter include:

1. The relationship of business ethics to personal ethics.
2. The relationship between law and ethics.
3. The contrast between duty-based ethics and utilitarian ethics.
4. Groups to whom corporations are perceived to owe duties.
5. Difficulties involved in measuring corporate social responsibility.

WHAT THIS CHAPTER IS ABOUT

The concepts set out in this chapter include the nature of business ethics and the relationship between ethics and business. Ultimately, the goal of this chapter is to provide you with basic tools for analyzing ethical issues in a business context.

CHAPTER OUTLINE

I. THE NATURE OF BUSINESS ETHICS

Ethics is the branch of philosophy that focuses on morality (right and wrong behavior) and the application of moral principles in everyday life.

A. BUSINESS ETHICS

Business ethics focuses on what constitutes ethical behavior in the world of business. Business ethics is *not* a separate kind of ethics.

B. BUSINESS ETHICS AND THE LAW

Because the law reflects society's ethical values, many ethical decisions are made for us. The law has limits, however, and ethical standards must sometimes guide the decision-making process.

II. SOURCES OF ETHICAL STANDARDS

A. DUTY-BASED ETHICS

1. Religious Standards

Religious standards provide that when an act is prohibited by religious teachings, it is unethical and should not be undertaken, regardless of the consequences. Religious standards also involve compassion.

2. **Philosophical Principles**
Immanual Kant believed that people should be respected because they are qualitatively different from other physical objects. Individuals should evaluate their actions in light of what would happen if everyone acted the same way.

B. OUTCOME-BASED ETHICS
Utilitarianism is a belief that an action is ethical if it produces the greatest good for the greatest number. This approach is often criticized, because it tends to reduce the welfare of people to plus and minus signs on a cost-benefit worksheet.

C. APPLYING ETHICAL STANDARDS
The impact of these value systems when actually put into practice illustrates their effect on business. The results of decisions based solely on utilitarianism would seem most open to public criticism.

III. OBSTACLES TO ETHICAL BUSINESS BEHAVIOR

A. ETHICS AND THE CORPORATE ENVIRONMENT
The corporate structure seems to shield corporate actors from responsibility or protect them from the consequences of their decisions (they do not witness or deal directly with the harm or injuries caused by their decisions).

B. ETHICS AND MANAGEMENT
A firm's policies may not be communicated clearly to employees. Management may indicate (by condoning or rewarding unethical conduct, or by setting unrealistic goals) that ethical considerations take second place.

C. ETHICS AND EMPLOYEES
Employees asked to commit unethical or illegal acts face a difficult ethical dilemma—participate in the act or inform the authorities and risk being fired (whistle-blowing is discussed in Chapter 22).

IV. CORPORATE SOCIAL RESPONSIBILITY

A. DUTY TO SHAREHOLDERS
Corporate directors and officers must act in the shareholders' interest. For example, they must act to maximize profits. Acting unethically could reduce profits in some circumstances.

B. DUTY TO EMPLOYEES

1. **Employment Discrimination**
Employers are prohibited from discriminating on the basis of race, color, national origin, sex, pregnancy, religion, age, or disability. For example, a fetal protection policy may discriminate against women.

2. **Sexual Harassment v. Wrongful Discharge**
Under some state laws and employment agreements, employers cannot fire employees without "just cause." An employee's illegal conduct (such as sexual harassment) may or may not constitute just cause.

3. **Corporate Restructuring and Employee Welfare**
Does an employer have an ethical duty to loyal, long-term employees not to replace them with workers who will accept lower pay? Should this duty prevail over a duty to improve profitability by restructuring?

C. DUTY TO CONSUMERS

1. Product Misuse
If a consumer is harmed by a product because he or she misused the product, should the manufacturer bear the responsibility?

2. Open and Obvious Risks
A firm must warn consumers of foreseeable risks associated with its products. No warning is needed for an open and obvious risk, but it can be difficult to predict when a risk will be considered open and obvious.

D. DUTY TO THE COMMUNITY
If a community in which a business is located has a stake in the firm, the firm may have to weigh community needs when making a decision.

E. DUTY TO SOCIETY
How can business best meet its duty to society? Making the most profit may be most beneficial in terms of use of resources to promote economic gains, an important social goal. Does business have a duty to use its wealth to further other social goals?

V. THE CORPORATE BALANCING ACT
Balancing profitability and ethical responsibility requires sacrificing some profits. Many firms thus aim for optimum, rather than maximum, profits.

VI. MEASURING CORPORATE RESPONSIBILITY

A. CORPORATE PHILANTHROPY
Business firms have long contributed to charitable causes. Sometimes, the particular cause and type of donation indicate a firm's social commitment.

B. CORPORATE PROCESS
How a corporation conducts its affairs at all levels inside and outside the firm can indicate how socially responsible it is.

C. IT PAYS TO BE ETHICAL
Behaving ethically can protect a firm's reputation and profits. Behaving ethically may also result in less harsh treatment by the government.

VII. ETHICS IN THE GLOBAL CONTEXT

A. WOMEN IN BUSINESS
Some countries reject any role for women professionals. Others impose cultural restrictions. Because of these restrictions, many U.S. companies are reluctant to assign women to work overseas. Equal employment opportunity is a fundamental policy in the United States, however.

B. BRIBERY OF FOREIGN OFFICIALS
In many countries, gift giving is common among companies or between companies and governments. U.S. firms are prohibited from offering payments to foreign officials to secure favorable contracts. Payments to minor officials to, for example, facilitate paperwork are not prohibited.

VIII. THE EVER-CHANGING ETHICAL LANDSCAPE
Our sense of what is ethical—what is fair or just or right in a given situation—changes over time. Conduct that was considered ethical ten years ago might be considered unethical today.

TRUE-FALSE QUESTIONS

___ 1. Ethics is the study of what constitutes right and wrong behavior.

___ 2. The study of business ethics is fundamentally different from the general study of ethics.

___ 3. According to religious standards, certain moral standards are universal.

___ 4. In determining how ethical an act is according to utilitarian standards, it does not matter how many people benefit from the act.

___ 5. A socially responsible firm will often aim for optimum profits instead of maximum profits.

___ 6. Ethical problems that arise in a business context normally involve clear-cut choices between good and bad alternatives.

___ 7. If a corporation fails to conduct itself ethically, its profits may suffer.

___ 8. A manufacturer is liable for an injury caused by a consumer's misuse of its product.

___ 9. In doing business internationally, a company must consider that what is prohibited in one country may be legal in another.

___ 10. Business conduct that was considered acceptable in the past is always acceptable today.

FILL-IN QUESTIONS

A law is what society considers ______________________ (proper behavior/a principle that never changes). An ethical value is an expression of what is considered ______________________ (proper behavior/a principle that never changes). Our sense of what is ethical ______________________ (changes/does not change) over time.

MULTIPLE-CHOICE QUESTIONS

___ 1. Business ethics focuses on the application of

a. moral principles.
b. business philosophies.
c. law.
d. none of the above.

___ 2. Which ethical standards derive from religious sources?

a. Duty-based ethics
b. Utilitarianism
c. Outcome-based ethics
d. None of the above

___ 3. Religious ethical standards are generally viewed as absolute but may also involve an element of

a. cost-benefit analysis.
b. discretion.
c. compassion.
d. none of the above.

___ 4. Which ethics is premised on acting so as to do the greatest good for the greatest number of people?

a. Duty-based ethics
b. Utilitarianism
c. Religious-based ethics
d. None of the above

___ 5. Which of the following is a criticism of utilitarianism?

a. It requires choosing among conflicting ethical principles.
b. It tends to focus on society as a whole rather than on individuals.
c. It is overly concerned with ideals of perfection.
d. It is an outdated philosophy.

___ 6. A corporate employer who responds to what the employer sees as a moral obligation to correct for past discrimination by adjusting pay differences raises an ethical conflict between which parties?

a. Employees only
b. Employer and employee only
c. Corporation and shareholder only
d. Employer and employee, and corporation and shareholder

___ 7. Employees who work for Chemco, a subsidiary of MegaCorp, must work with hazardous chemicals. To protect pregnant women and their fetuses, MegaCorp bars them from working for Chemco. Does this policy violate an ethical and legal duty to provide equal employment opportunity?

a. Yes. Equal employment opportunity is a "higher good."
b. Yes. Distinctions based on sex must relate to the ability to perform a job, and pregnant women can perform as well as anyone else.
c. No. Distinctions based on sex must relate to the ability to perform a job, and pregnant women cannot perform as well as men or non-pregnant women.
d. No. There is no "higher good" than protecting unborn children.

___ 8. When one ethical duty conflicts with another, a decision may have to be made as to which duty should prevail. Such a decision

a. does not normally have clear-cut answers.
b. may involve choices between equally good and bad alternatives.
c. both a and b.
d. none of the above.

___ 9. Ethical dilemmas in a business context can require determining

a. how much consideration to give to making a profit.
b. which law to obey.
c. whether to adhere to certain ethics.
d. all of the above.

____ **10.** To ensure that an action is profitable, legal, and ethical

a. some profit or ethical consideration may need to be traded off.
b. the religious implications must be considered.
c. the welfare of the people involved must be reduced to plus and minus signs on a cost-benefit worksheet.
d. none of the above.

SHORT ESSAY QUESTION

Discuss the difference between legal and ethical standards. How are legal standards affected by ethical standards?

ISSUE SPOTTERS

1. If, like Robin Hood, a person robs the rich to pay the poor, does his or her benevolent intent make his or her actions ethical?

2. When a manufacturer has to decide whether to close a plant, the costs of doing so may be weighed against the benefits. If the benefits are greater than the costs, can closing the plant be ethically justified, considering the effect on the employees?

3. When a corporate executive has to decide whether to market a product that might have undesirable side effects for a small percentage of users, what is the balance that must be struck?

4. Acme Corporation decides to respond to what it sees as a moral obligation to correct for past discrimination by adjusting pay differences among its employees. Does this raise an ethical conflict between Acme's employees? Between Acme and its employees? Between Acme and its shareholders?

5. Does a manufacturer owe an ethical duty to remove from the market a product that is capable of seriously injuring consumers, even if the injuries result from misuse?

★ **Learning Objectives**

The learning objectives in this chapter include:

1. How torts and crimes differ.
2. The purpose of tort law.
3. Some intentional torts against persons and property.
4. The four elements of negligence.
5. Circumstances in which strict liability applies.

Chapter 4: Torts

WHAT THIS CHAPTER IS ABOUT

Wrongful conduct by one person that causes injury to another is covered by the law of **torts**. *Tort* is French for "wrong." For acts that cause physical injury or that interfere with physical security and freedom of movement, tort law provides remedies, typically damages (money).

This chapter outlines intentional torts, negligence, and strict liability. Torts that are more specifically related to business are outlined in Chapter 6.

CHAPTER OUTLINE

I. THE BASIS OF TORT LAW

Two notions serve as the basis of all torts: wrongs and compensation. Tort law recognizes that some acts are wrong because they cause injuries to others. Most crimes involve torts, but not all torts are crimes. A tort action is a *civil* action in which one person brings a personal suit against another, usually for damages.

II. INTENTIONAL TORTS AGAINST PERSONS

Intentional torts involve acts that were intended or could be expected to bring about consequences that are the basis of the tort. A **tortfeasor** (one committing a tort) must intend to commit an act, the consequences of which interfere with the personal or business interests of another in a way not permitted by law.

A. ASSAULT AND BATTERY

1. Assault

An intentional act that creates in another person a reasonable apprehension or fear of immediate harmful or offensive contact.

2. **Battery**
An intentional and harmful or offensive physical contact. Physical injury need not occur. Whether the contact is offensive is determined by the reasonable person standard.

3. **Compensation**
A plaintiff may be compensated for emotional harm or loss of reputation resulting from a battery, as well as for physical harm.

4. **Defenses to Assault and Battery**

a. **Consent**
When a person consents to an act that damages him or her, there is generally no liability for the damage.

b. **Self-Defense**
An individual who is defending his or her life or physical well-being can claim self-defense.

c. **Defense of Others**
An individual can act in a reasonable manner to protect others who are in real or apparent danger.

d. **Defense of Property**
Reasonable force may be used in attempting to remove intruders from one's home, although force that is likely to cause death or great bodily injury can never be used just to protect property.

B. FALSE IMPRISONMENT

1. **What False Imprisonment Is**
The intentional confinement or restraint of another person without justification. The confinement can be accomplished through the use of physical barriers, physical restraint, or threats of physical force.

2. **The Defense of Probable Cause**
In some states, a merchant is justified in delaying a suspected shoplifter if the merchant has probable cause. The detention must be conducted in a reasonable manner and for only a reasonable length of time.

C. INFLICTION OF EMOTIONAL DISTRESS

Infliction of emotional distress is an intentional act that amounts to extreme and outrageous conduct resulting in severe emotional distress to another (a few states require physical symptoms). Stalking is one way to commit it. Repeated annoyance, with threats, is another.

D. DEFAMATION

Defamation is wrongfully hurting another's good reputation through false statements. Doing it orally is **slander**; doing it in writing is **libel**.

1. **Types of False Utterances That Are Torts *Per Se***
Proof of injury is not required when one falsely states that another has a loathsome communicable disease, has committed improprieties while engaging in a profession or trade, or has committed or been imprisoned for a serious crime, or that an unmarried woman is unchaste.

2. **The Publication Requirement**
The statement must be published (communicated to a third party). Anyone who republishes or repeats a defamatory statement is liable.

3. **Defenses against Defamation**

a. **Truth**
The statement is true. It must be true in whole, not in part.

b. **Privilege**
The statement is privileged: absolute (made in a judicial or legislative proceeding) or qualified (for example, made by one corporate director to another and was about corporate business).

c. **Public Figure**
The statement is about a public figure, made in a public medium, and related to a matter of general public interest. To recover damages, a public figure must prove a statement was made with **actual malice** (knowledge of its falsity or reckless disregard for the truth).

E. INVASION OF THE RIGHT TO PRIVACY
Four acts qualify as invasions of privacy:

1. The use of a person's name, picture, or other likeness for commercial purposes without permission. (This is **appropriation**—see Chapter 6.)

2. Intrusion on an individual's affairs or seclusion.

3. Publication of information that places a person in a false light.

4. Public disclosure of private facts about an individual that an ordinary person would find objectionable.

F. MISREPRESENTATION—FRAUD (DECEIT)
Fraud is the use of misrepresentation and deceit for personal gain. Puffery (seller's talk) is not fraud. The elements of fraudulent misrepresentation—

1. **Misrepresentation** of material facts or conditions with knowledge that they are false or with reckless disregard for the truth.

2. **Intent** to induce another to rely on the misrepresentation.

3. **Justifiable reliance** by the deceived party.

4. **Damages** suffered as a result of reliance.

5. **Causal connection** between the misrepresentation and the injury.

III. INTENTIONAL TORTS AGAINST PROPERTY

A. TRESPASS TO LAND
Trespass to land occurs if a person, without permission, enters onto, above, or below the surface of land owned by another; causes anything to enter onto the land; or remains on the land or permits anything to remain on it.

1. **Trespass Criteria, Rights, and Duties**
Posted signs *expressly* establish trespass. Entering onto property to commit an illegal act *impliedly* does so. Trespassers are liable for any property damage. Owners may have a duty to post notice of any danger.

2. **Defenses against Trespass to Land**
Defenses against trespass include that the trespass was warranted or that the purported owner had no right to possess the land in question.

B. TRESPASS TO PERSONAL PROPERTY
Occurs when an individual unlawfully harms the personal property of another or interferes with an owner's right to exclusive possession and enjoyment. Defenses include that the interference was warranted.

C. CONVERSION

1. **What Conversion Is**
An act depriving an owner of personal property without the owner's permission and without just cause. Conversion is the civil side of crimes related to theft. Buying stolen goods is conversion.

2. **Defenses**
Defenses to conversion include that the purported owner does not own the property or does not have a right to possess it that is superior to the right of the holder. Necessity is also a defense.

IV. UNINTENTIONAL TORTS (NEGLIGENCE)

A. THE ELEMENTS OF NEGLIGENCE

1. **What Negligence Is**
Someone's failure to live up to a required duty of care, causing another to suffer injury. The breach of the duty must create a risk of certain harmful consequences, whether or not that was the intent.

2. **The Elements of Negligence**
(1) A duty of care, (2) breach of the duty of care, (3) damage or injury as a result of the breach, and (4) the breach causes the damage or injury.

B. THE DUTY OF CARE AND ITS BREACH

1. **The Reasonable Person Standard**
The duty of care is measured by the **reasonable person standard** (how a reasonable person would have acted in the same circumstances).

2. **Duty of Landowners**
Owners are expected to use reasonable care (guard against some risks and warn of others) to protect persons coming onto their property.

3. **Duty of Professionals**
A professional's duty is consistent with his or her knowledge, skill, and intelligence, including what is reasonable for that professional.

4. **Factors for Determining a Breach of the Duty of Care**
The nature of the act (whether it is outrageous or commonplace), the manner in which the act is performed (cautiously versus heedlessly), and the nature of the injury (whether it is serious or slight). Note: Failing to rescue a stranger in peril is not a breach of a duty of care.

C. THE INJURY REQUIREMENT AND DAMAGES
To recover damages (receive compensation), the plaintiff must have suffered some loss, harm, wrong, or invasion of a protected interest. Punitive damages (to punish the wrongdoer and deter others) may also be awarded.

D. CAUSATION

1. Causation in Fact

The breach of the duty of care must cause the injury—that is, "but for" the wrongful act, the injury would not have occurred.

2. Proximate Cause

There must be a connection between the act and the injury strong enough to justify imposing liability. Generally, the harm or the victim of the harm must have been foreseeable in light of all of the circumstances.

3. Superseding Intervening Force

A superseding intervening force breaks the connection between the breach of the duty of care and the injury or damage. Taking a defensive action (such as swerving to avoid an oncoming car) does not break the connection. Nor does someone else's attempt to rescue the injured party.

E. DEFENSES TO NEGLIGENCE

1. Assumption of Risk

A plaintiff who voluntarily enters into a risky situation, knowing the risk, cannot recover. This does not include a risk different from or greater than the risk normally involved in the situation.

2. Contributory Negligence

In some states, a plaintiff cannot recover for an injury if he or she was negligent. The **last-clear-chance doctrine** allows a negligent plaintiff to recover if the defendant had the last chance to avoid the damage.

3. Comparative Negligence

In most states, the plaintiff's and the defendant's negligence is compared and liability prorated. Some states allow a plaintiff to recover even if his or her fault is greater than the defendant's. In many states, the plaintiff gets nothing if he or she is more than 50 percent at fault.

F. SPECIAL NEGLIGENCE DOCTRINES AND STATUTES

1. *Res Ipsa Loquitur*

If negligence is very difficult to prove, a court may infer it, and the defendant must prove he or she was *not* negligent. This is only if the event causing the harm is one that normally does not occur in the absence of negligence and is caused by something within the defendant's control.

2. Negligence *Per Se*

A person who violates a statute providing for a criminal penalty is liable when the violation causes another to be injured, if (1) the statute sets out a standard of conduct, and when, where, and of whom it is expected; (2) the injured person is in the class protected by the statute; and (3) the statute was designed to prevent the type of injury suffered.

3. Special Negligence Statutes

Good Samaritan statutes protect those who aid others from being sued for negligence. Dram shop acts impose liability on bar owners for injuries caused by intoxicated persons who are served by those owners. A statute may impose liability on social hosts for acts of their guests.

V. STRICT LIABILITY

Under this doctrine, liability for injury is imposed for reasons other than fault.

A. ABNORMALLY DANGEROUS OR EXCEPTIONAL ACTIVITIES

The basis for imposing strict liability on an abnormally dangerous activity is that the activity creates an extreme risk. Balancing the risk against the potential for harm, it is fair to ask the person engaged in the activity to pay for injury caused by that activity.

B. DANGEROUS ANIMALS

A person who keeps a dangerous animal is strictly liable for any harm inflicted by the animal.

C. PRODUCT LIABILITY

A significant application of strict liability is in the area of product liability—liability of manufacturers, sellers, and others for harmful or defective products. Product liability is outlined in Chapter 16.

TRUE-FALSE QUESTIONS

____ 1. One function of tort law is to provide an injured person with a remedy.

____ 2. To be guilty of an intentional tort, a person must intend the consequences of his or her act or know with substantial certainty that certain consequences will result.

____ 3. Immediate harmful or offensive contact is an element of assault.

____ 4. Immediate harmful or offensive contact is an element of battery.

____ 5. A single act, if it is extreme and outrageous, is enough to support an action for the infliction of emotional distress.

____ 6. The tort of defamation does not occur unless a defamatory statement is made in writing.

____ 7. Ed tells customers that he is "the best plumber in town." This is fraudulent misrepresentation, unless Ed actually believes that he is the best.

____ 8. A person who borrows a friend's car and fails to return it at the friend's request is guilty of conversion.

____ 9. To avoid liability for negligence, the same duty of care must be exercised by all individuals, regardless of their knowledge, skill, or intelligence.

____ 10. Under the doctrine of strict liability, liability is imposed for reasons other than fault.

FILL-IN QUESTIONS

1. Basic defenses to ____________________________ (negligence/intentional torts) include comparative negligence, contributory negligence, and assumption of risk.

2. One who voluntarily and knowingly enters into a risky situation normally cannot recover damages. This is the ____ (defense of contributory negligence/defense of assumption of risk).

3. When both parties' failure to use reasonable care combines to cause injury, in some states the injured party's recovery is precluded by his or her own negligence. This is the ________________ (comparative/contributory) negligence doctrine.

4. When both parties' failure to use reasonable care combines to cause injury, in most states damages are reduced by a percentage that represents the degree of the plaintiff's negligence. This is the ________________ (comparative/contributory) negligence doctrine.

MULTIPLE-CHOICE QUESTIONS

___ 1. Which of the following statements is TRUE?

a. Commission of a tort is always a crime.
b. The state prosecutes tortfeasors.
c. In a tort action, one person brings a suit of a personal nature against another.
d. A court may punish a tortfeasor with a jail term, a fine, or both.

___ 2. Joe, a 99-pound weakling, clenches his fist, stands as if ready to throw a punch, and orally threatens to hit a 360-pound lineman for the Chicago Bears. Joe is

a. not guilty of assault, because words alone are not enough.
b. not guilty of assault, because it is unlikely that the lineman is afraid of Joe.
c. guilty of assault, because the words are accompanied by a threatening act.
d. guilty of assault, because a professional football player is a public figure.

___ 3. Tonya owns Tonya's Ski Shop. One afternoon, Tonya sees Nancy, a customer, pick merchandise from a shelf and put it in her bag. As Nancy is about to leave the shop, Tonya tells her that she can't leave until Tonya checks her bag. If Nancy sues Tonya for false imprisonment, Nancy will

a. win, because a merchant cannot delay a customer on a mere suspicion.
b. win, because Nancy did not first commit a tort.
c. lose, because a merchant may delay a suspected shoplifter for a reasonable time based on probable cause.
d. lose, because Tonya did not intend to commit the tort of false imprisonment.

___ 4. A music critic writes in a review that Madonna performed drunk. If Madonna sues the critic for defamation, Madonna will

a. win, because Madonna is a public figure.
b. win, if Madonna can prove the statement was made with actual malice.
c. lose, because newspaper articles are absolutely privileged.
d. lose, because Madonna is a public figure.

___ 5. During a trial, a judge calls an attorney unethical. If the attorney sues the judge for defamation, the attorney will

a. win, because the attorney is a public figure.
b. win, if the attorney can prove the statement was made with actual malice.
c. lose, because the judge's statement was privileged.
d. lose, because the judge is a public figure.

___ **6.** Al, a landlord, installs two-way mirrors in his tenants' bedrooms through which he watches them without their knowledge. Al is guilty of which of the following categories of the tort of invasion of the right to privacy?

a. Using another's likeness for commercial purposes without permission
b. Public disclosure of private facts about another
c. Publication of information that places another in false lights
d. Intrusion into another's affairs or seclusion

___ **7.** Fred returns home from work to find Barney camped in Fred's backyard. Fred says, "Get off my property." Barney says, "I'm not leaving." Fred forcibly drags Barney off the property. If Barney sues Fred, Barney will

a. win, because Fred used too much force.
b. win, because Barney told Fred that he was not leaving.
c. lose, because Fred did not use deadly force.
d. lose, because Barney is a trespasser.

___ **8.** Gus sends a letter to Jose in which he accuses Jose of embezzling. Jose's secretary Tina reads the letter. If Jose sues Gus for defamation, Jose will

a. win, because Tina's reading of the letter satisfies the publication element.
b. win, because Gus's writing of the letter satisfies the publication element.
c. lose, because the letter is not proof that Jose is an embezzler.
d. lose, because the publication element is not satisfied.

___ **9.** Wandering through Don's air-conditioned market on a hot summer day with her sisters, seven-year-old Silvia drops her ice cream on the floor near the dairy case. Two hours later, Jan stops to buy milk, slips on the ice cream puddle, and breaks her arm. Don is

a. liable, because a merchant is always liable for customers' actions.
b. liable, if Don failed to take all reasonable precautions against Jan's injury.
c. not liable, because Jan's injury was her own fault.
d. not liable, because Jan's injury was the fault of Silvia's sisters.

___ **10.** Driving his car negligently, Paul crashes into an electrical pole. The pole falls, smashing through the roof of a house onto Karl, who is sitting inside. Karl dies. But for Paul's negligence, Karl would not have died. Regarding Karl's death, Paul's crash is the

a. cause in fact.
b. proximate cause.
c. intervening cause.
d. superseding cause.

___ **11.** Strict liability is applied to abnormally dangerous activities because of their extreme risk. Abnormally dangerous activities involve

a. potentially serious harm to persons or property.
b. a high degree of risk that cannot be completely guarded against by the exercise of reasonable care.
c. activities not commonly performed in the area.
d. all of the above.

___ 12. To be prepared to deal with potential legal problems, a retailer should

a. obtain liability insurance.
b. post warnings for all potential hazards.
c. not use accusatory words when questioning a suspected shoplifter.
d. all of the above.

SHORT ESSAY QUESTIONS

1. What is a *tort*?

2. Identify and describe the elements of a cause of action based on negligence.

ISSUE SPOTTERS

1. Adam kisses the sleeve of Eve's blouse, to which she did not consent. Is Adam guilty of a tort?

2. A bartender refuses to serve any more drinks to Andy, who has been drinking heavily in the bar. Andy argues with the bartender who tells two bouncers to "sober this guy up." The bouncers take Andy into the restroom and threaten him with physical harm if he doesn't stay there until he sobers up. Has a tort been committed against Andy?

3. If a student takes another student's business law textbook as a practical joke and hides it for several days before the final examination, has a tort been committed?

4. Standing next to a gasoline truck, Joe lights a cigarette and tosses the match into the tank. The ensuing explosion and fire ends in the evacuation and destruction of downtown Richmond. During the evacuation, eleven-year-old Mandy is trampled by a fleeing mob. Is Joe liable for Mandy's injuries?

5. Gary owns a pit bull that Gary knows can be unpredictably vicious. One afternoon while Gary is at work, nine-year-old Dennis is walking past Gary's house when the dog attacks Dennis, severely injuring the boy. Is Gary liable for Dennis's injuries?

 **Learning Objectives**

The learning objectives in this chapter include:

1. Circumstances in which a party is liable for the tort of wrongful interference.
2. How the tort of appropriation occurs.
3. The laws protecting trademarks, patents, and copyrights.
4. How trade secrets are protected by the law.
5. How the Racketeer Influenced and Corrupt Organizations Act is applied in civil cases.

Chapter 5: Business Torts, Intellectual Property, and Cyberlaw

WHAT THIS CHAPTER IS ABOUT

Business torts (wrongful interferences with others' business rights) include the torts discussed in the first part of this chapter. Intellectual property consists of the products of intellectual, creative processes. Many of these (inventions, books, movies, etc.) are protected by the law of trademarks, patents, copyrights, and related concepts outlined in the second part of this chapter. Finally, there is a section on the Racketeer Influenced and Corrupt Organizations Act (RICO) and fraud.

CHAPTER OUTLINE

I. WRONGFUL INTERFERENCE

Torts involving wrongful interference with another's business rights generally fall into the two categories outlined here.

A. WRONGFUL INTERFERENCE WITH A CONTRACTUAL RELATIONSHIP

Wrongful interference with a contractual relationship occurs when there is a contract between two parties, and a third party who knows of the contract intentionally causes either of the two parties to break it.

B. WRONGFUL INTERFERENCE WITH A BUSINESS RELATIONSHIP

If there are two yogurt stores in a mall, placing an employee of Store A in front of Store B to divert customers to Store A constitutes the tort of wrongful interference with a business relationship.

C. DEFENSES TO WRONGFUL INTERFERENCE

A person is not liable if the interference is justified or permissible (such as bona fide competitive behavior).

II. WRONGFUL ENTRY INTO BUSINESS

Opening a business for the sole purpose of driving another firm out of business is predatory. Business that is not normal competitive activity may be tortious.

III. APPROPRIATION

The use of one person's name or likeness by another, without permission and for the benefit of the user, constitutes the tort of **appropriation**. An individual's right to privacy includes the right to the exclusive use of his or her identity.

IV. DEFAMATION IN THE BUSINESS CONTEXT

The tort of defamation occurs when an individual makes a false statement that injures another's reputation. **Defamation** is a business tort when the defamatory matter injures someone in a profession, business, or trade, or when it adversely affects a business in its credit rating and other dealings.

V. DISPARAGEMENT OF PROPERTY

Disparagement of property occurs when economically injurious falsehoods are made about another's product or ownership of property. It is a general term for torts that can be specifically referred to as **slander of quality** (product) or **slander of title** (ownership of property).

VI. INTELLECTUAL PROPERTY PROTECTION

A. TRADEMARKS AND RELATED PROPERTY

1. Trademarks

Trademarks are protected at the federal level by the Lanham Act of 1946. Many states also have statutes that protect trademarks.

a. What a Trademark Is

A distinctive mark, motto, device, or emblem that a manufacturer stamps, prints, or otherwise affixes to the goods it produces to distinguish them from the goods of other manufacturers.

b. Trademark Registration

A trademark may be registered with a state or the federal government. Trademarks do not need to be registered to be protected.

1) Requirements for Federal Registration

A trademark may be filed with the U.S. Patent and Trademark Office on the basis of (1) use or (2) the intent to use the mark within six months (which may be extended to thirty months).

2) Renewal of Federal Registration

Registration is renewable between the fifth and sixth years and every twenty years thereafter.

c. Distinctiveness of Mark

The law protects a trademark to the extent that it is **distinctive**. This may depend on whether it has acquired a **secondary meaning** (do customers associate the mark with the source of a product?). Fanciful marks—even personal names used in fanciful ways—are considered the most distinctive.

d. Trademark Infringement

When a trademark is copied to a substantial degree or used in its entirety by another, the trademark is infringed.

2. Service, Certification, and Collective Marks
Laws that apply to trademarks normally also apply to—

a. Service Marks
Used to distinguish the services of one person or company from those of another. Registered in the same manner as trademarks.

b. Certification Marks
Used by one or more persons, other than the owner, to certify the region, materials, mode of manufacture, quality, or accuracy of the owner's goods or services.

c. Collective Marks
Certification marks used by members of a cooperative, association, or other organization.

3. Trade Names
Used to indicate part or all of a business's name. Trade names cannot be registered with the federal government but may be protected under the common law if they are used as trademarks or service marks.

B. PATENTS
A **patent** is a grant from the federal government that gives an inventor the exclusive right to make, use, and sell an invention for twenty years (fourteen years for a design).

1. Requirements for a Patent
An invention, discovery, or design must be genuine, novel, useful, and not obvious in light of current technology. A patent is given to the first person to invent a product, not to the first person to file for a patent.

2. Patent Infringement
Making, using, or selling another's patented design, product, or process without the patent owner's permission. The owner may obtain damages, an injunction, destruction of all infringing copies, and litigation costs.

3. Patents for Computer Software
The basis for software is often a mathematical equation or formula, which is not patentable, but a patent can be obtained for a process that incorporates a computer program.

C. COPYRIGHTS
A **copyright** is an intangible right granted by statute to the author or originator of certain literary or artistic productions. Protection is automatic; registration is not required.

1. Copyright Protection
Automatic for the life of the author plus fifty years. Copyrights owned by publishing houses expire seventy-five years from the date of publication or a hundred years from the date of creation, whichever is first. For works by more than one author, copyright expires fifty years after the death of the last surviving author.

2. What Is Protected Expression?
To be protected, a work must meet these requirements—

a. Must Fit a Certain Category
It must be a (1) literary work; (2) musical work; (3) dramatic work; (4) pantomime or choreographic work; (5) pictorial, graphic, or

sculptural work; (6) film or other audiovisual work; or (7) a sound recording. The Copyright Act also protects computer software and architectural plans.

b. **Must Be Fixed in a Durable Medium**
From which it can be perceived, reproduced, or communicated.

c. **Must Be Original**
A compilation of facts (formed by the collection and assembling of preexisting materials of data) is copyrightable if it is original.

3. **What Is Not Protected**
Ideas, facts, and related concepts. If an idea and an expression cannot be separated, the expression cannot be copyrighted.

4. **Copyright Infringement**
A copyright is infringed if a work is copied without the copyright holder's permission. A copy does not have to be exactly the same as the original—copying a substantial part of the original is enough.

a. **Penalties**
Actual damages (based on the harm to the copyright holder); damages under the Copyright Act, not to exceed $100,000; and criminal proceedings (which may result in fines or imprisonment).

b. **Exception—Fair Use Doctrine**
The Copyright Act permits the fair use of a work for purposes such as criticism, comment, news reporting, teaching (including multiple copies for classroom use), scholarship, or research.

5. **Copyright Protection for Computer Software**
The Computer Software Copyright Act of 1980 provides protection.

a. **What Is Protected**
The binary object code (the part of a software program readable only by computer); the source code (the part of a program readable by people); and the program structure, sequence, and organization.

b. **What May or May Not Be Protected**
The "look and feel"—the general appearance, command structure, video images, menus, windows, and other displays—of a program.

6. **The No Electronic Theft Act (NETA) of 1997**
Taking and distributing pirated, copyrighted works to others over the Internet is theft, even if there is no intent to profit. Penalties include fines of up to $250,000 and imprisonment of up to five years.

D. TRADE SECRETS

1. **What Trade Secrets Are**
Customer lists, formulas, plans, pricing information, marketing techniques, production techniques—anything that makes a company unique and would have value to a competitor.

2. **Trade Secret Protection**
Most law with respect to trade secrets is common law. Protection of trade secrets extends both to ideas and their expression. Liability extends to those who misappropriate trade secrets by any means.

E. CYBERLAW: PROTECTING INTELLECTUAL PROPERTY IN CYBERSPACE

1. Trademark Protection on the Internet—Domain Names

a. What a Domain Name Is

An address on the Internet, located by type of organization (such as .com) and the organization's name .

b. Domain Name Registration

Names are registered with Network Solutions, Inc. (a private firm), which requires a name to be used on the Internet on a regular basis. The use must not infringe on another's property rights.

c. Unauthorized Use of a Trademark as a Domain Name

Unauthorized use is trademark infringement; unauthorized commercial use violates the Federal Trademark Dilution Act.

2. Patent Protection for Cyberproducts

a. Cyberproducts

Cyberproducts include data-compression software, encryption programs, and software facilitating information linking and retrieval systems.

b. Licensing

In the context of a patent, a license is permission granted by a patent owner to another to make, sell, or use the patented item. A license can be limited to certain purposes and to the licensee only.

3. Copyrights in Cyberspace

a. Online Issues

How copyright law applies in cyberspace is still debated. Some courts hold that software stored in a computer constitutes a copy, as does digital storage of photographs, music, and other works.

b. Online Liability

Online providers (Internet access services, etc.) directly involved in the unauthorized copying, distribution, and performance or display of copyrighted work can be held liable for unauthorized use.

F. INTERNATIONAL PROTECTION

1. Copyright Protection

The United States is a party to international copyright treaties, such as the Berne Convention and the Universal Copyright Convention.

a. For Citizens of Countries That Have Signed the Berne Convention

If, for example, an American writes a book, the copyright in the book is recognized by every country that has signed the convention.

b. For Citizens of Other Countries

If a citizen of a country that has not signed the convention publishes a book first in a country that has signed, all other countries that have signed the convention recognize that author's copyright.

2. Trade-Related Aspects of Intellectual Property Rights

TRIPS is part of the agreement creating the World Trade Organization (WTO). Under TRIPS, each member nation must not discriminate (in the administration, regulation, or adjudication of intellectual property rights) against foreign owners of such rights.

VII. RICO

A person who commits two offenses under the Racketeer Influenced and Corrupt Organizations Act (RICO) of 1970 is guilty of "racketeering activity."

A. ACTIVITIES PROHIBITED BY RICO

1. Use income from racketeering to buy an interest in an enterprise.
2. Acquire or maintain such an interest through racketeering activity.
3. Conduct or participate in an enterprise through racketeering activity.
4. Conspire to do any of the above.

B. CIVIL LIABILITY UNDER RICO

Civil penalties include divestiture of a defendant's interest in a business or dissolution of the business. Private individuals can recover treble damages, plus attorneys' fees, for business injuries.

TRUE-FALSE QUESTIONS

___ 1. To commit wrongful interference with a contractual relationship, a party only needs to cause two parties to break a contract.

___ 2. There are no legitimate defenses to wrongful interference torts.

___ 3. Opening a business for the sole purpose of driving another firm out of business is a tort.

___ 4. To obtain a patent, an inventor must prove to the patent office that his or her invention is genuine, novel, useful, and not obvious in light of contemporary technology.

___ 5. To obtain a copyright, an author must prove to the copyright office that a work is genuine, novel, useful, and not a copy of another copyrighted work.

___ 6. Copyright infringement occurs if a computer program's structure, sequence, and organization is copied.

___ 7. A personal name can be trademarked if it has acquired a secondary meaning.

___ 8. Service, certification, and collective marks are covered by the same policies and restrictions that apply to copyrights.

___ 9. Protection of trade secrets extends only to the expression of ideas, not to the ideas themselves.

___ 10. The Racketeer Influenced and Corrupt Organizations Act (RICO) created no new types of crimes. It only increased penalties that could be applied to convictions for existing crimes.

FILL-IN QUESTIONS

RICO makes reference to twenty-six ________________________ (federal/state) crimes and nine ____________________ (federal/state) felonies. If a person commits

______________ (two/four) of these offenses, he or she is guilty of racketeering activity. Under RICO, it is a crime (1) to use income obtained from __________________ (racketeering/business) activity to buy an interest in any business, or (2) to acquire or ______________________ (maintain/sell) an interest in a business. It is also a crime (3) to conduct or ____________________________ (participate in/ignore) the affairs of an enterprise through racketeering activity. Finally, it is a crime (4) to conspire to do any of these things.

MULTIPLE-CHOICE QUESTIONS

___ **1.** Without Tom's permission, Mary makes and sells widgets identical to Tom's patented widget, except for slight differences in the handle. Tom's widget is not trademarked. Tom sues Mary for patent infringement. Mary is

a. liable, because she is making and selling Tom's widget without permission.
b. not liable, because Tom does not also have a trademark.
c. not liable, because of the differences between the widgets' handles.
d. not liable, because she is not stealing actual widgets that Tom made.

___ **2.** A salesperson for Woodco tells the owner of Pat's Lumber that Timber, Inc., does not sell mahogany. The salesperson knows that the statement is false. Pat had intended to buy mahogany from Timber, but instead buys it from Woodco. If Timber sues Woodco for slander of quality, Woodco will be held

a. liable, if Timber proves that it suffered damages from Pat's decision.
b. liable, if Timber proves that Pat did not see Timber's salesperson.
c. not liable, if Woodco proves that its prices are competitive.
d. not liable, if Woodco proves that it made no profit on the deal.

___ **3.** Big Food, Royal Dogs, and Giant Chicken are fast-food restaurants in a mall. Big's manager sends employees to Royal and Giant to divert customers with free samples. Royal and Giant sue Big for wrongful interference with a business relationship. If Big is held liable, it will be because it

a. interfered unreasonably with their attempts to do business.
b. wrongfully interfered with a contractual relationship.
c. wrongfully entered into business.
d. committed defamation.

___ **4.** RICO prohibits

a. wrongful interference with the business relationships of others.
b. the theft of trade secrets.
c. operation of an enterprise with income obtained from racketeering activity.
d. none of the above.

___ **5.** Under RICO, a convicted defendant may be

a. required to sell his or her interest in a business.
b. subject to fines or imprisonment.
c. both a and b.
d. none of the above.

___ 6. Mark Corporation uses a monkey symbol in marketing its Monkey brand jeans but has not registered the symbol with a government office. Quick, Inc., imports jeans made abroad and sells them with the monkey symbol, which it also has not registered. Mark sues Quick. Quick is

a. liable, because it had no right to trade on Mark's goodwill.
b. not liable, because Mark did not register the symbol with the government.
c. not liable, because it did not manufacture the jeans, it only imported them.
d. not liable, because a monkey symbol cannot be a trademark.

___ 7. Ken invents a light bulb that lasts longer than ordinary bulbs. To prevent others from making, using, or selling the bulb or its design, he should obtain

a. a trademark.
b. a copyright.
c. a patent.
d. none of the above.

___ 8. Joe is liable for the tort of appropriation if he

a. uses Grace's name or likeness, with Grace's permission, for Joe's benefit.
b. uses Grace's name or likeness, without Grace's permission, for Joe's benefit.
c. makes a false statement, with Grace's permission, that harms her reputation.
d. makes a false statement, without Grace's permission, that harms her reputation.

___ 9. Grace is liable for the tort of defamation when she

a. uses Joe's name or likeness, with Joe's permission, for Joe's benefit.
b. uses Joe's name or likeness, without Joe's permission, for Joe's benefit.
c. makes a false statement, with Joe's permission, that harms his reputation.
d. makes a false statement, without Joe's permission, that harms his reputation.

___ 10. The Computer Software Copyright Act of 1980 extended copyright protection to computer programs. This protection extends to

a. the source code and the binary code.
b. the structure, sequence, and organization.
c. a computer program's "look and feel"—the general appearance, command structure, video images, menus, windows, and other screen displays.
d. both a and b.

SHORT ESSAY QUESTIONS

1. What can a copyright protect and what can it not protect?

2. What constitutes civil liability under the Racketeer Influenced and Corrupt Organizations Act (RICO) and what are its penalties?

ISSUE SPOTTERS

1. After less than a year in business, Muscle Health Club surpasses Fitness Club in number of members. Muscle's advertising and marketing strategies attract many Fitness members, who then change clubs. Does Fitness have any recourse against Muscle?

2. A video game manufacturer develops a gladiators video game with distinctive graphics. Can the developer prevent a competitor from producing another game based on gladiators? Can the developer prevent competitors from copying the graphics?

3. Maldo writes, copyrights, and publishes in the United States a book in Spanish titled *En la Casa del Tigre*. What copyright protection does Maldo have in other countries?

4. Crabb's Apple Ball Company makes and sells "Crabb's Apple Balls," a distinctively flavored candy. Green Candy Corporation begins making and marketing "Green's Apple Balls." Can Crabb prevent Green from using the words "Apple Balls" for its candy?

5. Burley Seed Company discovers that it can extract data from the computer of North King Hybrids, Inc., its major competitor, by making a series of telephone calls over a high-speed modem. When Burley uses its discovery to extract North King's customer lists, without North King's permission, what recourse does North King have?

QUICKEN CD-ROM BUSINESS LAW PARTNER APPLICATIONS

Open **Quicken Business Law Partner**. Click on the *New Documents* icon. Select the *Confidentiality Agreement*, *Copyright Application Worksheet*, *License Agreement*, *Trademark Application Worksheet*, and *Trademark Violation Letter*. For each document, respond to the *Interview* questions with actual facts or hypothetical ones. For example, imagine that Alpha, Inc., is about to market a new computer and wants to include Beta Corporation's software on the computers as part of its marketing package. After you complete the *Interview* for each form, answer the following questions.

____ **1.** To grant Alpha permission to use its software, Beta should use

a. a licensing agreement.
b. a copyright application.
c. a confidentiality agreement.
d. a trademark application.

____ **2.** One of Alphas' employees, Carl, will be given the codes to Beta's software. To protect its codes, Beta should use

a. a licensing agreement.
b. a copyright application.
c. a confidentiality agreement.
d. a trademark application.

____ **3.** With each computer, Alpha includes a copy of *Alpha's Operating Guide*. To protect its rights in the guide, Alpha could use

a. a licensing agreement.
b. a copyright application.
c. a confidentiality agreement.
d. a trademark application.

____ **4.** To identify its products, Alpha uses a symbol of a miniature computer screen. To obtain protection for this symbol, Alpha could use

a. a licensing agreement.
b. a copyright application.
c. a confidentiality agreement.
d. a trademark application.

____ **5.** Gamma Company goes into business to market its own computer products, using a symbol almost identical to Alpha's miniature computer screen. To challenge this use, Alpha should send to Gamma

a. a licensing agreement.
b. a trademark violation letter.
c. a confidentiality agreement.
d. none of the above.

★ Learning Objectives

The learning objectives in this chapter include:

1. The difference between criminal offenses and other types of wrongful conduct.
2. The essential elements of criminal liability.
3. Constitutional safeguards that protect the rights of persons accused of crimes.
4. Crimes that affect business.
5. Defenses to criminal liability.

Chapter 6: Criminal Law

WHAT THIS CHAPTER IS ABOUT

This chapter defines what makes an act a crime, describes crimes that affect business, lists defenses to crimes, and outlines criminal procedure. Sanctions for crimes are different from those for torts or breaches of contract—this is just one difference between civil and criminal law. Another difference is that an individual can bring a civil suit, but only the government can prosecute a criminal.

CHAPTER OUTLINE

I. CIVIL LAW AND CRIMINAL LAW

A. CIVIL LAW

Civil law consists of the duties that exist between persons or between citizens and their governments, excluding the duty not to commit crimes.

B. CRIMINAL LAW

A **crime** is a wrong against society proclaimed in a statute and, if committed, punishable by society through fines, imprisonment, or death. Crimes are offenses against society as a whole and are prosecuted by public officials, not victims.

II. CLASSIFICATION OF CRIMES

Felonies are serious crimes punishable by death or by imprisonment in a federal or state penitentiary for more than a year. A crime that is not a felony is a **misdemeanor**—punishable by a fine or by confinement (in a local jail) for up to a year. Petty offenses are minor misdemeanors.

III. CRIMINAL LIABILITY

Two elements must exist for a person to be convicted of a crime:

A. A CRIMINAL ACT (*ACTUS REUS*)

A criminal statute prohibits certain behavior—an act of commission (doing something) or an act of omission (not doing something that is a legal duty).

B. AN INTENT TO COMMIT A CRIME (*MENS REA*)

The mental state required to establish criminal guilt depends on the crime.

IV. PROCEDURE IN CRIMINAL LAW

A. CONSTITUTIONAL SAFEGUARDS

Most of these safeguards apply not only in federal but also in state courts by virtue of the due process clause of the Fourteenth Amendment.

1. Fourth Amendment

Protection from unreasonable searches and seizures. No warrants for a search or an arrest can be issued without probable cause.

2. Fifth Amendment

No one can be deprived of "life, liberty, or property without due process of law." No one can be tried twice (double jeopardy) for the same offense. No one can be required to incriminate himself or herself.

3. Sixth Amendment

Guarantees a speedy trial, trial by jury, a public trial, the right to confront witnesses, and the right to a lawyer in some proceedings.

4. Eighth Amendment

Prohibits excessive bail and fines, and cruel and unusual punishment.

5. Exclusionary Rule

Evidence obtained in violation of the Fourth, Fifth, and Sixth Amendments, as well as all "fruit of the poisonous tree" (evidence derived from illegally obtained evidence), must be excluded.

6. *Miranda* Rule

A person in custody who is to be interrogated must be informed that he or she has the right to remain silent; anything said can and will be used against him or her in court; he or she has the right to consult with an attorney; and if he or she is indigent, a lawyer will be appointed.

B. CRIMINAL PROCESS

1. Arrest

Requires a warrant based on probable cause (a substantial likelihood that the person has committed or is about to commit a crime). To make an arrest without a warrant, an officer must also have probable cause.

2. Indictment or Information

A formal charge is called an **indictment** if issued by a grand jury and an **information** if issued by a public prosecutor.

3. Trial

Criminal trial procedures are similar to those of a civil trial, but the standard of proof is higher: the prosecutor must establish guilt beyond a reasonable doubt.

4. **Federal Sentencing Guidelines**
Federal sentencing guidelines set possible penalties for federal crimes. Judges impose a sentence based on a defendant's criminal record, the seriousness of the offense, and other factors.

V. CRIMES AFFECTING BUSINESS

A. FORGERY
Fraudulently making or altering any writing in a way that changes the legal rights and liabilities of another.

B. ROBBERY
Forcefully and unlawfully taking personal property from another.

C. BURGLARY
Unlawful entry into a building with the intent to commit a felony.

D. LARCENY
Wrongfully taking and carrying away another person's personal property with the intent of depriving the owner permanently of the property (without force or intimidation, which are elements of the crime of robbery).

1. **Property**
Property includes computer programs, computer time, trade secrets, cellular phone numbers, long-distance telephone time, and natural gas.

2. **Grand Larceny and Petit Larceny**
In some states, grand larceny is a felony and petit larceny a misdemeanor. The difference depends on the value of the property taken.

E. OBTAINING GOODS BY FALSE PRETENSES
Obtaining goods through fraud or deceit.

F. RECEIVING STOLEN GOODS
The recipient need not know the identity of the true owner of the goods.

G. EMBEZZLEMENT
Fraudulently appropriating another's property or money by one who has been entrusted with it (without force or intimidation).

H. ARSON
The willful and malicious burning, by fire or explosion, of a building (and in some states, personal property) owned by another. Every state has a statute that covers burning a building to collect insurance.

I. MAIL AND WIRE FRAUD

1. **The Crime**
It is a federal crime to (1) mail or cause someone else to mail something written, printed, or photocopied for the purpose of executing (2) a scheme to defraud. No one need actually be defrauded. It is also a crime to use wire, radio, or television transmissions to defraud.

2. **The Punishment**
Fine of up to $1,000, imprisonment for up to five years, or both. If the violation affects a financial institution, the fine may be up to $1 million, the imprisonment up to thirty years, or both.

J. COMPUTER CRIME

Computer crime is any act that is directed against computers or computer parts, that uses computers as instruments of crime, or that involves computers and constitutes abuse.

1. Types of Computer Crime

a. Financial Crimes
Unauthorized transfer of monies among accounts; unauthorized alteration of computer records.

b. Software Piracy
Theft of software; unauthorized copying of computer programs; rental, leasing, or lending of computer software without the express permission of the copyright holder.

c. Property Theft
Theft of computer equipment (hardware); theft of goods controlled or accounted for by means of a computer. Subject to the same criminal and tort laws as thefts of other property.

d. Vandalism and Destructive Programming
Smashing or damaging computer equipment; walking past computer storage banks with a large electromagnet; designing a computer program to rearrange, replace, or destroy data.

e. Theft of Data or Services
Using another's computer, computer information system, or data without authorization is larceny (theft).

2. Prosecuting Computer Crime

a. Federal Law
The Computer Access Device and Computer Fraud and Abuse Act of 1984 prohibits unauthorized use of certain information (restricted government info, info in a financial institution's records, info in a consumer reporting agency's files on consumers). Penalties include up to five years' imprisonment and a fine of up to $250,000, or twice the amount gained or lost from the crime.

b. State Law
Several states have laws addressing computer crime.

K. BRIBERY

1. Bribery of Public Officials

Attempting to influence a public official to act in a way that serves a private interest by offering the official a bribe. The crime is committed when the bribe (anything the recipient considers valuable) is offered.

2. Commercial Bribery

Attempting, by a bribe, to obtain proprietary information, cover up an inferior product, or secure new business.

3. Bribery of Foreign Officials

Attempting, by bribing foreign officials, to obtain business contracts. Prohibited by the Foreign Corrupt Practices Act of 1977 (see Chapter 3).

L. BANKRUPTCY FRAUD
Filing a false claim against a debtor; fraudulently transferring assets to favored parties; or fraudulently concealing property before or after a petition for bankruptcy is filed.

M. MONEY LAUNDERING
Transferring the proceeds of criminal acts through legitimate businesses.

N. INSIDER TRADING
Using inside information (information not available to the general public) about a publicly traded corporation to profit from the purchase or sale of the corporation's securities (see Chapter 27).

O. CRIMINAL RICO VIOLATIONS

1. The Crimes
The Racketeer Influenced and Corrupt Organizations Act (RICO) of 1970 prohibits (1) the use of legitimate business enterprises as shields for racketeering and (2) the purchase of a legitimate business interest with illegally obtained funds. (RICO is also discussed in Chapter 5.)

2. The Punishment
Fines of up to $25,000 per violation, imprisonment for up to twenty years, or both.

VI. DEFENSES TO CRIMES

A. INFANCY
In some states, children up to age seven are considered not to understand they are committing a crime. Children between seven and fourteen may be presumed incapable of committing a crime, but this can be rebutted.

B. INTOXICATION
Involuntary intoxication is a defense to a crime if it makes a person incapable of understanding that the act committed was wrong or incapable of obeying the law. *Voluntary* intoxication may be a defense if the person was so intoxicated as to lack the required state of mind.

C. INSANITY

1. The Model Penal Code Test
Most federal courts and some states use this test: A person is not responsible for criminal conduct if at the time, as a result of mental disease or defect, the person lacks substantial capacity either to appreciate the wrongfulness of the conduct or to conform his or her conduct to the law.

2. The *M'Naghten* Test
Some states use this test: A person is not responsible if at the time of the offense, he or she did not know the nature and quality of the act or did not know that the act was wrong.

3. The Irresistible Impulse Test
Some states use this test: A person operating under an irresistible impulse may know an act is wrong but cannot refrain from doing it.

D. MISTAKE

1. Mistake of Fact
Defense if it negates the mental state necessary to commit a crime.

2. **Mistake of Law**
A person not knowing a law was broken may have a defense if (1) the law was not published or reasonably made known to the public or (2) the person relied on an official statement of the law that was wrong.

E. **CONSENT**
Defense if it cancels the harm that the law is designed to prevent, unless the law forbids an act without regard to the victim's consent.

F. **DURESS**

1. **What Duress Is**
When a person's threat induces another person to perform an act that he or she would not otherwise perform.

2. **When Duress Is a Defense**
(1) The threat is one of serious bodily harm, (2) the threat is immediate and inescapable, (3) the threatened harm is greater than the harm caused by the crime, (4) the defendant is involved through no fault of his or her own, and (5) the crime is not murder.

G. **JUSTIFIABLE USE OF FORCE**

1. **Nondeadly Force**
People can use as much nondeadly force as seems necessary to protect themselves, their dwellings, or other property or to prevent a crime.

2. **Deadly Force**
Can be used in self-defense if there is a reasonable belief that imminent death or serious bodily harm will otherwise result, if the attacker is using unlawful force, and if the defender did not provoke the attack.

H. **ENTRAPMENT**
When a law enforcement agent suggests that a crime be committed, pressures or induces an individual to commit it, and arrests the individual for it.

I. **STATUTE OF LIMITATIONS**
Provides that the state has only a certain amount of time to prosecute a crime. Most statutes of limitations do not apply to murder.

J. **IMMUNITY**
A state can grant immunity from prosecution or agree to prosecute for a less serious offense in exchange for information. This is often part of a plea bargain between the defendant and the prosecutor.

TRUE-FALSE QUESTIONS

____ **1.** A crime is a wrong against society proclaimed in a statute.

____ **2.** A person can be convicted simply for intending to commit a crime.

____ **3.** If a crime is punishable by death, it must be a felony.

____ **4.** Children over age fourteen are presumed competent to stand trial.

____ **5.** Bill sees Tom sitting in Bill's car. Bill can tell Tom to get out of the car, but Bill may not normally use deadly force against Tom.

___ **6.** Under most statutes of limitations, states have only a certain amount of time to prosecute suspects on murder charges.

___ **7.** A person who has been granted immunity from prosecution cannot be compelled to answer any questions.

___ **8.** A person charged with a crime must prove his or her innocence beyond a reasonable doubt.

___ **9.** Burglary is the taking of another's personal property, from his or her person or immediate presence.

___ **10.** The willful and malicious burning of a building or some other structure owned by another is arson.

FILL-IN QUESTIONS

Specific constitutional safeguards for those accused of crimes apply in all federal courts, and most of them also apply in state courts under the due process clause of the Fourteenth Amendment. The safeguards include (1) the Fourth Amendment protection from ________________ (unexpected/unreasonable) searches and seizures, (2) the Fourth Amendment requirement that no warrants for a search or an arrest can be issued without ________________ (probable/possible) cause, (3) the Fifth Amendment requirement that no one can be deprived of "life, liberty, or property without ________________ (consent/due process of law)," (4) the Fifth Amendment prohibition against double ________________ (immunity/jeopardy), (5) the Sixth Amendment guaranties of a speedy ______________ (appeal/trial), ________________ (appeal to/trial by) a jury, a public trial, the right to confront ________________ (counsel/witnesses), and the right to legal counsel, and (6) the Eighth Amendment prohibitions against excessive ________________ (bail/bail and fines) and cruel and unusual punishment.

MULTIPLE-CHOICE QUESTIONS

___ **1.** Which of the following statements is TRUE?

a. Criminal defendants are prosecuted by the state.
b. Criminal defendants must prove their innocence.
c. Criminal law actions are intended to give the victims financial compensation.
d. A crime is never a violation of a statute.

___ **2.** Tina loans her skis to Doug. Tina's boy friend Tom sees a pair of skis in the back of Doug's truck and believes the skis are Tina's. He takes the skis to give to her. In fact, the skis belong to George. If arrested and charged with larceny, Tom may be acquitted because he acted under a mistake of

a. law.
b. fact.
c. both a and b.
d. none of the above.

___ **3.** Crime requires

a. the performance of a prohibited act.
b. the intent to commit a crime.
c. both a and b.
d. none of the above.

___ **4.** Karen kills Tony when she is drunk but sober enough to know what she is doing. If she is arrested and charged with murder, she will likely be

a. acquitted, because she was drunk when she killed Tony.
b. acquitted, because Tony should have recognized that she was drunk and avoided her.
c. acquitted, because intoxication negates an element of the crime of murder.
d. convicted.

___ **5.** Helen, an undercover police officer, pressures Pete to buy stolen goods. When he does so, he is arrested and charged with dealing in stolen goods. Pete will likely be

a. acquitted, because he was entrapped.
b. acquitted, because Helen was entrapped.
c. acquitted, because both parties were entrapped.
d. convicted.

___ **6.** Police officer Berry arrests John on suspicion of burglary. Berry advises John of his *Miranda* rights. These rights include that

a. John has the rights to remain silent and to consult with an attorney.
b. anything said can and will be used against John in court.
c. both a and b.
d. none of the above.

___ **7.** Probable cause means

a. a substantial likelihood.
b. a remote chance.
c. a certainty.
d. a better-than-even chance.

___ **8.** Sue is charged with car theft. Rob, the prosecutor, tells her that if she will inform on her criminal companions, he will grant her immunity. This is

a. an requisition.
b. an indictment.
c. a plea bargain.
d. none of the above.

___ **9.** In a jewelry store, April takes a diamond ring from the counter and puts it in her pocket. She walks three steps toward the door before the manager stops her. April is arrested and charged with larceny. She will likely be

a. acquitted, because she was entrapped.
b. acquitted, because she only took three steps.
c. acquitted, because she did not leave the store.
d. convicted.

___ **10.** Kevin takes home the company-owned laptop computer that he uses in his office. He has no intention of returning it. Kevin has committed

a. larceny.
b. embezzlement.
c. obtaining goods by false pretenses.
d. none of the above.

SHORT ESSAY QUESTIONS

What are some of the significant differences between criminal law and civil law?

ISSUE SPOTTERS

1. Bob drives off in Fred's car mistakenly believing that it is his. Is this theft?

2. Holding Gail's child by the arm, Frank threatens to kill the child unless Gail takes part in a convenience store robbery. If Gail participates, and is subsequently arrested and charged, could she be acquitted on the basis of Frank's threat to her child?

3. With Jim's permission, Lee signs Jim's name to several traveler's checks that were issued to Jim and cashes them. Jim reports that the checks were stolen and receives replacements. Has Lee committed forgery?

4. Jennifer takes her roommate's credit card, intending to charge expenses that she incurs on a vacation. Jennifer's first stop is a gas station, where she uses the card to pay for gas. With respect to the gas station, has Jennifer committed a crime? If so, what?

5. Carl appears on television talk shows touting a cure for AIDS that he knows is fraudulent, because it has no medical validity. He frequently mentions that he needs funds to make the cure widely available, and donations pour into local television stations to be forwarded to Carl. Has Carl committed a crime? If so, what?

★ **Learning Objectives**

The learning objectives in this chapter include:

1. The function of contract law.
2. The definition of the term *contract* and the basic elements that are required for contract formation.
3. The objective theory of contracts.
4. The types of contracts.
5. The rules that govern the courts' interpretation of contracts.

Chapter 7: Nature and Classification

WHAT THIS CHAPTER IS ABOUT

Contract law concerns the formation and keeping of promises, the excuses our society accepts for breaking such promises, and what promises are considered contrary to public policy and therefore legally void. This chapter introduces the basic terms and concepts of contract law, including the rules for interpreting contract language.

CHAPTER OUTLINE

I. THE FUNCTION OF CONTRACTS

A. ENFORCE PROMISES
Contract law assures the parties to private agreements that the promises they make will be enforceable.

B. AVOID PROBLEMS
The law of contracts is followed in business agreements to avoid problems.

C. SUPPORT THE EXISTENCE OF A MARKET ECONOMY
Businesspersons can usually rely on the good faith of others to keep their promises, but when price changes or adverse economic factors make it costly to comply with a promise, good faith may not be enough.

II. DEFINITION OF A CONTRACT

A. WHAT A CONTRACT IS
A **contract** is an agreement that can be enforced in court. It is formed by two or more parties who promise to perform or refrain from performing some act now or in the future.

B. THE OBJECTIVE THEORY OF CONTRACTS

Intention to enter into a contract is judged by objective (outward) facts as interpreted by a reasonable person, rather than by a party's subjective intention. Objective facts include (1) what the party said when entering into the contract, (2) how the party acted or appeared, and (3) the circumstances surrounding the transaction.

III. REQUIREMENTS OF A CONTRACT

A. THE ELEMENTS OF A CONTRACT

1. **Agreement**
   Includes an offer and an acceptance. One party must offer to enter into a legal agreement, and another party must accept the offer.

2. **Consideration**
   Promises must be supported by legally sufficient and bargained-for consideration.

3. **Contractual Capacity**
   Characteristics that qualify the parties to a contract as competent.

4. **Legality**
   A contract's purpose must be to accomplish a goal that is not against public policy.

B. DEFENSES TO THE ENFORCEMENT OF A CONTRACT

1. **Genuineness of Assent**
   The apparent consent of both parties must be genuine.

2. **Form**
   A contract must be in whatever form the law requires (some contracts must be in writing).

IV. FREEDOM OF CONTRACT AND FREEDOM FROM CONTRACT

A. FREEDOM OF CONTRACT

Generally, everyone may enter freely into contracts. This freedom is a strongly held public policy, and courts rarely interfere with contracts that have been voluntarily made.

B. FREEDOM FROM CONTRACT

Illegal bargains, agreements unreasonably in restraint of trade, and unfair contracts between one party with a great amount of bargaining power and another with little power are generally not enforced. Contracts are not enforceable if they are contrary to public policy, fairness, and justice.

V. TYPES OF CONTRACTS

A. BILATERAL VERSUS UNILATERAL CONTRACTS

1. **Bilateral Contract**
   A promise for a promise—to accept the offer, the offeree need only promise to perform.

2. **Unilateral Contract**
A promise for an act—the offeree can accept only by completing the contract performance. A problem arises when the promisor attempts to revoke the offer after the promisee has begun performance but before the act has been completed.

   a. **Revocation—Traditional View**
   The promisee can accept the offer only by performing fully. Offers are revocable until accepted.

   b. **Revocation—Modern View**
   The offer becomes irrevocable once performance begins. Thus, even though it has not yet been accepted, the offeror cannot revoke it.

B. EXPRESS VERSUS IMPLIED CONTRACTS

1. **Express Contract**
The terms of the agreement are fully and explicitly stated in words (oral or written).

2. **Implied-in-Fact Contract**
Implied from the conduct of the parties.

C. QUASI CONTRACTS—CONTRACTS IMPLIED IN LAW

In the absence of an actual contract, a quasi contract is imposed by a court to avoid the unjust enrichment of one party at the expense of another. Cannot be invoked if there is an actual contract that covers the area in controversy.

D. FORMAL VERSUS INFORMAL CONTRACTS

1. **Formal Contract**
Requires a special form or method of creation to be enforceable (such as a contract under seal, a formal writing with a special seal attached).

2. **Informal Contract**
All contracts that are not formal. Except for certain contracts that must be in writing, no special form is required.

E. EXECUTED VERSUS EXECUTORY CONTRACTS

1. **Executed Contract**
A contract that has been fully performed on both sides.

2. **Executory Contract**
A contract that has not been fully performed by one or more parties.

F. VALID, VOID, VOIDABLE, AND UNENFORCEABLE CONTRACTS

1. **Valid Contract**
Has all the elements necessary for contract formation.

2. **Void Contract**
Has no legal force or binding effect (for example, a contract is void if its purpose was illegal).

3. **Voidable Contract**
Valid contract that can be avoided by one or more parties (for example, contracts by minors are voidable at the minor's option).

4. **Unenforceable Contract**
Contract that cannot be enforced because of certain legal defenses (for example, if a contract that must be in writing is not in writing).

VI. INTERPRETATION OF CONTRACTS

Rules of contract interpretation provide guidelines for determining the meaning of contracts. The primary purpose of these rules is to determine the parties' intent from the language of their agreement and to give effect to that intent.

A. THE PLAIN MEANING RULE

When the writing is clear and unequivocal, it will be enforced according to its plain terms. The meaning of the terms is determined from the written document alone.

B. OTHER RULES OF INTERPRETATION

When the writing contains unclear terms, courts use the following rules—

1. A reasonable, lawful, and effective meaning is given to all terms.
2. A contract is interpreted as a whole; individual, specific clauses are considered subordinate to the contract's general intent. All writings that are part of the same transaction are interpreted together.
3. Terms that were negotiated separately are given greater consideration than standard terms and terms that were not negotiated separately.
4. A word is given its ordinary, common meaning, and a technical word its technical meaning, unless the parties clearly intended otherwise.
5. Specific, exact wording is given greater weight than general language.
6. Written or typewritten terms prevail over preprinted ones.
7. When the language has more than one meaning, it is interpreted against the party who drafted the contract.
8. Evidence of trade usage, prior dealing, and course of performance may be admitted to clarify meaning.

C. PLAIN-LANGUAGE LAWS

The federal government and most states require an agreement to be written clearly, coherently, and in words of common, everyday meaning.

TRUE-FALSE QUESTIONS

___ 1. All contracts involve promises, and every promise is a legal contract.

___ 2. An agreement includes an offer and an acceptance.

___ 3. Consideration, in contract terms, refers to the competency of a party to enter into a contract.

___ 4. A unilateral contract involves performance instead of promises.

___ 5. Formal contracts are contracts between parties who are in formal relationships—employer-employee relationships, for example.

___ 6. An unenforceable contract is a contract in which one or both of the parties has the option of avoiding his or her legal obligations.

___ 7. Under the plain meaning rule, a court will enforce a contract as it is written, regardless of any previous contracts between the parties.

___ 8. When the language in a contract has more than one meaning, it will be interpreted against the party who drafted the contract.

___ 9. If outside evidence is admissible to interpret an ambiguous contract, express terms are given the greatest weight.

___ 10. A quasi contract is imposed by a court to avoid the unjust enrichment of one party at the expense of another.

FILL-IN QUESTIONS

Whether or not a party intended to enter into a contract is determined by the ________________ (objective/subjective) theory of contracts. The theory is that a party's intention to enter into a contract is judged by ________________ (objective/subjective) facts as they would be interpreted by a reasonable person. Relevant facts include: (1) what the party said; (2) what the party ________________ (did/secretly believed); and (3) the ________________ (circumstances surrounding/party's personal thoughts concerning) the transaction. Generally, courts examine facts in ________________ (a particular transaction/similar transactions) to determine whether the parties made a contract and, if so, what its terms are.

MULTIPLE-CHOICE QUESTIONS

___ 1. Freedom of contract

a. refers to the right of certain persons to freely get out of their contracts.
b. refers to the right of most persons to freely enter into contracts.
c. is a concept no longer enforced by law.
d. is considered incompatible with public policy, fairness, and justice.

___ 2. Don contracts with Jan to paint Jan's townhouse while she's on vacation. By mistake, Don paints Mick's townhouse. Mick sees Don painting but says nothing. Who can Don recover from?

a. Jan, because she was the party with whom Don contracted
b. Jan, under the theory of quasi contract
c. Mick, because his house was painted
d. Mick, under the theory of quasi contract

___ 3. Brian offers to sell Ashley his CD-ROM collection, forgetting that he does not want to sell some of the disks. Unaware of Brian's forgetfulness, Ashley accepts. Is there a contract including all of Brian's disks?

a. Yes, according to the objective theory of contracts
b. Yes, according to the subjective theory of contracts
c. No, because Brian did not intend to sell his favorite disks
d. No, because Ashley had no reason to know of Brian's forgetfulness

___ **4.** Greg promises to imprint four thousand t-shirts with Rona's logo. Rona pays in advance. Before Greg delivers the shirts, the contract is classified as

a. executory, because it is executory on Greg's part.
b. executory, because it is executory on Rona's part.
c. executed, because it is executed on Greg's part.
d. none of the above.

___ **5.** Without agreeing as to payment, Mary accepts the services of Lee, an accountant, and is pleased with the work. Is there a contract between them?

a. Yes, there is an express contract.
b. Yes, there is an implied-in-fact contract.
c. No, because they made no agreement concerning payment
d. Yes, there is an implied-in-law contract.

___ **6.** The requirements of a contract include

a. agreement.
b. consideration.
c. both a and b.
d. none of the above.

___ **7.** When considering the rules that govern courts' interpretation of contracts, the most important principle to keep in mind is that

a. the law attempts to enforce the contract that the parties made.
b. when parties put their contract in writing, there is nothing to interpret.
c. if contract language is ambiguous, the law will void the contract.
d. specific clauses are more important than the contract as a whole.

___ **8.** If there is a conflict between a contract's standardized terms and terms that were the subject of separate negotiation

a. the standardized terms will prevail.
b. the terms that were the subject of separate negotiation will prevail.
c. a court will rewrite the terms to make them consistent.
d. none of the above.

___ **9.** Sam contracts with Hugo's Sports Equipment to buy a jet ski and to pay for it in installments. Sam is a minor, and so he can choose to avoid his contractual obligations. The contract between Sam and Hugo is

a. valid.
b. void.
c. voidable.
d. both a and c.

___ **10.** A contract consists of promises between two or more parties to

a. refrain from performing some act.
b. perform some act in the future.
c. perform some act now.
d. any of the above.

SHORT ESSAY QUESTIONS

1. List and define the basic elements of a contract.

2. What is the function of contract law?

ISSUE SPOTTERS

1. Shorty signs and returns a letter from Buck referring to a certain saddle and its price. When Buck delivers the saddle, Shorty sends it back, claiming that they have no contract. Buck claims that they do have a contract. Do they?

2. Alison receives from the local tax collector a notice of property taxes due. The notice is for tax on Jerry's property, but Alison believes that the tax is hers and pays it. Can Alison recover from Jerry the amount that she paid?

3. Dick tells Ben that he will pay Ben $1,500 to set fire to Dick's store, so that Dick can collect money under his fire insurance policy. Ben sets fire to the store, but Dick refuses to pay. Can Ben enforce this deal?

4. Henry and Rich negotiate an employment contract. The first draft is a standard printed contract. Clause 9 reads that no vacations can be taken in December. Beneath the clause in the final draft is written, in ink, "Only one-week vacations can be taken in December." If a dispute arises about December vacations, which term controls?

5. Lou applies for a credit card with the First National Bank under a contract specifying that the customer is liable for charges made on a lost or stolen card "until the card issuer is notified of the card's loss." Lou loses his card. When his bank statement shows purchases that he did not make, he tells the bank that he won't pay for any of those items. He contends that the contract means that once the bank is notified of a card's loss, a customer is no longer liable. Would a court agree with Lou?

QUICKEN CD-ROM
BUSINESS LAW PARTNER APPLICATIONS

Open **Quicken Business Law Partner**. Click on the *New Documents* icon. Choose the *Bill of Sale, Bill of Sale—Motor Vehicle,* and *General Receipt*. For each document, respond to the *Interview* questions with actual facts or hypothetical ones. For example, imagine that Ann wants to sell to Bob a personal computer and a sport-utility vehicle, and to give Bob temporary possession of her mountain bike. After you complete the *Interview* for each form, answer the following questions.

___ 1. To sell Bob the personal computer, Ann should use

a. a bill of sale.
b. a bill of sale for a motor vehicle.
c. a general receipt.
d. none of the above.

____ **2.** To give Bob temporary possession of the mountain bike, Ann should use

a. a bill of sale.
b. a bill of sale for a motor vehicle.
c. a general receipt.
d. none of the above.

____ **3.** A sale of personal property under a bill of sale is

a. an express contract.
b. an implied contract.
c. a quasi contract.
d. none of the above.

____ **4.** A general receipt for a gift is

a. an express contract.
b. an implied contract.
c. a quasi contract.
d. none of the above.

____ **5.** A sale of personal property in which the parties orally agree to the terms but do not put anything in writing is

a. an express contract.
b. an implied contract.
c. a quasi contract.
d. none of the above.

QUICKEN BUSINESS LAW PARTNER ENHANCEMENT: EXPLORING THE PERSONAL LAW HANDBOOK

Personal Law Handbook, within Topic 4, Owning and Operating Motor Vehicles, the first three sections (*Buying a New Car, Buying or Selling a Used Car,* and *Renting or Leasing a Car*) give you a useful review of the law behind buying, selling, renting, and leasing a car.

★ Learning Objectives

The learning objectives in this chapter include:

1. The elements of contractual agreement.
2. The requirements of an offer.
3. How an offer is accepted.
4. The elements of consideration.
5. Circumstances in which a promise is enforced despite a lack of consideration.

Chapter 8: Agreement and Consideration

WHAT THIS CHAPTER IS ABOUT

An agreement is the essence of every contract. The parties to a contract are the **offeror** (who makes an offer) and the **offeree** (to whom the offer is made). If, through the process of offer and acceptance, an agreement is reached, and the other elements are present (consideration, capacity, legality), a valid contract is formed.

Good reasons for enforcing promises include a benefit that the promisor received and a detriment that the promisee incurred. These are referred to as *consideration*. No contract is enforceable without it. This chapter outlines the concepts and principles of agreement and consideration.

CHAPTER OUTLINE

I. AGREEMENT

The elements of an agreement are an offer and an acceptance—one party offers a bargain to another, who accepts.

A. REQUIREMENTS OF THE OFFER

An **offer** is a promise or commitment to do or refrain from doing some specified thing in the future. An offer has three elements—

1. Intention

The offeror must intend to be bound by the offer.

a. How to Determine the Offeror's Intent

The offeror's intent is what a reasonable person in the offeree's position would conclude the offeror's words and actions meant. Offers in obvious anger, jest, or undue excitement do not qualify.

b. What Does Not Constitute an Offer?
Nonoffers include: (1) expressions of opinion, (2) statements of intention, (3) preliminary negotiations, and (4) advertisements, catalogues, price lists, and circulars. Auctions are a special situation—the bidder is the offeror; the seller is the offeree.

c. Agreements to Agree
Agreements to agree to a material term of a contract at some future date may be enforced if the parties clearly intended to be bound.

2. Definiteness
All of the major terms must be stated with reasonable definiteness in the offer (or, if the offeror directs, in the offeree's acceptance).

3. Communication
The offeree must know of the offer.

B. TERMINATION OF THE OFFER

1. Termination by Action of the Parties

a. Revocation of the Offer
The offeror usually can revoke the offer (even if he or she has promised to keep it open), by express repudiation or by acts that are inconsistent with the offer and that are made known to the offeree.

1) Communicated to the Offeree
A revocation becomes effective when the offeree or offeree's agent receives it.

2) Offers to the General Public
An offer made to the general public can be revoked in the same manner the offer was originally communicated.

b. Irrevocable Offers

1) When an Offeree Changes Position in Justifiable Reliance
The offer may not be revoked, under the doctrine of promissory estoppel (see below).

2) A Merchant's Firm Offer
The offer may be irrevocable (see Chapter 13).

3) Option Contract
An option contract is a promise to hold an offer open for a period of time. If no time is specified, a reasonable time is implied.

c. Rejection of the Offer by the Offeree
An offer may be rejected by the offeree by words or conduct evidencing an intent not to accept. A rejection is effective on receipt. Asking about an offer is not a rejection.

d. Counteroffer by the Offeree
The offeree's attempt to include different terms is a rejection of the original offer and a simultaneous making of a new offer. The **mirror image rule** requires the acceptance to match the offer exactly.

2. **Termination by Operation of Law**

   a. **Lapse of Time**
   An offer terminates automatically when the period of time specified in the offer has passed.

      1) **When the Time Begins to Run**
      When the offer is received by the offeree. If it is delayed, the period runs from the date the offeree would have received it (if the offeree knows or should know of the delay).

      2) **If No Time Is Specified**
      If no time is specified , a reasonable time is implied.

   b. **Destruction of the Subject Matter**
   An offer is automatically terminated.

   c. **Death or Incompetence of the Offeror or Offeree**
   An offeree's power of acceptance is terminated. Exceptions include irrevocable offers (see above).

   d. **Supervening Illegality of the Proposed Contract**
   When a statute or court decision makes an offer illegal, the offer is automatically terminated.

C. ACCEPTANCE

1. **Who Can Accept?**
Usually, only the offeree (or the offeree's agent) can accept.

2. **Unequivocal Acceptance**
The offeree must accept the offer unequivocally. This is the mirror image rule (see above).

3. **Silence as Acceptance**
Ordinarily, silence cannot operate as an acceptance. Silence or inaction can constitute acceptance in the following circumstances—

   a. **Receipt of Offered Services**
   If an offeree receives the benefit of offered services even though he or she had an opportunity to reject them and knew that they were offered with the expectation of compensation.

   b. **Prior Dealings**
   The offeree had prior dealings with the offeror that lead the offeror to understand silence will constitute acceptance.

4. **Communication of Acceptance**

   a. **Bilateral Contract**
   A bilateral contract is formed when acceptance is communicated. The offeree must use reasonable efforts to communicate acceptance.

   b. **Unilateral Contract**
   Communication is normally unnecessary, unless the offeror requests it or has no way of knowing the act has been performed.

5. **Mode and Timeliness of Acceptance in Bilateral Contracts**
Acceptance is timely if it is made before the offer is terminated.

a. **Authorized Means of Acceptance**
If an offeree uses a mode of communication expressly or impliedly authorized by the offeror, acceptance is effective on dispatch. This is the **mailbox rule** (deposited acceptance rule).

1) **Express**
When an offeror specifies how acceptance should be made and the offeree uses that mode, the acceptance is effective even if the offeror never receives it.

2) **Implied**
When an offeror does not specify how acceptance should be made, the offeree may use the same means the offeror used to make the offer or a faster means.

3) **Exceptions**

a) If an acceptance is not properly dispatched, in most states it will not be effective until it is received.

b) If an offeror conditions an offer on receipt of acceptance by a certain time, acceptance is effective only on timely receipt.

c) If both a rejection and an acceptance are sent, whichever is received first is effective.

b. **Unauthorized Means of Acceptance**
If an offeree uses a mode of communication that was not authorized by the offeror, acceptance is effective when received.

II. CONSIDERATION AND ITS REQUIREMENTS

Consideration is the value given in return for a promise.

A. ELEMENTS OF CONSIDERATION

There are two elements to consideration—

1. **Something of Legal Value**
Something of legal value must be given in exchange for a promise.

a. **Promise, Act, or Forbearance**
It may be (1) a promise to do something that one had no legal duty to do, (2) performing an act that one had no legal duty to perform, or (3) refraining from doing something that one could otherwise do.

b. **Legal Sufficiency**
What is exchanged for a promise must be (1) legally detrimental to the promisee or (2) legally beneficial to the promisor.

2. **A Bargained-for Exchange**
The consideration given by the promisor must induce the promisee to incur legal detriment, and the detriment incurred must induce the promisor to make the promise. A gift does not have this element.

B. ADEQUACY OF CONSIDERATION

Adequacy of consideration refers to the fairness of a bargain. Normally, a court will not question the adequacy of consideration.

1. **Extreme Cases**
Extremely inadequate consideration may indicate fraud, duress, incapacity, undue influence, or a lack of bargained-for exchange.

2. **Unconscionability**
A contract may be unconscionable (and unenforceable) if consideration is so one-sided under the circumstances as to be unfair. (See Chapter 9.)

C. CONTRACTS THAT LACK CONSIDERATION

1. **Preexisting Duty**
A promise to do what one already has a legal duty to do does not constitute consideration (no legal detriment is incurred). Exceptions include—

   a. **Unforeseen Difficulties**
   If a party runs into extraordinary difficulties that were unforeseen when a contract was formed, some courts will enforce an agreement to pay more. Ordinary business risks are not included.

   b. **Rescission and New Contract**
   The parties can rescind a contract to the extent that it is executory.

2. **Past Consideration**
An act already done cannot be consideration for a later promise.

3. **Illusory Promises**
If a contract expresses such uncertainty of performance that the promisor has not definitely promised anything, it is unenforceable.

D. SETTLEMENT OF CLAIMS

1. **Accord and Satisfaction**
Concerns a debtor's offer of payment and a creditor's acceptance of a lesser amount than the creditor originally purported to be owed.

   a. **Accord**
   The agreement under which one of the parties undertakes to give or perform, and the other to accept, in satisfaction of a claim, something other than that which was originally agreed on.

   b. **Satisfaction**
   Takes place when the accord is executed.

   c. **The Amount of the Debt Must Be Unliquidated (in Dispute)**

      1) **Unliquidated Debt—Consideration**
      When the amount of a debt is in dispute, acceptance of a lesser sum discharges the debt. Consideration is given by the parties' giving up a legal right to contest the amount of debt.

      2) **Liquidated Debt—No Consideration**
      Acceptance of less than the entire amount of a liquidated debt is not satisfaction, and the balance of the debt is still owed. No consideration is given by the debtor, because he or she has a preexisting obligation to pay the entire debt.

2. **Release**
A **release** (a promise to refrain from pursuing a valid claim) bars any further recovery beyond the terms stated in the release. Releases are

generally binding if they are (1) given in good faith, (2) stated in a signed writing, and (3) accompanied by consideration.

3. **Covenant Not to Sue**
The parties substitute a contractual obligation for some other type of legal action based on a valid claim. If the obligation is not met, an action can be brought for breach of contract.

E. **PROMISES ENFORCEABLE WITHOUT CONSIDERATION**
Under the doctrine of **promissory estoppel** (detrimental reliance), a person who relies on the promise of another may be able to recover if—

1. The promise was clear and definite.
2. The reliance is justifiable.
3. The reliance is of a substantial and definite character.
4. Justice will be better served by enforcement of the promise.

TRUE-FALSE QUESTIONS

___ 1. The seriousness of an offeror's intent is determined by what a reasonable offeree would conclude the offeror's words and actions meant.

___ 2. A contract providing that Joe is to pay Bill "a fair share of the profits" will be enforced.

___ 3. A simple rejection of an offer will terminate it.

___ 4. Offers that must be kept open for a period of time include advertisements.

___ 5. The mirror image rule is an old common law rule that no longer applies.

___ 6. If an offeree is silent, he or she can never be considered to have accepted an offer.

___ 7. Ordinarily, courts evaluate the adequacy or fairness of consideration even if the consideration is legally sufficient.

___ 8. A promise to do what one already has a legal duty to do is not legally sufficient consideration under most circumstances.

___ 9. Promises made with consideration based on events that have already taken place are fully enforceable.

___ 10. Rescission is the unmaking of a contract so as to return the parties to the positions they occupied before the contract was made.

FILL-IN QUESTIONS

The elements necessary for an effective offer are (1) a ______________ (serious/subjective) intent by the ______________ (offeror/offeree) to be bound by the offer; (2) ______________ (detailed/reasonably definite) contractual terms; and (3) communication of the offer to the ______________ (offeror/offeree).

MULTIPLE-CHOICE QUESTIONS

___ 1. Kelly mails to Pat an offer to sell her computer, stating that Pat has thirty days to accept. Pat immediately mails a letter of rejection. After reconsidering, Pat mails a letter of acceptance within the time permitted by the offer. Which of the following is TRUE?

a. The rejection is effective because Pat mailed it first.
b. The acceptance is effective if Kelly receives it first.
c. The acceptance has no effect, because a rejection, whenever mailed, voids a deal.
d. None of the above

___ 2. Before opening her new sports merchandise store, Kate places an ad in the newspaper showing cross-training shoes at certain prices. Within hours of opening for business, the store is sold out of some of the shoes. Gene arrives later and is angry that a specific shoe is sold out. Gene sues Kate. Kate will

a. win, because the ad was only an invitation seeking offers.
b. lose, because the ad was an offer that Gene accepted.
c. lose, because anyone who offered money for the shoes was entitled to buy.
d. win, because the ad was run before she was open for business.

___ 3. Icon Properties, Inc., makes an offer in a letter to Bob to sell a certain lot for $30,000, with the offer to stay open for thirty days. Bob would prefer to pay $25,000, if Icon would sell at that price. What should Bob reply to Icon to leave room for negotiation without rejecting the offer?

a. "I will not pay $30,000."
b. "Will you take $25,000?"
c. "I will pay $25,000."
d. "I will pay $27,500."

___ 4. Julio offers to sell Christine a used computer for $400. Which of the following replies would constitute an acceptance?

a. "I accept. Please send a written contract."
b. "I accept, if you send a written contract."
c. "I accept, if I can pay in monthly installments."
d. None of the above

___ 5. John's car is hit by Ben's truck. A doctor tells John that he will be disabled only temporarily. Ben's insurance company offers John $5,000 to settle his claim. John accepts and signs a release. Later, John learns that he is permanently disabled. John sues Ben and the insurance company. John will

a. win, because John did not know when he signed the release that the disability was permanent.
b. win, because Ben caused the accident.
c. lose, because John signed a written release—no fraud was involved, and consideration was given.
d. none of the above.

____ **6.** Bill makes an offer to Ann. If Bill dies before Ann can reply, the offer

a. remains open.
b. remains open until Ann learns of Julio's death.
c. terminates immediately.
d. none of the above.

____ **7.** Dwight offers to buy a book owned by Lee for $40. Lee accepts and hands the book to Dwight. The transfer and delivery of the book constitute performance. Is this performance consideration for Dwight's promise?

a. Yes, because performance always constitutes consideration.
b. Yes, because Dwight sought it in exchange for his promise, and Lee gave it in exchange for that promise.
c. No, because performance never constitutes consideration.
d. No, because Lee already had a duty to hand the book to Dwight.

____ **8.** Max agrees to supervise a construction project for Al for a certain fee. In mid-project, without an excuse, Max removes the plans from the site and refuses to continue. Al promises to increase Max's fee. Max returns to work. Is going back to work consideration for the promise to increase the fee?

a. Yes, because performance always constitutes consideration.
b. Yes, because Al sought it in exchange for his promise.
c. No, because performance never constitutes consideration.
d. No, because Max already had a duty to supervise the project.

____ **9.** Shannon contracts with Dan to build two houses on two lots. After building the first house, they decide that they would prefer to build a garage instead of a house on the second lot. Under these circumstances

a. they must build the second house—a contract must be fully executed.
b. they can rescind their contract and make a new contract to build a garage.
c. the contract to build two houses is illusory.
d. none of the above.

____ **10.** Mike promises that next year he will sell Kim a certain house, allowing her to live in it until then. Kim puts a new roof on the house, repairs the heating system, and landscapes the property. The next year, Mike tells Kim he's decided to keep the house. Who is entitled to the house?

a. Kim, under the doctrine of promissory estoppel.
b. Kim, because Mike's decision to keep the house is an unforeseen difficulty.
c. Mike, because his promise to sell Kim the house was illusory.
d. Mike, because he initially stated only his intention to sell.

SHORT ESSAY QUESTIONS

1. Define "offer" and state the elements necessary for an effective offer.

2. Define "consideration," list its elements, and explain what, in this context, is "legal sufficiency."

ISSUE SPOTTERS

1. One morning, when Jane's new car—with an $18,000 market value—doesn't start, she yells in anger, "I'd sell this car to anyone for $5." If you drop $5 in her lap, is the car yours?

2. Fidelity Corporation offers to hire Ron to replace Monica, who has given Fidelity a month's notice of intent to quit. Fidelity gives Ron a week to decide whether to accept. Two days later, Monica signs an employment contract with Fidelity for another year. The next day, Monica tells Ron of the new contract. Ron immediately sends a formal letter of acceptance to Fidelity. Do Fidelity and Ron have a contract?

3. In September, Sharon agrees to work for Cole Productions, Inc., at $500 a week for a year beginning January 1. In October, Sharon is offered the same work at $600 a week by Quintero Shows, Ltd. When Sharon tells Cole about the other offer, they tear up their contract and agree that Sharon will be paid $575. Is the new contract binding?

4. Rick, the president of Pye Corporation, announces to Pye employees that "if you work hard, and profits remain high, you'll get a bonus, if management thinks it's warranted." Profits remain high, but no bonus is paid. If the employees sue, would a court enforce the promise?

5. Before Mary starts her first year of college, Fred promises to give her $5,000 when she graduates. She goes to college, borrowing and spending far more than $5,000. At the beginning of the spring semester of her senior year, she reminds Fred of the promise. Fred sends her a note that says, "I revoke the promise." Is Fred's promise binding?

★ **Learning Objectives**

The learning objectives in this chapter include:

1. The contractual rights and obligations of minors.
2. How intoxication affects contractual liability.
3. The effects of mental incompetency on contractual liability.
4. Some contracts that are contrary to state or federal statutes.
5. The enforceability of contracts and clauses that are contrary to public policy.

Chapter 9: Capacity and Legality

WHAT THIS CHAPTER IS ABOUT

If a party to a contract lacks capacity, an essential element for a valid contract is missing, and the contract is void. Some persons have capacity to enter into a contract, but if they wish, they can avoid liability under the contract. Also, to be enforceable, a contract must not violate any statutes or public policy.

CHAPTER OUTLINE

I. CONTRACTUAL CAPACITY

A. MINORS

A minor can enter into any contract that an adult can enter into, as long as it is not prohibited by law (for example, the sale of alcoholic beverages).

1. Right to Disaffirm

A minor can disaffirm a contract by manifesting an intent not to be bound. A contract can ordinarily be disaffirmed at any time during minority or for a reasonable time after a minor comes of age.

2. Duty of Restitution

A minor cannot disaffirm a fully executed contract without returning whatever goods have been received or paying their reasonable value.

a. What the Adult Recovers

1) In Most States

If the goods (or other consideration) are in the minor's control, the minor must return them (without added compensation).

2) **In a Growing Number of States**
If the goods have been used, damaged, or ruined, the adult must be restored to the position he or she held before the contract.

b. **What the Minor Recovers**
All property that a minor has transferred to an adult as consideration, even if it is in the hands of a third party. If the property cannot be returned, the adult must pay the minor its value.

3. **Disaffirmance and Misrepresentation of Age**

a. **In Most States**
A minor who misrepresents his or her age can still disaffirm a contract. In some states, he or she is not liable for fraud, because indirectly that might force the minor to perform the contract.

b. **In Some States**
Some states prohibit disaffirmance; some courts refuse to allow minors to disaffirm executed contracts unless they can return the consideration; some courts allow a minor to disaffirm but hold the minor liable for damages for fraud.

4. **Liability for Necessaries**
Necessaries are food, clothing, shelter, medicine, and hospital care—whatever a court believes is necessary to maintain a person's status. A minor may disaffirm a contract for necessaries but will be liable for the reasonable value.

5. **Ratification**
Ratification is the act of accepting and thereby giving legal force to an obligation that was previously unenforceable.

a. **Express Ratification**
When a minor states orally or in writing that he or she intends to be bound by a contract.

b. **Implied Ratification**
When a minor performs acts inconsistent with disaffirmance or fails to disaffirm an executed contract within a reasonable time after reaching the age of majority.

6. **Parents' Liability**
Generally, parents are not liable for contracts made by their minor children acting on their own.

7. **Emancipation**
Minors, over whom parents have relinquished control, have full contractual capacity and do not have the right to disaffirm.

B. INTOXICATED PERSONS

1. **If a Person Is Sufficiently Intoxicated to Lack Mental Capacity**
Any contract he or she enters into is voidable at the option of the intoxicated person, even if the intoxication was voluntary.

2. **If a Person Understands the Legal Consequences of a Contract**
Despite intoxication, the contract is usually enforceable.

C. MENTALLY INCOMPETENT PERSONS

1. Persons Adjudged Mentally Incompetent by a Court
If a person has been adjudged mentally incompetent by a court of law and a guardian has been appointed, a contract by the person is void.

2. Incompetent Persons Not So Adjudged by a Court

a. Those Who Do Not Understand Their Contracts
A contract is voidable (at the option of the person) if a person does not know he or she is entering into the contract or lacks the capacity to comprehend its nature, purpose, and consequences.

b. Those Who Understand Their Contracts
If a mentally incompetent person understands the nature and effect of entering into a certain contract, the contract will be valid.

II. LEGALITY

A. CONTRACTS CONTRARY TO STATUTE

1. Usury
All states limit the rate of interest that may be charged for a loan.

2. Gambling
All states regulate gambling.

3. Sabbath (Sunday) Laws

a. Prohibited Contracts
In some states, all contracts entered into on a Sunday are illegal. Other states prohibit only the sale of certain merchandise (such as alcoholic beverages) on a Sunday.

b. Exceptions
Contracts for necessities and works of charity; executed contracts.

4. Licensing Statutes
In some states, the lack of a required business license bars the enforcement of work-related contracts.

a. Illegal Contracts
If the statute's purpose is to protect the public from unauthorized practitioners, a contract with an unlicensed individual is illegal.

b. Enforceable Contracts
If the purpose of the statute is to raise revenue, a contract entered into with an unlicensed practitioner is enforceable.

B. CONTRACTS CONTRARY TO PUBLIC POLICY

1. Contracts in Restraint of Trade
Competition in the economy is favored so contracts that restrain trade or violate an antitrust statute are prohibited.

a. Covenant Not to Compete
Enforceable if it is reasonable, determined by the length of time and the size of the area in which the party agrees not to compete.

b. **Reformation of an Illegal Covenant Not to Compete**
A court may reform an unreasonable covenant not to compete by changing it to reflect the true intentions of the parties.

2. **Unconscionable Contracts or Clauses**
A bargain that is unfairly one-sided is **unconscionable**.

a. **Procedural Unconscionability**
Relates to a party's lack of knowledge or understanding of contract terms because of small print, "legalese," etc. An **adhesion contract** (drafted by one party for his benefit) may be held unconscionable.

b. **Substantive Unconscionability**
Relates to the parts of a contract that are so unfairly one-sided they "shock the conscience" of the court.

3. **Exculpatory Clauses**
Contract clauses attempting to release parties of negligence or other wrongs. Usually held to be contrary to public policy.

C. THE EFFECT OF ILLEGALITY

1. **The General Rule**
An illegal contract is void. No party can sue to enforce it and no party can recover for its breach.

2. **Exceptions**

a. **Justifiable Ignorance of the Facts**
A party who is innocent may recover benefits conferred in a partially executed contract or enforce a fully performed contract.

b. **Members of Protected Classes**
When a statute is designed to protect a certain class of people, a member of that class can enforce a contract in violation of the statute (the other party to the contract cannot enforce it).

c. **Withdrawal from an Illegal Agreement**
If the illegal part of an agreement has not been performed, the party rendering performance can withdraw and recover the performance or its value.

d. **Fraud, Duress, or Undue Influence**
A party induced to enter into an illegal bargain by fraud, duress, or undue influence can enforce the contract or recover for its value.

TRUE-FALSE QUESTIONS

___ 1. An adult who enters into a contract with a minor cannot generally avoid the contract.

___ 2. When a minor disaffirms a contract, whatever the minor transferred as consideration (or its value) normally must be returned.

___ 3. A person who is so intoxicated as to lack mental capacity when he or she enters into a contract must perform the contract even if the other party has reason to know of the intoxication.

___ **4.** Emancipation has no effect on a minor's contractual capacity.

___ **5.** If an individual who has not been judged mentally incompetent understands the nature and effect of entering into a certain contract, the contract is normally valid.

___ **6.** An exculpatory clause may not be enforced.

___ **7.** An adhesion contract will never be deemed unconscionable.

___ **8.** An illegal contract is valid unless it is executory.

___ **9.** If the purpose of a licensing statute is to protect the public from unlicensed practitioners, a contract entered into with an unlicensed practitioner is unenforceable.

___ **10.** Covenants not to compete are never enforceable.

FILL-IN QUESTIONS

The act of accepting and giving legal force to an obligation that previously was not enforceable is ______________________ (disaffirmance/ratification). In relation to contracts entered into by minors or persons who are intoxicated or mentally incompetent, this is an act or an expression in words by which the person, on or after reaching majority or regaining sobriety or mental competence, indicates intent to be bound by a contract.

Disaffirmance or ratification may be express or implied. For example, a person's continued use and payments on something bought when he or she was incompetent is inconsistent with a desire to ______________________ (disaffirm/ratify) and ______________________ (indicates/does not indicate) an intent to be bound by the contract. In general, any act or conduct showing an intent to affirm the contract will be deemed ______________________ (disaffirmance/ratification).

MULTIPLE-CHOICE QUESTIONS

___ **1.** On May 1, Ellen, a seventeen-year-old minor, misrepresents her age as twenty to buy a used car from Don. On May 5, Ellen has an accident and the car is destroyed. The next day, Ellen tells Don that she is disaffirming the contract. In most states, Ellen could

a. disaffirm, but could be held liable in tort for damage to the car.
b. disaffirm only if she could return the consideration received (the car).
c. not disaffirm.
d. all of the above.

___ **2.** Troy, a minor, sells to Vern his collection of sports memorabilia for $250. On his eighteenth birthday, Troy learns that the collection may have been worth at least $2,500. Troy can

a. disaffirm, because the contract has not been fully performed.
b. disaffirm, if Troy does so within a reasonable time of attaining majority.
c. not disaffirm, because Troy has already attained majority.
d. not disaffirm, because the contract has been fully performed.

___ **3.** Doug has been drinking heavily. Joe offers to buy Doug's farm for a fair price. Believing the deal is a joke, Doug writes and signs an agreement to sell and gives it to Joe. Joe believes the deal is serious. The contract is

a. enforceable, if the circumstances indicate Doug understands what he did.
b. enforceable, because Joe believes that the transaction is serious.
c. unenforceable, because the intoxication permits Doug to avoid the contract.
d. unenforceable, because Doug thinks it is a joke.

___ **4.** Ed is adjudged mentally incompetent. Irwin is appointed to act as Ed's guardian. Irwin signs a contract to sell some of Ed's property to pay for Ed's care. On regaining competency, Ed can

a. disaffirm, because he was mentally incompetent.
b. disaffirm, because he is no longer mentally incompetent.
c. not disaffirm, because Irwin could enter into contracts on his behalf.
d. not disaffirm, because he may become mentally incompetent again.

___ **5.** Al sells his business to Dan and as part of the agreement promises not to engage in a business of the same kind within thirty miles for three years. Competition within thirty miles would hurt Dan's business. Al's promise

a. violates public policy, because it is part of the sale of a business.
b. violates public policy, because it unreasonably restrains Al from competing.
c. does not violate public policy, because it is no broader than necessary.
d. none of the above.

___ **6.** If a contract has been executed, the fact that it was entered into on a Sunday means that it normally

a. must be rescinded.
b. may be rescinded.
c. is unconstitutional.
d. none of the above.

___ **7.** At the start of the football season, Jim bets Murray about the results of the next SuperBowl. Adam holds their money. By the time of the divisional play-offs, Jim changes his mind and asks for his money back. Gambling on sports events is illegal in their state. Can Jim be held to the bet?

a. Yes. It would be unconscionable to let Jim to back out so late in the season.
b. Yes. No party to the contract is innocent, and thus, no party can withdraw.
c. No. If an illegal agreement is still executory, either party can withdraw.
d. No. The only party who can be held to the bet is Murray.

___ **8.** Luke practices law without an attorney's license. The state requires a license to protect the public from unauthorized practitioners. Clark hires Luke to handle a legal matter. Luke cannot enforce their contract because

a. it is illegal.
b. Luke has no contractual capacity.
c. Luke did not give consideration.
d. none of the above.

___ 9. Amy contracts to buy Kim's business. Kim agrees not to compete with Amy for one year in the same county. Six months later, Kim opens a competing business six blocks away. Amy

a. cannot enforce the contract because it is unconscionable.
b. cannot enforce the contract because it is a restraint of trade.
c. can enforce the contract because all covenants not to compete are valid.
d. can enforce the contract because it is reasonable in scope and duration.

___ 10. Sam signs an employment contract that contains a clause absolving the employer of any liability if Sam is injured on the job. If Sam is injured on the job due to the employer's negligence, the clause will

a. protect the employer from liability.
b. likely not protect the employer from liability.
c. likely be held unconscionable.
d. both b and c.

SHORT ESSAY QUESTIONS

1. State which parties are afforded special protection under the law relating to contractual capacity and what protection they are afforded.

2. What makes an agreement illegal? What is the effect of an illegal agreement?

ISSUE SPOTTERS

1. Joan, who is sixteen years old, moves out of her parents' home and signs a one-year lease for an apartment at Kenwood Apartments. Joan's parents tell her that she can return to live with them at any time. Unable to pay the rent, Joan moves to her parents' home two months later. Can Kenwood enforce the lease against Joan?

2. Nick buys a franchise from Dave for $24,000. Later, while extremely drunk, Nick sells the franchise back to Dave, at Dave's urging, for $10,000. On becoming sober, Nick cannot remember selling the franchise back to Dave. Can Nick cancel the sale?

3. Pam is mentally incompetent. She signs a contracts to sell land to Marion, who is unaware of the incompetency. Before the deal is completed, Pam regains her competency and decides not to go through with it. Can she disaffirm the contract?

4. Diane bets Tex $1,000 that the Dallas Cowboys will win the SuperBowl. A state law prohibits gambling. Do Diane and Tex have an enforceable contract?

5. Potomac Airlines prints on the backs of its tickets that it is not liable for any injury to a passenger caused by Potomac's negligence. Ron buys a ticket and boards the plane. On takeoff, the plane crashes, and Ron is injured. If the cause of the accident is found to be Potomac's negligence, can Potomac use the clause as defense to liability?

Learning Objectives

The learning objectives in this chapter include:

1. The difference between a mistake of value or quality and a mistake of fact.
2. Fraudulent misrepresentation and its elements.
3. The effects of undue influence and duress on contract enforceability.
4. The types of contracts that must be in writing to be enforceable.
5. The parol evidence rule and when parol evidence is admissible.

Chapter 10: Assent and Form

WHAT THIS CHAPTER IS ABOUT

A contract may be unenforceable if the parties have not genuinely assented to its terms. Under the Statute of Frauds, certain types of contracts must be in writing to be enforceable. This chapter covers both of those topics and the parol evidence rule.

CHAPTER OUTLINE

I. GENUINENESS OF ASSENT

In most cases in which assent is not genuine, the innocent party can choose to rescind the contract, or enforce it and seek damages.

A. MISTAKES

1. Unilateral Mistakes

When *one* contracting party makes a mistake as to some material fact, he or she is *not* entitled to relief from the contract. Exceptions are—

a. Other Party's Knowledge

A contract may not be enforceable if the other party to the contract knows or should have known that a mistake was made.

b. Mathematical Mistakes

A contract may not be enforceable if a mistake in addition, subtraction, division, or multiplication was inadvertent.

2. Mutual Mistakes of Material Fact

When *both* parties make a mistake as to some *material fact,* the contract can be rescinded by either party.

3. Mutual Mistakes in Value

When *both* parties make a mistake as to the *market value* or quality of the object of the contract, the contract can be *enforced* by either party.

B. FRAUDULENT MISREPRESENTATION

1. The Elements of Fraud

(1) Misrepresentation of a material fact, (2) an intent to deceive, and (3) an innocent party's justifiable reliance on the misrepresentation.

2. Misrepresentation Must Occur

a. Statements of Opinion

Statements of opinion are generally not subject to claims of fraud. But when a naïve purchaser relies on an expert's opinion, the innocent party may be entitled to rescission or reformation.

b. Misrepresentation by Conduct

Misrepresentation can occur by, for example, concealment, which prevents the other party from learning of a material fact.

c. Misrepresentation of Law

Misrepresentation of law does not entitle a party to relief, unless the misrepresenting party is in a profession that is known to require greater knowledge of the law than the average person has.

d. Misrepresentation by Silence

No party to a contract has a duty to disclose facts, unless a serious defect known to one could not reasonably be suspected by the other.

3. Intent to Deceive (*Scienter*)

The misrepresenting party must know that facts have been falsely represented. This occurs when a party (1) knows a fact is not as stated; (2) makes a statement that he or she believes not to be true or makes it recklessly, without regard to the truth; or (3) says or implies that a statement is made on a basis such as personal knowledge when it is not.

4. Reliance on the Misrepresentation

The misrepresentation must be an important factor in inducing the party to contract. Reliance is not justified if the party knows the true facts or relies on obviously extravagant statements, or the defect is obvious.

5. Injury to the Innocent Party

To rescind a contract, most courts do not require proof of injury. To recover damages, proof of injury is required.

C. UNDUE INFLUENCE

If a contract enriches a party at the expense of another who is dominated by the enriched party, the contract is voidable. The essential feature is that the party taken advantage of does not exercise free will.

D. DURESS

Duress involves coercive conduct—forcing a party to enter into a contract by threatening the party with a wrongful act. Economic need is not enough.

II. THE STATUTE OF FRAUDS—REQUIREMENT OF A WRITING

The Statute of Frauds stipulates what types of contracts must be in writing to be enforceable. If one of these contracts is not in writing, it is not void but the Statute of Frauds is a defense to its enforcement.

A. CONTRACTS INVOLVING INTERESTS IN LAND

Land includes all objects permanently attached, such as trees. Contracts for transfer of interests in land (such as leases) must be in writing.

B. THE ONE-YEAR RULE

1. Performance Objectively Impossible Must Be in Writing

A contract must be in writing if performance is objectively impossible within a year of the date of the contract's formation.

2. Possibility of Performance Need Not Be in Writing

A contract need not be in writing if performance within one year is possible—even if it is improbable, unlikely, or takes longer.

C. COLLATERAL PROMISES

1. What Collateral Promises Must Be in Writing

A promise ancillary to a principal transaction and made by a third party to assume the debts or obligations of the primary party (only if the primary party does not perform).

2. Exception—"Main Purpose" Rule

An oral promise to answer for the debt of another is enforceable if the guarantor's main purpose is to secure a personal benefit.

D. PROMISES MADE IN CONSIDERATION OF MARRIAGE

Prenuptial agreements must be in writing to be enforceable.

E. CONTRACTS FOR SALES OF GOODS

The Uniform Commercial Code (UCC) requires a writing for a sale of goods priced at $500 or more [UCC 2–201].

F. EXCEPTIONS TO THE STATUTE OF FRAUDS

1. Partial Performance

a. Contracts for the Transfer of Interests in Land

If a buyer pays part of the price, takes possession, and makes permanent improvements and the parties cannot be returned to their pre-contract status quo, a court may grant specific performance.

b. Contracts Covered by the UCC

Under the UCC, an oral contract is enforceable to the extent that a seller accepts payment or a buyer accepts delivery of the goods.

2. Admissions

In some states, if a party admits in pleadings, testimony, or in court that a contract was made, the contract will be enforceable.

3. Promissory Estoppel

An oral contract may be enforced if (1) a promisor makes a promise on which the promisee justifiably relies to his or her detriment, (2) the reliance was foreseeable to the promisor, and (3) injustice can be avoided only by enforcing the promise.

4. **Special Exceptions under the UCC**
Oral contracts that may be enforceable under the UCC include those for customized goods and those between merchants that have been confirmed in writing (see Chapter 13).

III. THE STATUTE OF FRAUDS—SUFFICIENCY OF A WRITING

There must be at least a memo, confirmation, invoice, sales slip, check, fax, or several documents stapled together or in the same envelope that include—

A. SIGNATURE OF THE PARTY TO BE CHARGED

The writing must be signed (initialed) by the party who refuses to perform. The signature can be anywhere in the writing.

B. ESSENTIAL TERMS

1. **Contracts Covered by the UCC**
The writing must include a quantity term. Other terms need not be stated exactly, if they adequately reflect the parties' intentions.

2. **Other Contracts**
The writing must name the parties, subject matter, consideration, and quantity. In some states, a sale of land must include the price and a description of the property.

IV. THE PAROL EVIDENCE RULE

A. THE RULE

If the parties' written contract is integrated (the final expression of their agreement), evidence of their prior negotiations, prior agreements, or contemporaneous oral agreements that contradicts or varies the terms of their contract is not admissible at trial.

B. EXCEPTIONS

Parol evidence is admissible to show—

1. **Subsequent Modification of a Contract**
Evidence of subsequent modification (oral or written) of a written contract is admissible (but oral modifications may not be enforceable if they bring the contract under the Statute of Frauds).

2. **A Contract Is Voidable or Void**

3. **Meaning of Ambiguous Terms**

4. **Essential Term Lacking in an Incomplete Contract**

5. **Prior Dealing, Course of Performance, or Usage of Trade**
Under the UCC, evidence can be introduced to explain or supplement a contract by showing a prior dealing, course of performance, or usage of trade (see Chapter 13).

6. **Orally Agreed-on Condition**
Proof of such a condition is admissible if it does not modify the written terms but involves the enforceability of the written contract.

7. **An Obvious or Gross Clerical Error**

TRUE-FALSE QUESTIONS

___ 1. Under a mistake of fact, a contract can sometimes be avoided.

___ 2. When parties to both sides of a contract are mistaken as to the same fact, the contract cannot be rescinded by either party.

___ 3. To commit fraudulent misrepresentation, one party must intend to mislead another.

___ 4. In an action to rescind a contract for fraudulent misrepresentation, proof of injury is required to collect damages.

___ 5. Threatening a civil suit does not normally constitute duress.

___ 6. Contracts for transfers, other than sales, of interests in land need not be in writing to be enforceable under the Statute of Frauds.

___ 7. A contract for a sale of goods of over $300 must be in writing to be enforceable under the Statute of Frauds.

___ 8. An oral contract that should be in writing to be enforceable under the Statute of Frauds may be enforceable if it has been partially performed.

___ 9. The only writing sufficient to satisfy the Statute of Frauds is a typewritten form, signed at the bottom by all parties, with the heading "Contract" at the top.

___ 10. Under the parol evidence rule, virtually any evidence is admissible to prove or disprove the terms of a contract.

FILL-IN QUESTIONS

A collateral promise is a promise that is ______________________ (superior/ancillary) to a ______________________ (primary/secondary) contractual relationship.

A promise by one person to pay the debts or discharge the duties of another person if the other fails to perform ______________________ (must/need not) be in writing to be enforceable under the Statute of Frauds. If the main purpose of a promise to pay another's debts or perform another's duties is to benefit the promisor, however, the agreement ______________________ (must/need not) be in writing to be enforceable.

MULTIPLE-CHOICE QUESTIONS

___ 1. Metro Transport asks for bids on a construction project. Metro estimates that the cost will be $200,000. Most bids are about $200,000, but A&B Construction bids $150,000. In adding a column of figures, A&B mistakenly omitted a $50,000 item. Because Metro had reason to know of the mistake

a. Metro can enforce the contract.
b. A&B can increase the price and enforce the contract at the higher price.
c. A&B can avoid the contract.
d. none of the above.

___ **2.** To induce Sam to buy a lot in a Mel's development, Mel tells Sam that he intends to add a golf course. The terrain is suitable, and there is enough land, but Mel has no intention of adding a golf course. Sam is induced by the statement to buy a lot. Sam's reliance on Mel's statement is justified because

a. Mel is the owner of the development.
b. Sam does not know the truth and has no way of finding it out.
c. Sam did not buy the golf course.
d. the golf course had obviously not been built yet.

___ **3.** Bob agrees to sell to Pam ten shares of Mina Corporation stock. Neither party knows whether the stock will increase or decrease in value. Pam believes that it will increase in value. If she is mistaken, her mistake will

a. justify voiding the contract.
b. not justify voiding the contract.
c. warrant a refund to her from Bob of the difference.
d. warrant a payment from her to Bob of the difference.

___ **4.** Ken, who is not a real estate broker, sells Cathy some land. Which of the following statements by Ken, with the accompanying circumstance, would be a fraudulent misrepresentation in that sale?

a. "This acreage offers the most spectacular view of the valley." From higher up the mountain, more of the valley is visible.
b. "You can build an office building here." The county requires the property to be exclusively residential, but neither Ken nor Cathy know that.
c. "This property includes ninety acres." Ken knows it is only eighty acres.
d. "The value of this property will triple in five years." Ken does not know whether the value of the property will triple in five years.

___ **5.** In a letter offering to sell amplifiers to Gina for her theater, Dick describes the 120-watt amplifiers as "210 watts per channel." This is fraudulent misrepresentation if

a. the number of watts is a material fact.
b. Dick intended to deceive Gina.
c. Gina relies on the description.
d. all of the above.

___ **6.** Fern is an eighty-year-old widow with no business experience. Mark, Fern's nephew, urges Fern to sell some of her stock at a price below market value to Tab, Mark's "business" partner. Fern, relying on Mark, agrees to sell the stock to Tab. She may avoid the contract on the ground of

a. duress.
b. mistake.
c. undue influence.
d. all of the above.

___ **7.** Hans owes Bell Credit Company $10,000. Chris orally promises Bell that he will pay Hans' debt if Hans does not. This promise is

a. not enforceable because it is not in writing.
b. enforceable under the "main purpose rule" exception.
c. not enforceable because the debt is Hans'.
d. enforceable under the part performance exception.

___ **8.** Jim orally promises to work for Pat, and Pat orally promises to employ Jim at a rate of $500 a week. This contract must be in writing to be enforceable if Jim promises to work for

a. his entire life.
b. at least five years.
c. five years, but either party may terminate the contract on thirty-days' notice.
d. both a and c.

___ **9.** On March 1, the chief engineer for the software design division of Uni Products orally contracts to hire Lee for one year, beginning March 4. Lee works for Uni for five months. When sales decline, Lee is discharged. Lee sues Uni for reinstatement or seven months' salary. Lee will

a. win, because the contract can be performed within one year.
b. win, because employment contracts need not be in writing to be enforceable.
c. lose, because the contract cannot be performed within one year.
d. lose, because employment contracts must be in writing to be enforceable.

___ **10.** Under a written agreement, Calvin sells a motel to Hobbes. When Calvin removes the motel furniture, Hobbes sues. Calvin claims that they orally agreed he would keep the furniture. If the court decides that the written agreement includes everything that the parties intended, evidence of an oral agreement about the furniture is

a. not admissible.
b. admissible to contradict the terms of the written agreement.
c. admissible for any purpose.
d. both b and c.

SHORT ESSAY QUESTIONS

1. Define "fraudulent misrepresentation." What are its elements?

2. What is required to satisfy the writing requirement of the Statute of Frauds?

ISSUE SPOTTERS

1. Michael, a famous and wealthy musician, dies. Michael's wife Jessy sells their farm to Carl, who asks what should be done with all the "junk" on the property. Jessy says that Carl can do whatever he wants with it. Unknown to Jessy or Carl, in a cabinet in the house are the master tapes for an unreleased album. Can Carl keep the tapes?

2. Brad, an accountant, files Dina's tax returns. When the Internal Revenue Service assesses a large tax against Dina, she retains Brad to resist the assessment. The day before the deadline for replying to the IRS, Brad tells Dina that unless she pays a higher fee, he will withdraw. If Dina agrees to pay, is the contract enforceable?

3. GamesCo orders $800 worth of game pieces from Midstate Plastic, Inc. Midstate delivers, and GamesCo pays for, $450 worth. GamesCo then says it wants no more pieces from Midstate. GamesCo and Midstate have never dealt with each other before and have nothing in writing. Can Midstate enforce a deal for $350 more?

4. Paula orally agrees with Next Corporation to work in New York City for Next for two years. Paula moves her family to New York and begins work. Three months later,

Paula is fired for no stated cause. She sues for reinstatement or pay. Next argues that there is no written contract between them. What will the court say?

5. Under a written agreement, Walt sells his pick-up truck to Bob. When Walt starts to remove the camper, Bob says, "Wait. We agreed that the camper was included." Walt points to their written agreement and says, "No, we didn't. Our contract says nothing about the camper." If Bob sues, what will the court say?

QUICKEN CD-ROM
BUSINESS LAW PARTNER APPLICATIONS

Open **Quicken Business Law Partner**. Click on the *New Documents* icon. Select the *Guaranty Agreement*. Respond to the *Interview* questions with actual facts or hypothetical ones. For example, imagine that José loans money to Erin, and Frank signs the guaranty agreement. As you complete the *Interview*, answer the following questions.

___ **1.** In the guaranty agreement, in writing, the parties can agree to limit

a. the amount of the guaranty.
b. the duration of the guaranty.
c. the guarantor's obligation if the debt is unenforceable against the debtor.
d. all of the above.

___ **2.** A guaranty does not have to be in writing to be enforceable if its main purpose is to benefit

a. the creditor.
b. the debtor.
c. the guarantor.
d. none of the above.

___ **3.** In the guaranty agreement, in which clause could the parties agree that José could lend more money to Erin without notifying Frank and Frank would remain liable?

a. II. Limitation of Amount.
b. V. Authority to Lend More.
c. VI. Creditor Provisions.
d. VII. Authority to Alter Obligation.

___ **4.** Unless the guaranty agreement provides otherwise, in seeking payment of the debt, José

a. must proceed against Erin first.
b. must proceed against Frank first.
c. can proceed against either Erin or Frank.
d. none of the above.

___ **5.** In the guaranty agreement, in which clause could the parties agree that the terms could later be modified without notifying Frank and Frank would remain liable?

a. VII. Authority to Alter Obligation.
b. XIII. Amendment.
c. XIV. Severability.
d. XV. Waiver of Contractual Right.

QUICKEN BUSINESS LAW PARTNER ENHANCEMENT: EXPLORING THE PERSONAL LAW HANDBOOK

Personal Law Handbook, within Topic 3, Consumer Law, the *Consumer Contract* section gives you a brief review of the law concerning fraud, unconscionability, and adhesion contracts.

Learning Objectives

The learning objectives in this chapter include:

1. Noncontracting parties who have rights under a contract.
2. Assignments of contract rights.
3. The different kinds of contract conditions.
4. How contract obligations are commonly discharged.
5. The difference between complete and substantial performance of a contract.

Chapter 11: Third Party Rights and Discharge

WHAT THIS CHAPTER IS ABOUT

A party to a contract can assign the rights arising from it to another party or delegate the duties of the contract by having another person perform them. A third party also acquires rights to enforce a contract when the contracting parties intend that the contract benefit the third party (who is known as an *intended* beneficiary). This chapter also discusses performance and discharge of contracts.

CHAPTER OUTLINE

I. ASSIGNMENTS AND DELEGATIONS

Assignment and delegation occur after the original contract is made, when one of the parties transfers to another party an interest or duty in the contract.

A. ASSIGNMENTS

1. What an Assignment Is

Parties to a contract have rights and duties. One party has a *right* to require the other to perform, and the other has a *duty* to perform. The transfer of the *right* to a third person is an assignment.

2. Rights That Cannot Be Assigned

a. Statute Prohibits Assignment

(Such as assignment of future workers' compensation benefits.)

b. Contract Is Personal

The rights under the contract cannot be assigned unless all that remains is a money payment.

c. **Assignment Materially Increases or Alters Risk or Duties of Obligor**

d. **Contract Provides That It Cannot Be Assigned**
Exceptions: a contract cannot prevent an assignment of (1) a right to receive money, (2) rights in real property (known as restraints against alienation), (3) rights in negotiable instruments (see Chapter 17), or (4) a right to receive damages for breach of a sales contract or for payment of an amount owed under the contract.

3. **Notice of Assignment**
An assignment is effective immediately, with or without notice.

a. **Same Right Assigned to More Than One Party**
If the assignor assigns the same right to different persons, in most states, the first assignment in time is the first in right. In some states, priority is given to the first assignee who gives notice.

b. **Discharge before Notice**
Until an obligor has notice, his or her obligation can be discharged by performance to the assignor. Once the obligor has notice, only performance to the assignee can act as a discharge.

B. DELEGATIONS

Duties are delegated. The party making the delegation is the delegator; the party to whom the duty is delegated is the delegatee.

1. **Duties That Cannot Be Delegated**
Any duty can be delegated, unless (1) performance depends on the personal skill or talents of the obligor, (2) special trust has been placed in the obligor, (3) performance by a third party will vary materially from that expected by the obligee (the one to whom performance is owed) under the contract, or (4) the contract expressly prohibits it.

2. **Effect of a Delegation**
The obligee (the one to whom performance is owed) must accept performance from the delegatee, unless the duty is one that cannot be delegated. If the delegatee fails to perform, the delegator is still liable.

3. **Liability of the Delegatee**
If the delegatee makes a promise of performance that will directly benefit the obligee, there is an "assumption of duty." Breach of this duty makes the delegatee liable to the obligee, and the obligee can sue both the delegatee and the delegator.

C. ASSIGNMENT OF ALL RIGHTS

A contract that provides in general words for an assignment of all rights (for example, "I assign the contract" or "I assign all my rights under the contract") is both an assignment of rights and a delegation of duties.

II. THIRD PARTY BENEFICIARIES

Only intended beneficiaries acquire legal rights in a contract.

A. INTENDED BENEFICIARIES

An intended beneficiary is one for whose benefit a contract is made. If the contract is breached, he or she can sue the promisor.

1. **Types of Intended Beneficiaries**

   a. **Creditor Beneficiaries**
   A creditor beneficiary benefits from a contract in which a promisor promises to pay a debt that the promisee owes to him or her.

   b. **Donee Beneficiaries**
   A donee beneficiary benefits from a contract made for the express purpose of giving a gift to him or her.

2. **When the Rights of an Intended Beneficiary Vest**
To enforce a contract against the original parties, the rights of the third party must first vest (take effect). The rights vest when (1) the third party manifests assent to the contract or (2) the third party materially alters his or her position in detrimental reliance

3. **Modification or Rescission of the Contract**
Until the third party's rights vest, the others can modify or rescind the contract without the third party's consent. If the contract reserves the power to rescind or modify, vesting does not terminate the power.

B. INCIDENTAL BENEFICIARIES
The benefit that an incidental beneficiary receives from a contract between other parties is unintentional. An incidental beneficiary cannot enforce a contract to which he or she is not a party.

C. INTENDED OR INCIDENTAL BENEFICIARY?

1. **Reasonable Person Test**
A beneficiary is intended if a reasonable person in his or her position would believe that the promisee intended to confer on the beneficiary the right to sue to enforce the contract.

2. **Other Factors Indicating an Intended Beneficiary**
(1) Performance is rendered directly to the third party, (2) the third party has the right to control the performance, or (3) the third party is expressly designated as beneficiary in the contract.

III. CONTRACT DISCHARGE

A. CONDITIONS OF PERFORMANCE
If performance is contingent on a condition and it is not satisfied, a party does not have to perform.

1. **Condition Precedent**
A condition that must be fulfilled before a party's performance can be required. Such conditions are common.

2. **Condition Subsequent**
A condition that operates to terminate an obligation to perform. The condition follows a duty to perform. Such conditions are rare.

3. **Concurrent Condition**
When each party's duty to perform is conditioned on the other party's duty to perform. Occurs only when the parties are to perform their duties simultaneously (for example, paying for goods on delivery). No party can recover for breach unless he or she first tenders performance.

B. DISCHARGE BY PERFORMANCE

Most contracts are discharged by the parties' doing what they promised to do. Discharge can be accomplished by tender. If performance has been tendered and the other party refuses to perform, the party making the tender can sue for breach.

1. Complete versus Substantial Performance

a. Complete Performance

Express conditions fully occur in all aspects. Any deviation is a breach of contract and discharges the other party.

b. Substantial Performance

Performance that does not vary greatly from the performance promised in the contract. If one party fulfills the terms of the contract with substantial performance, the other party is obligated to perform (but may obtain damages for the minor deviations).

2. Performance to the Satisfaction of Another

a. Personal Satisfaction of One of the Parties

When the subject matter of the contract is personal, performance must actually satisfy the party (a condition precedent).

b. Satisfaction of a Reasonable Person

Contracts involving mechanical fitness, utility, or marketability need only be performed to the satisfaction of a reasonable person.

c. Satisfaction of a Third Party

When the satisfaction of a third party is required, most courts require the work to be satisfactory to a reasonable person.

3. Material Breach of Contract

A **breach of contract** is the nonperformance of a contractual duty. A breach is material when performance is not at least substantial. The nonbreaching party is excused from performing.

4. Anticipatory Repudiation

Occurs when, before either party has a duty to perform, one party refuses to perform. This can discharge the nonbreaching party, who can sue to recover damages and can also seek a similar contract elsewhere.

C. DISCHARGE BY AGREEMENT

Any contract can be discharged by an agreement of the parties.

1. Discharge by Rescission

Rescission is the process by which a contract is canceled and the parties are returned to the positions they occupied prior to forming it.

a. Executory Contracts

Can be rescinded. The parties must make another agreement, which must satisfy the legal requirements for a contract. Their promises not to perform are consideration for the second contract.

b. Enforceable Even if Made Orally

Unless the new agreement falls within the Statute of Frauds, or the original contract was subject to the UCC and required a writing.

c. **Executed Contracts**
Can be rescinded only if the party who has performed receives consideration to call off the deal.

2. **Discharge by Novation**
Occurs when the parties to a contract and a new party get together and agree to substitute the new party for one of the original parties. Requirements are (1) a previous valid obligation, (2) an agreement of all the parties to a new contract, (3) the extinguishment of the old obligation (discharge of the prior party), and (4) a new, valid contract .

3. **Discharge by Accord and Satisfaction**
The parties agree to accept performance that is different from the performance originally promised.

a. **Accord**
An executory contract to perform an act that will satisfy an existing duty. An accord suspends, but does not discharge, the duty.

b. **Satisfaction**
The performance of the accord discharges the original contract.

c. **If the Obligor Refuses to Perform**
The obligee can sue on the original obligation or seek a decree for specific performance on the accord.

D. **WHEN PERFORMANCE IS IMPOSSIBLE**

1. **Objective Impossibility**
Performance becomes objectively impossible in the event of (1) the death or incapacity of a party, (2) the destruction of the specific subject matter of the contract, or (3) a change in the law that makes performance illegal.

2. **Commercial Impracticability**
Performance may be excused if it becomes much more difficult or expensive than contemplated when the contract was formed.

3. **Temporary Impossibility**
An event that makes it temporarily impossible to perform will suspend performance until the impossibility ceases.

TRUE-FALSE QUESTIONS

___ 1. Intended beneficiaries have no legal rights under a contract.

___ 2. A third party can enforce a contract against the original parties when the third party's rights in the contract vest.

___ 3. The party who makes an assignment is the obligor.

___ 4. All rights can be assigned.

___ 5. If a contract contains a clause that prohibits assignment of the contract, then ordinarily the contract cannot be assigned.

____ **6.** If performance of a contract is contingent on a condition and it is not satisfied, a party does not have to perform.

____ **7.** Complete performance occurs when a contract's conditions fully occur.

____ **8.** A material breach of contract does not discharge the other party's duty to perform.

____ **9.** An executory contract cannot be rescinded.

____ **10.** Performance may be excused if it becomes much more difficult or expensive than contemplated when the contract was formed under the doctrine of commercial impracticability.

FILL-IN QUESTIONS

The transfer of rights to a third person is ______________________ (an assignment/a delegation) and the transfer of duties to a third person is ______________________ (an assignment/a delegation). Probably the most common contractual right that is ______________________ (assigned/delegated) is the right to the payment of money. For instance, Fidelity Computer Corporation sells its computers on credit. Fidelity has the right to installment payments from its customers. To obtain funds to buy more inventory, Fidelity can ______________ (assign/delegate) the right to the payments to a financing agency, which will pay Fidelity for the right.

MULTIPLE-CHOICE QUESTIONS

____ **1.** Gary contracts with Dan to buy Dan a new car manufactured by General Motors Corporation (GMC). GMC is

a. an intended beneficiary.
b. an incidental beneficiary.
c. not a third party beneficiary.
d. both a and b.

____ **2.** Frank owes Jim $100. Frank contracts with Ron to pay the $100 and notifies Jim of the contract by mail. Jim replies by mail that he agrees. After Frank receives Jim's reply, Ron and Frank send Jim a letter stating that they decided to rescind their contract. Jim's rights under the contract

a. vested when Jim learned of the contract and manifested assent to it.
b. vested when Frank and Ron formed their contract.
c. will not vest because Ron and Frank rescinded their contract.
d. could never vest because Jim is an incidental beneficiary.

____ **3.** Bernie has a right to $100 against Holly. Bernie assigns the right to Tom. Tom's rights against Holly

a. include the right to demand performance from Holly.
b. are subject to any defenses Holly has against Bernie.
c. do not vest until Holly assents to the assignment.
d. both a and b.

___ **4.** Jenny sells her Value Auto Parts store to Burt and makes a valid contract not to compete. Burt wants to sell the store to Discount Auto Centers and assign to Discount the right to have Jenny not compete. Burt can

a. sell the business and assign the right.
b. sell the business but not assign the right.
c. assign the right but not sell the business.
d. neither assign the right nor sell the business.

___ **5.** Dick contracts with Jane to cut the grass on Jane's lawn. Dick delegates performance of the duty to Sally with Jane's assent. Who owes Jane a duty to cut her grass?

a. Dick, but not Sally
b. Sally, but not Dick
c. Both Dick and Sally
d. Neither Dick nor Sally

___ **6.** Don contracts to build a store for Logan for $500,000, with payments to be in installments of $50,000 as building progresses. Don finishes the store except for a cover over a compressor on the roof. A cover can be installed for $500. Logan refuses to pay the last installment. If Don's breach is not material

a. Don has a claim against Logan for $50,000.
b. Logan has a claim against Don for damages for Don's breach of his duty to put a cover over the compressor.
c. both a and b.
d. none of the above.

___ **7.** Gil contracts to produce a movie for Big Pictures, Inc. As Big knows, Gil's only source of funds for the film is a $500,000 deposit in Commerce Bank (CB). CB fails. Gil loses $400,000 and fails to produce the film. Gil's duty to produce the movie is

a. discharged on the ground of impossibility.
b. discharged on the ground of commercial impracticability.
c. suspended on the ground of temporary impossibility.
d. not discharged, and Gil is liable to Big for breach of contract.

___ **8.** Lee contracts to repair Al's building for $30,000. Payment is to be made "on the satisfaction of Will, Al's architect." To save money, Al tells Will not to approve the repairs. If Lee sues Al for $30,000, Lee will

a. win, because Will is Al's architect.
b. win, because Al is not acting reasonably.
c. lose, because Lee is not acting reasonably, honestly, and in good faith.
d. lose, because Will has not expressed satisfaction with the work.

___ **9.** Sam owes Lyle $10,000. Sam promises, in writing, to give Lyle a "Destroyers" video-game machine in lieu of payment of the debt. Lyle agrees and Sam delivers the machine. Substituting and performing one duty for another is called

a. rescission.
b. accord and satisfaction.
c. novation.
d. none of the above.

___ **10.** On May 1, Val agrees to work for Babcott, Inc., for four months beginning June 1. On May 15, Babcott tells Val that it doesn't need her after all. Val's duty to work for Babcott

a. was discharged on May 15.
b. was discharged on May 16.
c. will be discharged on June 1.
d. will be discharged on September 30.

SHORT ESSAY QUESTIONS

1. Who are the parties in an assignment? What are their respective rights and duties?

2. Define "material breach of contract." What effect does a material breach and a nonmaterial breach have on the nonbreaching party?

ISSUE SPOTTERS

1. Brian owes Jeff $100. Ed tells Brian to give him the money and he'll pay Jeff. Brian gives Ed the money. Ed never pays Jeff. Can Jeff successfully sue Ed for the money?

2. Abby owes Penny $100. Penny assigns her right to the money to Charlie. Can Charlie successfully sue Abby for the money?

3. Lani Construction contracts with Ho to build a store on Ho's lot. The work is to begin on May 1 and be completed by November 1, so that Ho can open for the Christmas buying season. Lani does not finish until November 6. Ho opens, but due to the delay Ho loses some sales. Is Ho's duty to pay for the construction of the store discharged?

4. Red Tiger Foods contracts to buy from Bree Distributors two hundred carloads of frozen pizzas. Before Red Tiger or Bree start performing, can they call off the deal? What if Bree has already shipped the pizzas?

5. The Ramrods contract with Howard to perform the last concert of their current tour in Indianapolis. The night before the concert, the Ramrods are killed in a plane crash. How do their deaths affect the contract?

★ **Learning Objectives**

The learning objectives in this chapter include:

1. The different types of damages.
2. Measures of damages for breach of different types of contracts.
3. The difference between liquidated damages and penalties.
4. Equitable remedies and when they are granted.
5. The doctrine of election of remedies.

Chapter 12: Breach and Remedies

WHAT THIS CHAPTER IS ABOUT

Breach of contract is the failure to perform what a party is under a duty to perform. When this happens, the nonbreaching party can choose one or more remedies. Unless damages would be inadequate, that is usually what a court will award.

CHAPTER OUTLINE

I. DAMAGES

Damages compensate a nonbreaching party for the loss of a bargain and, under special circumstances, for additional losses. Generally, the party is placed in the position he or she would have occupied if the contract been performed.

A. TYPES OF DAMAGES

1. Compensatory Damages
Damages compensating a party for the *loss* of a bargain—the difference between the promised performance and the actual performance.

a. Incidental Damages
Expenses that are caused directly by a breach of contract (such as those incurred to obtain performance from another source).

b. Measurement of Compensatory Damages

1) Contract for a Sale of Goods
The usual measure is the difference between the contract price and the market price. If the buyer breaches and the seller has not yet made the goods, the measure is lost profits on the sale.

2) **Contract for a Sale of Land**

a) **Majority Rule**
If specific performance (see below) is unavailable, or if the buyer breaches, the measure of damages is the difference between the land's contract price and its market price.

b) **Minority Rule**
If the seller breaches and the breach is not deliberate, the buyer recovers any down payment, plus expenses.

3) **Construction Contracts**

a) **Owner's Breach Before, During, or After Construction**
Contractor can recover (1) before construction: only profits (contract price, less cost of materials and labor); (2) during construction: profits, plus cost of partial construction; (3) after construction: the contract price, plus interest.

b) **Contractor's Breach**
Owner can recover, before construction is complete, the cost of completion.

2. **Consequential Damages**
Damages giving an injured party the entire *benefit* of the bargain—foreseeable losses caused by special circumstances beyond the contract. The breaching party must know (or have reason to know) that special circumstances will cause the additional loss.

3. **Punitive Damages**
Damages punishing a guilty party and making an example to deter similar, future conduct. Awarded for a tort, but not for a contract breach.

4. **Nominal Damages**
Damages (such as $1) establishing, when no actual loss resulted, that a defendant acted wrongfully.

B. MITIGATION OF DAMAGES

An injured party has a duty to mitigate damages. For example, persons whose jobs have been wrongfully terminated have a duty to seek other jobs. The damages they receive are their salaries, less the income they received (or would have received) in similar jobs.

C. LIQUIDATED DAMAGES VERSUS PENALTIES

1. **Liquidated Damages Provision**
Specifies a certain amount to be paid in the event of a breach to the nonbreaching party for the loss. Such provisions are enforceable.

2. **Penalty Provision**
Specifies a certain amount to be paid in the event of a breach *to penalize the breaching party*. Such provisions are *not* enforceable.

3. **How to Determine If a Provision Will Be Enforced**
Ask: (1) When the contract was made, was it clear that damages would be difficult to estimate in the event of a breach? (2) Was the amount set as damages a reasonable estimate? If either answer is "no," the provision will not be enforced.

II. RESCISSION AND RESTITUTION

A. RESCISSION

Rescission is an action to undo, or cancel, a contract—to return nonbreaching parties to the positions they occupied prior to the transaction. Rescission is available if fraud, mistake, duress, or failure of consideration is present. The rescinding party must give prompt notice to the breaching party.

B. RESTITUTION

To rescind a contract, the parties must make **restitution** by returning to each other goods, property, or money previously conveyed.

III. SPECIFIC PERFORMANCE

This remedy calls for the performance of the act promised in the contract.

A. WHEN SPECIFIC PERFORMANCE IS AVAILABLE

Damages must be an inadequate remedy. If goods are unique, a court will decree specific performance. Specific performance is granted to a buyer in a contract for the sale of land (every parcel of land is unique).

B. WHEN SPECIFIC PERFORMANCE IS NOT AVAILABLE

Contracts for sale of goods (other than unique goods) rarely qualify, because substantially identical goods can be bought or sold elsewhere. Courts normally refuse to grant specific performance of personal service contracts.

IV. REFORMATION

Used when the parties have imperfectly expressed their agreement in writing. Allows the contract to be rewritten to reflect the parties' true intentions.

A. WHEN REFORMATION IS AVAILABLE

(1) In cases of fraud or mutual mistake; (2) to prove the correct terms of an oral contract; (3) if a covenant not to compete is for a valid purpose (such as the sale of a business), but the area or time constraints are unreasonable, some courts will reform the restraints to make them reasonable.

B. WHEN REFORMATION IS NOT AVAILABLE

If the area or time constraints in a covenant not to compete are unreasonable, some courts will throw out the entire covenant.

V. RECOVERY BASED ON QUASI CONTRACT

When there is no enforceable contract, quasi contract prevents unjust enrichment. The law implies a promise to pay the reasonable value for benefits received.

A. WHEN QUASI-CONTRACTUAL RECOVERY IS USEFUL

A party has partially performed under a contract that is unenforceable. The party may recover the reasonable value (fair market value).

B. ELEMENTS TO RECOVER IN QUASI CONTRACT

The party seeking recovery must show (1) he or she conferred a benefit on the other party, (2) he or she had the reasonable expectation of being paid, (3) he or she did not act as a volunteer in conferring the benefit, and (4) the other party would be unjustly enriched by retaining it without paying.

VI. ELECTION OF REMEDIES

A nonbreaching party must choose which remedy to pursue. The purpose of the doctrine is to prevent double recovery. The doctrine has been eliminated in contracts for sales of goods—UCC remedies are cumulative (see Chapter 15).

VII. PROVISIONS LIMITING REMEDIES

A. EXCULPATORY CLAUSES

A provision excluding liability for fraudulent or intentional injury or for illegal acts will not be enforced. An exculpatory clause for negligence contained in a contract made between parties who have roughly equal bargaining positions usually will be enforced.

B. LIMITATION-OF-LIABILITY CLAUSES

Provide that the only remedy for breach is replacement, repair, or refund of the purchase price (or some other limit). Such clauses may be enforced.

C. CONTRACTS FOR SALES OF GOODS

Remedies can be limited (see Chapter 15).

TRUE-FALSE QUESTIONS

___ **1.** Normal damages compensate a nonbreaching party for the loss of the contract or give a nonbreaching party the benefit of the contract.

___ **2.** Punitive damages are usually not awarded for a breach of contract.

___ **3.** Nominal damages are awarded when it cannot be proved that a party actually breached a contract.

___ **4.** Liquidated damages are uncertain in amount.

___ **5.** Reformation allows a contract to be rewritten to reflect the contracting parties' true intention.

___ **6.** Limitation-of-liability clauses are never enforced.

___ **7.** A covenant not to compete that is for a valid purpose and has reasonable area and time constraints will usually be enforced by the courts.

___ **8.** Quasi contract provides relief only when there is an enforceable contract.

___ **9.** Consequential damages are awarded for foreseeable losses caused by special circumstances beyond the contract.

___ **10.** Specific performance is available only when damages are also an adequate remedy.

FILL-IN QUESTIONS

The usual measure of compensatory damages under a contract for a sale of goods is the difference between ______________________________ (the contract price and the market price/the market price and lost profits on the sale). The usual remedy for a seller's breach of a contract for a sale of real estate is ______________________________ (specific performance/rescission and restitution). If this remedy is unavailable or if the buyer breaches, in most states the measure of damages is the difference between ______________________________ (the contract price and the market price/the market price and lost profits on the sale).

MULTIPLE-CHOICE QUESTIONS

___ 1. Larry contracts to send his daughter Ann to Quality School for $10,000 tuition. After the school year begins, he withdraws Ann from Quality, refuses to pay, and enrolls Ann in ABC School for $5,000. Quality, which cannot find another student to replace Ann, has a right to damages equal to

a. $15,000.
b. $10,000.
c. $5,000.
d. $0.

___ 2. Sam contracts to sell several rendering tanks to Bob for $10,000, payable in advance. Bob pays the money, which Sam deposits in the First National Bank. The bank goes out of business. Sam refuses to perform. Bob can

a. rescind the contract.
b. get restitution of the $10,000 but may not rescind the contract.
c. rescind the contract and get restitution of the $10,000.
d. do nothing.

___ 3. Mix Corporation contracts to sell to Frosty Malts, Inc., eight steel mixers. When Mix refuses to deliver, Frosty buys mixers from MaxCo, for 25 percent more than the contract price. Frosty is entitled to damages equal to

a. what Mix's profits would have been.
b. the price Frosty would have had to pay Mix.
c. the difference between what Frosty would have had to pay Mix and what Frosty did pay MaxCo.
d. what Frosty paid MaxCo.

___ 4. BuildRite Construction contracts to build a store for Boutique Stores for $1 million. In mid-project, Boutique repudiates the contract, and BuildRite stops working. BuildRite, which incurred costs of $600,000 and would have made a profit of $100,000, has a right to damages equal to

a. $1 million.
b. $700,000.
c. $100,000.
d. $0.

___ 5. Dave contracts with Paul to buy six computers. Dave tells Paul that if the goods are not delivered on Monday, he will lose $12,000 in business. Paul does not deliver the goods on Monday. Dave is forced to rent computers on Tuesday. Paul delivers four computers on Friday. Dave is entitled to

a. compensatory damages.
b. incidental damages.
c. consequential damages.
d. all of the above.

___ **6.** Jay agrees in writing to sell a warehouse and the land on which it is located to Nora. When Jay refuses to go through with the deal, Nora sues. Jay must transfer the land and warehouse to Nora if she is awarded

a. rescission and restitution.
b. specific performance.
c. reformation.
d. quasi-contractual recovery.

___ **7.** Ken orally agrees to work for Jennifer for two years. He works for her for six months when, because she hasn't paid him, he quits and files a suit. He is entitled to the reasonable value of his services for the work if he obtains

a. rescission and restitution.
b. specific performance.
c. reformation.
d. quasi-contractual recovery.

___ **8.** Jake agrees to hire Teresa. Their contract provides that if Jake fires Teresa, she is to be paid whatever amount would have been payable if she had worked for the full term. This clause is

a. a liquidated damages clause.
b. a penalty clause.
c. both a and b.
d. none of the above.

___ **9.** Joe signs a contract to work for NuCorp. The contract provides that if he quits, he cannot work in the same business anywhere in North America for ten years. Joe quits. NuCorp files a suit to enforce the clause. If the court decides that the clause is unreasonable, the clause may be subject to

a. rescission and restitution.
b. specific performance.
c. reformation.
d. quasi-contractual recovery.

___ **10.** Brenda agrees to sell her house to Carl. Under the contract, he gives her a deposit, which she can keep if he breaches. Carl breaches. Brenda keeps the deposit and files a suit, asking the court for damages. If the court refuses to give Brenda damages, it may be because

a. the election of remedies doctrine applies.
b. the election of remedies doctrine does not apply.
c. the appropriate remedy is quasi-contractual recovery.
d. none of the above.

SHORT ESSAY QUESTIONS

1. What are damages designed to do in a breach of contract situation?

2. Define "rescission." What must parties do to rescind a contract?

ISSUE SPOTTERS

1. George contracts to build a storage shed for Ron. Ron pays George in full, but George completes only half the work. Ron pays Paula $500 to finish the shed. If Ron sues George, what would be the measure of recovery?

2. Amy contracts to sell her ranch to Mark, who is to take possession on June 1. Amy delays the transfer until August 1. Mark incurs expenses in providing for cattle that he bought to stock the ranch. When they made the contract, Amy had no reason to know of the cattle. Is Amy liable for Mark's expenses in providing for the cattle?

3. Jack contracts to sell his art collection to Dean. The collection includes original works of art that cannot be obtained anywhere else at any price. When Jack refuses to go through with the deal, Dean sues. Can Dean be awarded the collection?

4. A doctor is passing the scene of a car accident when she notices that several people are unconscious and injured. She stops and renders assistance. Under what legal doctrine can the doctor recover for the medical services rendered?

5. MCT Engineering signs a contract to design a jet for the Clark Company. In the contract is a clause that excludes liability for errors in design and construction of the jet. An error in design causes the jet to crash, killing the pilot and the president of Clark. Is the clause that excluded liability enforceable?

Learning Objectives

The learning objectives in this chapter include:

1. The scope of UCC Article 2, on sales of goods, and Article 2A, on leases of goods.
2. How the UCC differs from the common law of contracts.
3. How the UCC attempts to avoid the "battle of the forms."
4. Rules that apply only to contracts between merchants.
5. Laws governing contracts for the international sale of goods.

Chapter 13: The Formation of Sales and Lease Contracts

WHAT THIS CHAPTER IS ABOUT

This chapter introduces two parts of the Uniform Commercial Code: Article 2, which covers sales of goods, and Article 2A, which covers leases. The chapter also includes a section on contracts for an international sale of goods.

CHAPTER OUTLINE

I. THE SCOPE OF THE UCC

The UCC provides rules to deal with all phases of a commercial sale: Articles 2 and 2A cover contracts for sales or leases of goods; Articles 3, 4, and 4A cover payments by checks, notes, and other means; Article 7 covers warehouse documents; and Article 9 covers transactions that involve collateral.

II. THE SCOPE OF ARTICLE 2—SALES

Article 2 governs contracts for sales of goods.

A. WHAT IS A SALE?

A **sale** is "the passing of title from the seller to the buyer for a price" [UCC 2–106(1)]. The price may be payable in money, goods, services, or land.

B. WHAT ARE GOODS?

Goods are tangible and movable. Legal disputes concern the following—

1. Goods Associated with Real Estate

Goods include minerals or the like and structures, if severance from the land is by the seller (but not if the buyer is to do it); growing crops or timber to be cut; and other "things attached" to realty but capable of severance without material harm to the land [UCC 2–107].

2. Goods and Services Combined

a. General Rule

Services are not included in the UCC. If a transaction involves both goods and services, a court determines which aspect is dominant.

b. Special Cases

Serving food or drink is a sale of goods [UCC 2–314(1)]. Other goods include unborn animals and rare coins.

C. WHO IS A MERCHANT?

UCC 2–104: Special rules apply to those who (1) deal in goods of the kind involved; (2) by occupation, hold themselves out as having knowledge and skill peculiar to the practices or goods involved in the transaction; (3) employ a merchant as a broker, agent, or other intermediary.

III. THE SCOPE OF ARTICLE 2A—LEASES

Article 2A governs contracts for leases of goods.

A. DEFINITION OF A LEASE

A **lease agreement** is the lessor and lessee's bargain, in their words and deeds, including course of dealing, usage of trade, and course of performance [UCC 2A–103(k)].

B. CONSUMER LEASES

Special provisions apply to leases involving (1) a lessor who regularly leases or sells, (2) a lessee who leases for a personal, family, or household purpose, and (3) total payments of less than $25,000 [UCC 2A–103(1)(e)].

C. FINANCE LEASES

A finance lease involves a lessor (financier) who buys or leases goods from a supplier and leases or subleases them to a lessee [UCC 2A–103(g)]. The lessee must perform, whatever the financier does [UCC 2A–407].

IV. THE FORMATION OF SALES AND LEASE CONTRACTS

The following summarizes how the UCC *changes* the common law of contracts.

A. OFFER

An agreement sufficient to constitute a contract can exist even if verbal exchanges, correspondence, and conduct do not reveal exactly when it became binding [UCC 2–204(2), 2A–204(2)].

1. Open Terms

A sales or lease contract will not fail for indefiniteness even if one or more terms are left open, as long as (1) the parties intended to make a contract and (2) there is a reasonably certain basis for the court to grant an appropriate remedy [UCC 2–204(3), 2A–204(3)].

a. Open Price Term

1) If the parties have not agreed on a price, a court will determine "a reasonable price at the time for delivery" [UCC 2–305(1)].

2) If either the buyer or the seller is to determine the price, the price is to be fixed in good faith [UCC 2–305(2)].

3) If a price is not fixed through the fault of one party, the other can cancel the contract or fix a reasonable price [UCC 2–305(3)].

b. **Open Payment Term**
When parties do not specify payment terms—

1) Payment is due at the time and place at which the buyer is to receive the goods [UCC 2–310(a)].

2) The buyer can tender payment in cash or a commercially acceptable substitute (a check or credit card) [UCC 2–511(2)].

c. **Open Delivery Term**
When no delivery terms are specified—

1) The buyer normally takes delivery at the seller's place of business [UCC 2–308(a)]. If the seller has no place of business, the seller's residence is used. When goods are located in some other place and both parties know it, delivery is made there.

2) If the time for shipment or delivery is not clearly specified, a court will infer a "reasonable" time [UCC 2–309(1)].

d. **Duration of an Ongoing Contract**
A party who wishes to terminate an indefinite but ongoing contract must give reasonable notice to the other party [UCC 2–309(2), (3)].

e. **Options and Cooperation Regarding Performance**

1) When no specific shipping arrangements have been made but the contract contemplates shipment of the goods, the seller has the right to make arrangements [UCC 2–311].

2) When terms relating to an assortment of goods are omitted, the buyer can specify the assortment [UCC 2–311].

f. **Open Quantity Term**
If parties do not specify a quantity, there is no basis for a remedy. Exceptions include [UCC 2–306]—

1) **Requirements Contract**
The buyer agrees to buy and the seller agrees to sell all or up to a stated amount of what the buyer needs or requires. There is consideration: the buyer gives up the right to buy from others.

2) **Output Contract**
The seller agrees to sell and the buyer agrees to buy all or up to a stated amount of what the seller produces. Because the seller forfeits the right to sell goods to others, there is consideration.

3) **The UCC Imposes a Good Faith Limitation**
The quantity under these contracts is the amount of requirements or output that occurs during a normal production year.

2. **Merchant's Firm Offer**
If a merchant gives assurances in a signed writing that an offer will remain open, the offer is irrevocable, without consideration, for the stated period, or if no definite period is specified, for a reasonable period (neither to exceed three months) [UCC 2–205, 2A–205].

a. The offer must be written and signed by the offeror. When a firm offer is contained in a form contract prepared by the offeree, a separate firm offer assurance must be signed as well.

b. The other party need not be a merchant.

B. ACCEPTANCE

1. Any Reasonable Means

When an offeror does not specify a means of acceptance, acceptance can be by any reasonable means [UCC 2–206(1), 2A–206(1)].

2. Promise to Ship or Prompt Shipment

a. Promise or Shipment of Conforming Goods

An offer to buy goods for current or prompt shipment can be accepted by a promise to ship or by a prompt shipment [UCC 2–206(1)(b)].

b. Shipment of Nonconforming Goods

Prompt shipment of nonconforming goods is both an acceptance and a breach, unless the seller (1) seasonably notifies the buyer that it is offered only as an accommodation and (2) indicates clearly that it is not an acceptance.

3. Notice of Acceptance

To accept a unilateral offer, the offeree must notify the offeror of performance if the offeror would not otherwise know [UCC 2–206(2)].

4. Additional Terms

If the offeree's response indicates a definite acceptance of the offer, a contract is formed, even if the acceptance includes terms in addition to, or different from, the original offer [UCC 2–207(1)].

a. Subject to the Offeror's Assent

If the additional terms are conditioned on the offeror's assent, the offeree's response is not an acceptance.

b. Not Subject to the Offeror's Assent—Battle of the Forms

Does the contract include the additional terms?

1) When the Seller or Buyer Is a Nonmerchant

Additional terms are considered proposals and not part of the contract. The contract is on the offeror's terms [UCC 2–207(2)].

2) When Both Parties Are Merchants

Additional terms are part of the contract unless (1) the offer expressly states no other terms; (2) they materially alter the original contract; or (3) the offeror objects to the modified terms in a timely fashion [UCC 2–207(2)].

3) When the Parties Act As If They Have a Contract

Regardless of what parties write down, they have a contract according to their conduct [UCC 2–207(3)]. If they do not act in accord with added terms, the terms are not part of a contract.

C. CONSIDERATION

An agreement modifying a sales or lease contract needs no consideration to be binding [UCC 2–209(1), 2A–208(1)].

1. **Modification Must Be Sought in Good Faith [UCC 1–203]**

2. **When a Modification Must Be in Writing to Be Enforceable**

   a. Contract prohibits changes except by a signed writing.

   b. If a consumer (nonmerchant) is dealing with a merchant, and the merchant's form prohibits oral modification, the consumer must sign a separate acknowledgment [UCC 2–209(2), 2A–208(2)].

   c. Any modification that brings a *sales* contract under the Statute of Frauds must be in writing to be enforceable [UCC 2–209(3)].

D. STATUTE OF FRAUDS

To be enforceable, a sales contract must be in writing if the goods are $500 or more and a lease if the payments are $1,000 or more [UCC 2–201, 2A–201].

1. **Sufficiency of the Writing**
   A writing is sufficient if it indicates the parties intended to form a contract and is signed by the party against whom enforcement is sought. A sales contract is not enforceable beyond the quantity stated. A lease must identify and describe the goods and the lease term.

2. **Transactions Between Merchants**
   The requirement of a writing is satisfied if one merchant sends a signed written confirmation to the other.

   a. **Contents of the Confirmation**
      The confirmation must indicate the terms of the agreement, and the merchant receiving it must have reason to know of its contents.

   b. **Objection Within Ten Days**
      Unless the merchant who receives the confirmation objects in writing within ten days, the confirmation is enforceable [UCC 2–201(2)].

3. **Exceptions**
   An oral contract for a sale or lease that should otherwise be in writing will be enforceable in cases of [UCC 2–201(3), 2A–201(4)]—

   a. **Specially Manufactured Goods**
      The seller (or lessor) makes a substantial start on the manufacture of the goods, or makes commitments for it, and the goods are unsuitable for resale to others in the ordinary course of the business.

   b. **Admissions**
      The party against whom enforcement of a contract is sought admits in pleadings or court proceedings that a contract was made.

   c. **Partial Performance**
      Some payment has been made and accepted or some goods have been received and accepted (enforceable to that extent).

E. PAROL EVIDENCE

1. **The Rule**
   If the parties to a contract set forth its terms in a writing intended as their final expression, the terms cannot be contradicted by evidence of any prior agreements or contemporaneous oral agreements.

2. **Exceptions [UCC 2–202, 2A–202]**
A court may accept evidence of the following—

a. **Consistent Additional Terms**
Such terms clarify or remove ambiguities in a writing.

b. **Course of Dealing and Usage of Trade**
The meaning of an agreement is interpreted in light of commercial practices and other surrounding circumstances [UCC 1–205].

c. **Course of Performance**
Conduct that occurs under the agreement indicates what the parties meant by the words in their contract [UCC 2–208(1), 2A–207(1)].

3. **Rules of Construction**
Express terms, course of performance, course of dealing, and usage of trade are to be construed together when they do not contradict one another. If that is unreasonable, the priority is: (1) express terms, (2) course of performance, (3) course of dealing, and (4) usage of trade [UCC 1–205(4), 2–208(2), 2A–207(2)].

F. UNCONSCIONABILITY

1. **What an Unconscionable Contract (or Clause) Is**
A contract so one-sided and unfair (at the time it was made) that enforcing it would be unreasonable.

2. **What a Court Can Do**
A court can (1) refuse to enforce the contract, (2) enforce the contract without the unconscionable clause, or (3) limit the clause to avoid an unconscionable result [UCC 2–302, 2A–108].

V. CONTRACTS FOR THE INTERNATIONAL SALE OF GOODS

Contracts for the international sale of goods are governed by the 1980 United Nations Convention on Contracts for the International Sale of Goods (CISG).

A. APPLICABILITY OF THE CISG

The CISG is to international sales contracts what UCC Article 2 is to domestic sales contracts (except the CISG does not apply to consumer sales). The CISG applies when the parties to an international sales contract do not specify in writing the precise terms of their contract.

B. COMPARISON OF CISG AND UCC PROVISIONS

1. **Statute of Frauds**
International contracts need not be in writing to be enforceable [Art. 11].

2. **Price Term**
Must be specified or be determinable from the contract.

3. **Mirror Image Rule**
The terms of the acceptance must mirror those of the offer [Art. 19].

4. **Acceptance**
When an acceptance is sent, an offer becomes irrevocable, but the acceptance is not effective until it is received. Acceptance by performance does not require notice to the offeror.

TRUE-FALSE QUESTIONS

___ 1. If the subject of a sale is goods, Article 2 of the UCC applies.

___ 2. A contract for a sale of goods is subject to the same traditional principles that apply to all contracts.

___ 3. If the subject of a transaction is a service, Article 2 of the UCC applies.

___ 4. The UCC requires that an agreement modifying a contract must be supported by new consideration to be binding.

___ 5. Under the UCC's Statute of Frauds, a writing must include all material terms except quantity.

___ 6. An unconscionable contract is a contract so one-sided and unfair, at the time it is made, that enforcing it would be unreasonable.

___ 7. Under the CISG, if the parties to a contract have not agreed on a price, a court will supply one.

___ 8. Under the CISG, a writing for a contract for a sale of goods is not required.

___ 9. A lease agreement is a bargain between a lessor and a lessee, as shown by their words and conduct.

___ 10. A consumer lease involves a lessee who leases for a personal, family, or household purpose.

FILL-IN QUESTIONS

________________________________ (Course of dealing/Usage of trade) is a sequence of conduct between the parties that occurred before their agreement and establishes a common basis for their understanding. ________________ ____________ (Course of dealing/Usage of trade) is any practice or method of dealing having regularity of observance in a place, vocation, or ______________ (deal/trade) so as to justify an expectation that it will be observed with respect to the transaction in question. The express terms of an agreement, the course of dealing, and the usage of trade will be construed to be ________________(consistent/ inconsistent) with each other whenever reasonable. When that is not possible, the ________________ _______________ (course of dealing/usage of trade/terms in the agreement) prevail.

MULTIPLE-CHOICE QUESTIONS

___ 1. Under UCC Article 2, the price of a sale may be payable in

a. money only.
b. goods only.
c. money or goods only.
d. money, goods, services, or real estate.

___ **2.** Morro Beverage Company has a surplus of carbon dioxide (which is what puts the bubbles in Morro beverages). Morro agrees to sell the surplus to the Rock Ale Company. Morro is a merchant with respect to

a. carbon dioxide but not Morro beverages.
b. Morro beverages but not carbon dioxide.
c. both Morro beverages and carbon dioxide.
d. neither Morro beverages nor carbon dioxide.

___ **3.** Marina Shipyard agrees to build a barge for MaxCo Shipping. The contract includes an option for up to five more barges, but states that the prices of the other barges could be higher. Marina and MaxCo have

a. a binding contract for at least one barge and up to six barges.
b. a binding contract for one barge only.
c. no contract, because the terms of the option are too indefinite.
d. no contract, because both parties are merchants with respect to barges.

___ **4.** Dina Labs sends Kraft Instruments a purchase order for scalpels. The order states that Dina will not be bound by any additional terms. Kraft ships the scalpels with an acknowledgment that includes an additional, materially different term. Dina is

a. not bound by the term, because the offer expressly states that no other terms will be accepted.
b. not bound by the term, because the additional term constitutes a material alteration.
c. both a and b.
d. bound by the term.

___ **5.** Mike and Rita orally agree to a sale of 100 pair of hiking boots at $50 each. Rita gives Mike a check for $500 as a down payment. Mike takes the check. At this point, the contract is enforceable

a. to the full extent because it is for specially made goods.
b. to the full extent because it is oral.
c. to the extent of $500.
d. none of the above.

___ **6.** Gary leases a construction crane from Able Machinery and subleases it to Baker Contractors. This arrangement is

a. a consumer lease.
b. a finance lease.
c. a sale of goods, not a lease.
d. none of the above.

___ **7.** Barb is an uneducated consumer with low income. After a hard-sell sales presentation, Barb buys a home entertainment center from Don for $2,000, payable in monthly installments of $150. After ten payments, Barb learns that she could have bought the same system at a store for $800. In deciding whether the contract is unconscionable, a court may consider that

a. Barb is an uneducated consumer with low income.
b. Don sold Barb the home entertainment center for more than twice what she could have paid elsewhere for the same system.
c. both a and b.
d. none of the above.

___ **8.** Under the parol evidence rule, evidence of contradictory prior agreements or contemporaneous oral agreements is inadmissible EXCEPT

a. that consistent terms can clarify or remove an ambiguity in the writing.
b. that commercial practices can be used to interpret the contract.
c. both a and b.
d. none of the above.

___ **9.** Stron Computers agrees to buy and SmartCorp agrees to sell all of the microchips that Stron needs this year. The quantity of microchips that Stron must buy under this contract is the amount that

a. SmartCorp would sell during a normal year.
b. Stron would buy during a normal year.
c. SmartCorp actually makes this year.
d. none of the above.

___ **10.** Diana, in Great Britain, and Maria, in Mexico, orally agree to a sale of 100 VCRs at $125 each. Both Britain and Mexico have adopted the CISG. The contract is

a. enforceable because the CISG does not require that a contract be in writing.
b. unenforceable because the CISG requires that a contract be in writing..
c. enforceable because the UCC does not require that a contract be in writing..
d. unenforceable because the UCC requires that a contract be in writing..

SHORT ESSAY QUESTIONS

1. UCC Article 2 deals with sales of goods. What is a sale? What are goods?

2. In certain phases of sales transactions involving merchants, the UCC imposes special standards. Who, for these purposes, is a merchant?

ISSUE SPOTTERS

1. Chuck orally agrees to sell a tool shed to Ron for $450. Chuck removes the shed from his property and takes it to Ron's place. Ron does not pay, and Chuck sues. Ron claims that the sale of the shed was an oral contract that is not enforceable under the Statute of Frauds. What will the court say?

2. Lena, a car dealer, writes to Sam that "I have a 1992 Honda Civic that I will sell to you for $4,000. This offer will be kept open for one week." Six days later, Pam tells Sam that Lena sold the car that morning for $5,000. Did Lena breach any contract?

3. Brad orders 150 computer desks. Fred ships 150 printer stands. Is this an acceptance of Brad's offer or a counteroffer? If it is an acceptance, is it a breach of the contract? What if Fred told Brad, "I'm sending printer stands as an accommodation"?

4. Smith & Sons, Inc., sells truck supplies to J&B, which services trucks. Over the phone, J&B and Smith negotiate for the sale of eighty-four sets of tires. Smith sends a letter to J&B detailing the terms. Smith ships the tires two weeks later. J&B refuses to pay. Is there an enforceable contract between them?

5. Under three contracts for the delivery of 23-inch steel, the United Steel Company delivers, and City Construction accepts, 23-inch and 24-inch steel. Under a new contract for the delivery of 24-inch steel, City rejects United's tender of 23-inch steel. In light of their course of dealing under the other contracts, was City's rejection proper?

QUICKEN CD-ROM
BUSINESS LAW PARTNER APPLICATIONS

Open **Quicken Business Law Partner**. Click on the *New Documents* icon. Choose the *General Contract for Products*. Respond to the *Interview* questions with actual facts or hypothetical ones. For example, imagine that National Connection, Inc., orders fifty hard drives at $400 each from Wong Computers, and they fill out and sign this form. As you complete the *Interview*, answer the following questions.

____ **1.** National and Wong will have an enforceable contract even if they do *not* state in writing

a. the number of hard drives ordered.
b. the terms of payment.
c. both a and b.
d. none of the above.

____ **2.** If, in this form, the parties do not specify in detail exactly what will constitute "conforming" goods, then the goods must satisfy

a. the seller's subjective belief in their quality.
b. the buyer's subjective expectations of their quality.
c. the seller's description of the goods in ads, on labels, and so on.
d. none of the above.

____ **3.** In this form, the clause that gives National (the buyer) an incentive to pay on time is

a. 4. Payment.
b. 5. Delivery.
c. 6. Payment of Taxes.
d. 8. Inspection.

____ **4.** In this form, the clause that gives Wong (the seller) an incentive to deliver goods that conform to the contract is

a. 4. Payment.
b. 5. Delivery.
c. 6. Payment of Taxes.
d. 8. Inspection.

____ **5.** In this form, the clause that allows for the suspension of performance, if performance is prevented by causes beyond a party's reasonable control, is

a. 7. Warranties.
b. 9. Termination.
c. 10. Force Majeure.
d. 11. Dispute Resolution.

★ **Learning Objectives**

The learning objectives in this chapter include:

1. When title to goods passes from seller to buyer.
2. Problems that can arise when persons who acquire goods with imperfect title attempt to resell the goods.
3. Contract terms that help to determine when the risk of loss passes from a seller or lessor to a buyer or lessee.
4. Who bears the risk of loss when a contract is breached.
5. When a party to a sales or lease contract has an insurable interest in the goods.

Chapter 14: Title and Risk of Loss

WHAT THIS CHAPTER IS ABOUT

The UCC has special rules involving title, which may determine the rights and remedies of the parties to a sales contract. In most situations, however, issues concerning the rights and remedies of parties to sales or lease contracts are controlled by three other concepts: (1) identification, (2) risk of loss, and (3) insurable interest.

CHAPTER OUTLINE

I. IDENTIFICATION

For an interest in goods to pass from seller to buyer or lessor to lessee, the goods must (1) exist and (2) be identified as the goods subject to the contract.

A. WHAT IDENTIFICATION IS

Designation of goods as the subject matter of a sales or lease contract.

B. THE SIGNIFICANCE OF IDENTIFICATION

Identification gives the buyer (1) the right to obtain insurance and (2) the right to obtain the goods from the seller.

C. WHEN IDENTIFICATION OCCURS

1. According to the Parties' Agreement

Parties can agree when identification will occur [UCC 2–501, 2A–217].

2. If the Parties Do Not Specify a Time in Their Contract

a. Existing Goods

If the contract calls for a sale of specific goods already existing, identification occurs when the contract is made.

b. **Future Goods**
If a sale involves unborn animals or crops to be harvested within twelve months of the contract (or, for crops, during the next harvest season, whichever is further in the future), identification occurs when the goods are conceived, planted, or begin to grow.

c. **Goods That Are Part of a Larger Mass**
Identification occurs when—

1) **Goods Are Marked, Shipped, or Otherwise Designated**

2) **Exception—Fungible Goods**
A buyer can acquire rights to goods that are alike by physical nature, agreement, or trade usage and that are held by owners in common by replacing the seller as owner [UCC 2–105(4)].

II. PASSAGE OF TITLE

A. WHEN TITLE PASSES

1. **According to the Parties' Agreement**
Parties can agree on when and under what conditions title will pass.

2. **At the Time and Place at Which the Seller Performs**
If the parties do not specify a time, title passes on delivery [UCC 2–401(2)]. The delivery terms determine when this occurs.

a. **Shipment Contracts**
If the seller is required or authorized to ship goods by carrier, title passes at time and place of shipment [UCC 2–401(2)(a)]. All contracts are shipment contracts unless they say otherwise.

b. **Destination Contracts**
If the seller is required to deliver goods to a certain destination, title passes when the goods are tendered there [UCC 2–401(2)(b)].

c. **Delivery without Movement of the Goods**
If a buyer is to pick up goods, passing title turns on whether a seller must give a document of title (bill of lading, warehouse receipt).

1) **When a Document of Title Is Required**
Title passes when and where the document is delivered. The goods do not need to move (for example, they can stay in a warehouse).

2) **When No Document of Title Is Required**
If the goods have been identified, title passes when and where the contract was made. If the goods have not been identified, title does not pass until identification [UCC 2–401(3)].

B. SALES OR LEASES BY NONOWNERS

Generally, a buyer acquires whatever title the seller has to the goods sold [UCC 2–402, 2–403]. A lessee acquires whatever title a lessor could transfer, subject to the lease [UCC 2A–303, 2A–304, 2A–305].

1. **Void Title**
If the seller or lessor stole the goods, the buyer or lessee acquires nothing; the real owner can reclaim the goods.

2. **Voidable Title**
A seller or lessor has voidable title if goods were obtained by fraud, paid for with a check that is later dishonored, bought on credit when the seller was insolvent, or bought from a minor.

a. **The Real Owner Can Reclaim the Goods**

b. **Exception—Good Faith Purchaser or Lessee for Value**
The real owner cannot recover the goods [UCC 2–403(1)].

3. **The Entrustment Rule**
Entrustment includes both delivering goods to a merchant and leaving goods with the merchant for later delivery or pickup [UCC 2–403(3)].

a. **Entrusting Goods to a Merchant Who Deals in Goods of the Kind**
The merchant can transfer all rights to a buyer or sublessee in the ordinary course of business [UCC 2–403(2), 2A–305(2)].

b. **What a Buyer or Sublessee in the Ordinary Course Gets**
Only those rights held by the person who entrusted the goods.

III. RISK OF LOSS

The question of who suffers a financial loss if goods are damaged, destroyed, or lost (who bears the *risk of loss*) is determined by the parties' contract. If the contract does not state who bears the risk, the UCC has rules to determine it.

A. DELIVERY WITH MOVEMENT OF THE GOODS—CARRIER CASES

When goods are to be delivered by truck or other paid transport—

1. **Contract Terms**

a. **F.O.B.** (Free on board)—delivery is at seller's expense to a specific location. Risk passes at the location [UCC 2–319(1)].

b. **F.A.S.** (Free alongside)—seller delivers goods next to the ship that will carry them, and risk passes to buyer [UCC 2–319(2)].

c. **C.I.F. or C.&F.** (Cost, insurance, and freight)—seller puts goods in possession of a carrier before risk passes [UCC 2–320(2)].

d. **Delivery Ex-ship** (From the carrying vessel)—risk passes to buyer when goods leave the ship or are unloaded [UCC 2–322].

2. **Shipment Contracts**
Risk passes to the buyer or lessee when the goods are delivered to a carrier [UCC 2–509(1)(a), 2A–219(2)(a)].

3. **Destination Contracts**
Risk passes to the buyer or lessee when the goods are tendered to the buyer at the destination [UCC 2–509(1)(b), 2A–219(2)(b)].

B. DELIVERY WITHOUT MOVEMENT OF THE GOODS

When goods are to be picked up by the buyer or lessee—

1. **If the Seller or Lessor Is a Merchant**
Risk passes only on the buyer's or lessee's taking possession of the goods.

2. **If the Seller or Lessor Is Not a Merchant**
Risk passes on tender of delivery [UCC 2–509(3), 2A–219(c)].

3. If a Bailee Holds the Goods

Risk passes when (1) the buyer receives a negotiable document of title for the goods, (2) the bailee acknowledges the buyer's (or in the case of a lease, the lessee's) right to the goods, or (3) the buyer receives a nonnegotiable document of title, presents the document to the bailee, and demands the goods. If the bailee refuses to honor the document, the risk remains with the seller [UCC 2–503(4)(b), 2–509(2), 2A–219(2)(b)].

C. CONDITIONAL SALES

1. Sale or Return (or Sale and Return)

A seller delivers goods to a buyer who may retain any part and pay accordingly. The balance is returned or held by the buyer as a bailee.

a. Title and Risk Pass to the Buyer with Possession

Title and risk stay with the buyer until he or she returns the goods to the seller within the specified time. A sale is final if the buyer fails to return the goods in time. Goods in the buyer's possession are subject to the claims of the buyer's creditors.

b. Consignment

A consignment is a sale or return. Goods in the consignee's (buyer's) possession are subject to his or her creditors' claims [UCC 2–326(3)].

2. Sale on Approval

A seller offers to sell goods, and the buyer takes them on a trial basis. Title and risk remain with the seller until the buyer accepts the goods.

a. What Constitutes Acceptance

Any act inconsistent with the trial purpose or the seller's ownership; or by the buyer's choice not to return the goods on time.

b. Return

Return is at the seller's expense and risk [UCC 2–327(1)]. Goods are not subject to the claims of the buyer's creditors until acceptance.

D. RISK OF LOSS WHEN A SALES OR LEASE CONTRACT IS BREACHED

Generally, the party in breach bears the risk of loss.

1. When the Seller or Lessor Breaches

Risk passes to the buyer or lessee when the defects are cured or the buyer or lessee accepts the goods in spite of the defects. If, after acceptance, a buyer discovers a latent defect, acceptance can be revoked and the risk goes back to the seller [UCC 2–510(2), 2A–220(1)].

2. When the Buyer or Lessee Breaches

Risk shifts to the buyer or lessee (if the goods have been identified), where it stays for a commercially reasonable time after the seller or lessor learns of the breach. The buyer or lessee is liable to the extent of any deficiency in seller or lessor's insurance [UCC 2–510(3), 2A–220(2)].

IV. INSURABLE INTEREST

A party buying insurance must have a "sufficient interest" in the insured item (see Chapter 30). More than one party can have an interest at the same time.

A. INSURABLE INTEREST OF THE BUYER OR LESSEE
A buyer or lessee has an insurable interest in goods the moment they are identified, even before risk of loss passes [UCC 2–501(1), 2A–218(1)].

B. INSURABLE INTEREST OF THE SELLER OR LESSOR
A seller or lessor has an insurable interest in goods as long as he or she holds title or a security interest in the goods [UCC 2–501(2), 2A–218(3)].

V. BULK TRANSFERS

A. WHAT A BULK TRANSFER IS
A transfer of more than half of a seller's inventory not made in the ordinary course of business [UCC 6–102(1)]. Subject to UCC Article 6.

B. BULK TRANSFER RULES UNDER ARTICLE 6
For the buyer to acquire title to goods free of all claims of the seller's creditors, the seller and buyer must comply with certain notice requirements [UCC 6–104, 6–105]. If the requirements are not met, the goods are subject to the claims of the seller's unpaid creditors for six months [UCC 6–111].

C. REPEAL AND REVISION OF ARTICLE 6
Article 6 has been repealed or replaced with revised Article 6 in most states. Revised Article 6 applies only to bulk sales of property valued between $10,000 and $25 million by sellers whose principal business is the sale of inventory from bulk stock. If a seller has more than two hundred creditors, a buyer can give notice by public filing. The notice period is forty-five days. The statute of limitations is one year.

TRUE-FALSE QUESTIONS

___ **1.** Identification occurs when goods are shipped by the seller.

___ **2.** Unless the parties agree otherwise, title passes at the time and place that the buyer accepts the goods.

___ **3.** Unless a contract provides otherwise, it is normally assumed to be a shipment contract.

___ **4.** A sale on approval occurs when a coin dealer mails coins to a prospective buyer to examine for fourteen days to decide whether to buy or return them.

___ **5.** A buyer and a seller cannot both have an insurable interest in the same goods at the same time.

___ **6.** A bulk transfer is a transfer of a major part of the inventory not made in the ordinary course of the transferor's business.

___ **7.** In a sale on approval, the risk of loss passes to the buyer as soon as the buyer takes possession.

___ **8.** A buyer can acquire valid title to stolen goods if he or she does not know that the goods are stolen.

___ **9.** Under a destination contract, title passes at time and place of shipment.

___ **10.** If a seller is a merchant, the risk of loss passes when a buyer takes possession of the goods.

FILL-IN QUESTIONS

______________ (F.A.S./F.O.B.) means that delivery is at a seller's expense to a specific location—the place of shipment or a place of destination. When the term is ____________ (F.A.S./F.O.B.) place of *shipment*, risk passes when the seller puts the goods into a carrier's possession. When the term is ______________ (F.A.S./F.O.B.) place of *destination*, risk passes when the seller tenders delivery. ______________ (F.A.S./ F.O.B.) requires a seller at his or her own expense and risk to deliver goods alongside the ship that will transport them at which point risk passes.

MULTIPLE-CHOICE QUESTIONS

___ **1.** Bob contracts to sell to the Marcos University Book Store 10,000 black felt-tipped pens. Bob identifies the pens by boxing the order, attaching labels with Marcos's address to the cartons, and leaving the boxes on the loading dock for shipping. Between Bob and Marcos,

a. the risk of loss has passed with respect to all of the pens.
b. the risk of loss has passed with respect to half of the pens.
c. the risk of loss has passed with respect to the pens with labels on the boxes.
d. none of the above.

___ **2.** Popco in Akron agrees to ship one hundred popcorn poppers to Fine Stores in Dayton under a shipment contract. On Monday, Popco delivers the poppers to Capitol Transport to take to Dayton, where they arrive on Tuesday. On Wednesday, Capitol tells Fine that it can pick the goods up at Capitol's warehouse. On Thursday, the warehouse burns to the ground. On Friday, Fine learns about the fire. The risk of loss passed to Fine on

a. Monday.
b. Tuesday.
c. Friday.
d. none of the above.

___ **3.** On Monday, Stan buys a mountain bike from Tom, his neighbor, who says, "Take the bike." Stan says, "I'll leave it in your garage until Friday." On Tuesday, Rosie steals the bike from Tom's garage. Who bore the risk?

a. Stan
b. Tom
c. Both a and b
d. None of the above.

___ **4.** Pat's goods are in Andy's warehouse. Pat has a negotiable document of title for the goods. On Tuesday, she sells the goods to Nick and gives him the title document. On Friday, the warehouse collapses in an earthquake. The goods are destroyed. Who suffers the loss?

a. Pat
b. Andy
c. Nick
d. Both b and c

___ **5.** Jay steals a car from Diamond Car Rental in Arizona. Jay leaves the car with Bull's Sales in North Carolina, for repairs. Bull's sells the car to Darryl, who does not know that Bull's has no right to sell the car. Against whom does Darryl have good title?

a. Jay
b. Diamond
c. Bull's
d. Both a and c

___ **6.** Suzy buys a jeep from Sheridan Jeep Sales. Suzy says, "I'll pick up the jeep Monday." On Sunday, Sheridan sells the jeep to Pam, who does not know Sheridan has no right to sell it. Against whom does Pam have good title?

a. Suzy
b. Sheridan
c. Both a and b
d. None of the above

___ **7.** On Monday, Craft Computers in Seattle delivers five hundred keyboards to Pac Transport to take to Portland under a destination contract with Comp Stores. The keyboards arrive in Portland on Tuesday, and Pac tells Comp they are at Pac's warehouse. On Thursday, the warehouse burns down. On Friday, Comp learns of the fire. The risk of loss passed to Comp on

a. Monday.
b. Tuesday.
c. Friday.
d. none of the above.

___ **8.** Alpha Comm agrees to sell one hundred cellular phones to Beta Electronics. Alpha identifies the goods by marking the crates with red stripes. Title has not yet passed to Beta. Who has an insurable interest in the goods?

a. Only Alpha
b. Only Beta
c. Both Alpha and Beta
d. None of the above

___ **9.** Under a contract with QT Corp., Gold Media ships sixty hard drives. When QT opens the crates, it discovers that the drives are the wrong model, but agrees to accept them anyway. The risk of loss passed to QT when

a. Gold shipped the drives.
b. QT opened the crates.
c. QT discovered that the goods were the wrong model.
d. QT accepted the drives.

___ **10.** Apple Bike Makers agrees to sell forty mountain bikes to Orange Mountain Recreation, under a shipment contract. Apple delivers the goods to Sugar Trucking to take to Orange Mountain. Sugar delivers the goods. Title to the goods passed when

a. Apple agreed to sell the goods.
b. Apple delivered the goods to Sugar.
c. Sugar delivered the goods to Orange Mountain.
d. none of the above.

SHORT ESSAY QUESTIONS

1. Define "risk of loss" under the UCC.

2. Discuss when risk passes: (a) under a shipment contract; (b) under a destination contract; (c) when the buyer is to pick up the goods and (1) the seller is a merchant and (2) the seller is not a merchant; and (d) when a bailee holds the goods.

ISSUE SPOTTERS

1. Adams Textiles in Kansas City sells certain fabrics to Silk n' Satin Stores in Oklahoma City. Adams packs the fabric and ships it by rail to Silk. In transit across Kansas, a tornado derails the train and scatters and shreds the fabric across miles of cornfields. What are the consequences if Silk bore the risk? If Adams bore the risk?

2. Under a contract between a seller in New York and a buyer in Dallas, if delivery is "F.O.B. New York," the risk passes when the seller puts the goods in the carrier's hands. If delivery is "F.O.B. Dallas," the risk passes when the goods reach Dallas. What if the contract says only that the seller is "to ship goods at seller's expense"?

3. Butler Farms in Washington sells Astor Produce in Alaska a certain size of apples to be shipped "F.O.B. Seattle." The apples Butler delivers to the shipping company for transport are too small. The apples are lost in transit. Who suffers the loss?

4. Paula boards her horse Blaze at Gold Spur Stables. She sells the horse to George and calls Gold Spur to say, "I sold Blaze to George." Gold Spur says, "Ok." That night, Blaze is kicked in the head by another horse and dies. Who pays for the loss?

5. Chocolate, Inc., sells five hundred cases of cocoa mix to Dan's Food Company, which pays with a bad check. Chocolate does not discover that the check is bad until after Dan sells the cocoa to Chip's Food Stores, which suspects nothing. Can Chocolate recover the cocoa from Chip's?

QUICKEN CD-ROM BUSINESS LAW PARTNER APPLICATIONS

Open **Quicken Business Law Partner**. Click on the *New Documents* icon. Select the *Consignment Agreement*. Respond to the *Interview* questions with actual facts or hypothetical ones. For example, imagine that Home Stores, Inc., agrees to accept a variety of items from Smith Craftworks to sell on consignment. As you complete the *Interview*, answer the following questions.

____ **1.** Unless the parties provide otherwise, the risk of loss is with

a. Smith (the consignor).
b. Home (the consignee).
c. Home's customers, before they buy the goods.
d. none of the above.

____ **2.** In this form, the risk of loss is spelled out in the clause titled

a. IV. Title to Merchandise.
b. VI. Defaults.
c. VIII. Warranties.
d. none of the above.

___ **3.** In this form, Smith (the consignor) can grant to Home (the consignee)

a. only exclusive rights to sell the goods.
b. only territorial rights to sell the goods.
c. exclusive or territorial rights to sell the goods.
d. none of the above.

___ **4.** A consignment agreement may terminate on

a. the consignee's failure to make payments when due.
b. notice by either party.
c. a specified date automatically.
d. any of the above.

___ **5.** In this form, a clause that can be excluded without voiding the contract is

a. XI. Entire Agreement.
b. XIV. Waiver of Contractual Right.
c. both a and b.
d. none of the above.

 **Learning Objectives**

The learning objectives in this chapter include:

1. The obligations of sellers and lessors under the UCC.
2. The perfect tender rule and its exceptions.
3. The obligations of buyers and lessees under the UCC.
4. The options available if a party to a sales or lease contract repudiates the contract before the time for performance.
5. The remedies available to when a sales or lease contract is breached.

Chapter 15: Performance and Breach of Sales and Lease Contracts

WHAT THIS CHAPTER IS ABOUT

This chapter examines the basic obligations of a seller and a buyer under a sales contract, and a lessor and a lessee under a lease contract, and the remedies each party has if the contract is breached. The general purpose of the remedies is to put a nonbreaching party "in as good a position as if the other party had fully performed."

CHAPTER OUTLINE

I. PERFORMANCE OBLIGATIONS

The obligations of good faith and commercial reasonableness underlie every contract within the UCC [UCC 1–203]. The obligation of the seller or lessor is to tender conforming goods. The obligation of the buyer or lessee is to pay for the goods [UCC 2–301, 2A–516(1)].

II. OBLIGATIONS OF THE SELLER OR LESSOR

The seller or lessor must have and hold conforming goods at the disposal of the buyer or lessee and give whatever notice is reasonably necessary to enable the buyer or lessee to take delivery [UCC 2–503(1), 2A–508(1)].

A. TENDER OF DELIVERY

At a reasonable hour, in a reasonable manner, and the goods must be kept available for a reasonable time [UCC 2–503(1)(a)]. Goods must be tendered in a single delivery unless parties agree otherwise [UCC 2–612, 2A–510] or, under the circumstances, a party can request delivery in lots [UCC 2–307].

B. PLACE OF DELIVERY

The parties may agree on a particular destination, or their contract or the circumstances may indicate a place.

1. **Noncarrier Cases**

   a. **Seller's Place of Business**
   If the contract does not designate a place of delivery, and the buyer is to pick up the goods, the place is the seller's place of business or if none, the seller's residence [UCC 2–308].

   b. **Identified Goods That Are Not at the Seller's Place of Business**
   Wherever they are is the place of delivery [UCC 2–308].

2. **Carrier Cases**

   a. **Shipment Contract**
   The seller must [UCC 2–504]—

      1) Put the goods into the hands of a carrier.

      2) Make a contract for the transport of the goods that is reasonable according to their nature and value.

      3) Tender to the buyer any documents necessary to obtain possession of the goods from the carrier.

      4) Promptly notify the buyer that shipment has been made.

      5) If a seller fails to meet these requirements, and this causes a material loss or a delay, the buyer can reject the shipment.

   b. **Destination Contract**
   The seller must give the buyer appropriate notice and any necessary documents of title [UCC 2–503].

C. **THE PERFECT TENDER RULE**
A seller or lessor must deliver goods in conformity with every detail of the contract. If goods or tender fail in any respect, the buyer or lessee can accept the goods, reject them, or accept part and reject part [UCC 2–601, 2A–509].

D. **EXCEPTIONS TO THE RULE**

1. **Agreement of the Parties**
Parties can agree in their contract that, for example, the seller can repair or replace any defective goods within a reasonable time.

2. **Cure**

   a. **Within the Contract Time for Performance**
   If nonconforming goods are rejected, the seller or lessor can notify the buyer or lessee of an intention to repair, adjust, or replace the goods and can then do so within the contract time for performance [UCC 2–508, 2A–513].

   b. **After the Time for Performance Expires**
   The seller or lessor can cure if there were reasonable grounds to believe the nonconformance would be acceptable.

   c. **Substantially Restricts the Buyer's Right to Reject**
   If the buyer or lessee refuses goods but does not disclose the nature of the defect, he or she cannot later assert the defect as a defense if it is one that could have been cured [UCC 2–605, 2A–514].

3. **Substitution of Carriers**
If, through no fault of either party an agreed manner of delivery is not available, a substitute is sufficient [UCC 2–614(1)].

4. **Installment Contracts**

a. **Substantial Nonconformity**
A buyer or lessee can reject an installment only if a nonconformity substantially impairs the value of the installment and cannot be cured [UCC 2–612(2), 2–307, 2A–510(1)].

b. **Breach of the Entire Contract**
A breach occurs if one or more nonconforming installments substantially impair the value of the whole contract. If the buyer or lessee accepts a nonconforming installment, the contract is reinstated [UCC 2–612(3), 2A–510(2)]

5. **Commercial Impracticability**
No breach if performance is impracticable by the occurrence of an unforeseen contingency. If the event allows for partial performance, the seller or lessor must do so, in a fair manner (with notice to the buyer or lessee) [UCC 2–615, 2A–405]

6. **Destruction of Identified Goods**
When goods are destroyed (through no fault of a party) before risk passes to the buyer or lessee, the parties are excused from performance [UCC 2–613, 2A–221]. If goods are only partially destroyed, a buyer can treat a contract as void or accept damaged goods with a price credit.

III. OBLIGATIONS OF THE BUYER OR LESSEE

The buyer or lessee must make payment at the time and place he or she receives the goods unless the parties have agreed otherwise [UCC 2–310(a), 2A–516(1)].

A. PAYMENT

Payment can be by any means agreed on between the parties [UCC 2–511].

B. RIGHT OF INSPECTION

The buyer or lessee can verify, before making payment, that the goods are what were contracted for. The buyer has no duty to pay if the goods are not what were ordered [UCC 2–513(1), 2A–515(1)].

1. **Time, Place, and Manner**
Inspection can be in any reasonable place, time and manner, determined by custom of the trade, practice of the parties, and so on [UCC 2–513(2)].

2. **C.O.D. Shipments**
If a buyer agrees to a C.O.D. shipment or to pay for goods on presentation of a bill of lading, no right of inspection exists [UCC 2–513(3)].

3. **Payment Due—Documents of Title (C.I.F. and C.&F. Contracts)**
Payment is required on receipt of documents of title, before inspection, and must be made unless the buyer knows the goods are nonconforming [UCC 2–310(b), 2–513(3)].

C. ACCEPTANCE

Acceptance is presumed if a buyer or lessee has a reasonable opportunity to inspect and fails to reject in a reasonable time [UCC 2–606, 2–602, 2A–515].

1. **How a Buyer or Lessee Can Accept**
A buyer or lessee can accept by words or conduct. Under a sales contract, a buyer can accept by any act (such as using or reselling the goods) inconsistent with the seller's ownership [UCC 2–606(1)(c)].

2. **A Buyer or Lessee Can Accept Only Some of the Goods**
But not less than a single commercial unit [UCC 2–601(c), 2A-509(1)].

IV. ANTICIPATORY REPUDIATION

The nonbreaching party can (1) treat the repudiation as a final breach by pursuing a remedy or (2) wait, hoping that the repudiating party will decide to honor the contract [UCC 2–610, 2A–402]. If the party decides to wait, the breaching party can retract the repudiation [UCC 2–611, 2A–403].

V. REMEDIES OF THE SELLER OR LESSOR

A. WHEN THE GOODS ARE IN POSSESSION OF THE SELLER OR LESSOR

1. **The Right to Cancel the Contract**
A seller or lessor can cancel a contract (with notice to the buyer or lessee) if the other party breaches it [UCC 2–703(f), 2A–523(1)(a)].

2. **The Right to Withhold Delivery**
A seller or lessor can withhold delivery if a buyer or lessee wrongfully rejects or revokes acceptance, fails to pay, or repudiates [UCC 2–703(a), 2A–523(1)(c)]. If a buyer or lessee is insolvent, a seller or lessor can refuse to deliver unless a buyer pays cash [UCC 2–702(1), 2A–525(1)].

3. **The Right to Resell or Dispose of the Goods**

   a. **When a Seller or Lessor Can Resell Goods**
   A seller or lessor still has the goods and the buyer or lessee wrongfully rejects or revokes acceptance, fails to pay, or repudiates the contract [UCC 2–703(d), 2–706(1), 2A–523(1)(e), 2A–527(1)].

   b. **Unfinished Goods**
   A seller or lessor can (1) resell the goods as scrap or (2) finish and resell them (buyer or lessee is liable for any difference in price). The goal is to obtain maximum value [UCC 2–704(2), 2A–524(2)].

4. **The Right to Recover the Purchase Price or Lease Payments Due**
A seller or lessor can bring an action for the price if the buyer or lessee breaches after the goods are identified to the contract and the seller or lessor is unable to resell [UCC 2–709(1), 2A–529(1)].

5. **The Right to Recover Damages**
If a buyer or lessee repudiates a contract or wrongfully refuses to accept, the seller or lessor can recover the difference between the contract price and the market price (at the time and place of tender), plus incidental damages. If the market price is less than the contract price, the seller or lessor gets lost profits [UCC 2–708, 2A–528].

B. WHEN THE GOODS ARE IN TRANSIT

A seller or lessor can stop delivery of goods if (1) the buyer or lessee is insolvent or (2) the buyer or lessee is solvent but in breach (if the quantity shipped is a carload, a truckload, or larger) [UCC 2–705, 2A–526].

C. WHEN THE GOODS ARE IN POSSESSION OF THE BUYER OR LESSEE

1. **The Right to Recover the Purchase Price or Lease Payments Due**
A seller or lessor can bring an action for the price if the buyer or lessee accepts the goods but refuses to pay [UCC 2–709(1), 2A–529(1)].

2. **The Right to Reclaim the Goods**

a. **Sales Contracts—Buyer's Insolvency**
If an insolvent buyer gets goods on credit, the seller can (within ten days) reclaim them. A seller can reclaim any time if a buyer misrepresents solvency in writing within three months before delivery [UCC 2–702(2)].

b. **Sales Contracts—A Buyer in the Ordinary Course of Business**
A seller cannot reclaim goods from such a buyer.

c. **Sales Contracts—Bars the Pursuit of Other Remedies**
A seller who reclaims gets preferential treatment over a buyer's other creditors (but cannot pursue other remedies) [UCC 2–702(3)].

d. **Lease Contracts**
A lessor can reclaim goods from a lessee in default [UCC 2A–525(2)].

VI. REMEDIES OF THE BUYER OR LESSEE

A. WHEN THE SELLER OR LESSOR REFUSES TO DELIVER THE GOODS

When a seller or lessor fails to deliver or repudiates the contract, the buyer or lessee has the following rights.

1. **The Right to Cancel the Contract**
The buyer or lessee can rescind (cancel) the contract. On notice to the seller, the buyer or lessee is discharged [UCC 2–711(1), 2A–508(1)(a).

2. **The Right to Recover the Goods**
A buyer or lessee who paid for goods in the hands of the seller or lessor can recover them if the seller or lessor becomes insolvent within ten days of receiving payment and the goods are identified to the contract. Buyer or lessee must tender any unpaid balance [UCC 2–502, 2A–522].

3. **The Right to Obtain Specific Performance**
A buyer or lessee can obtain specific performance if goods are unique or damages would be inadequate [UCC 2–716(1), 2A–521(1)].

4. **The Right of Cover**
The measure of damages is the difference between the cost of cover and the contract price, plus incidental and consequential damages, less expenses saved by the breach [UCC 2–712, 2–715, 2A–518, 2A–520].

5. **The Right to Replevy the Goods**
A buyer or lessee can use replevin if seller or lessor fails to deliver or repudiates and buyer or lessee cannot cover [UCC 2–716(3), 2A–521(3)].

6. **The Right to Recover Damages**
The measure of damages is the difference between the contract price and, when the buyer or lessee learned of the breach, the market price (at the place of delivery), plus incidental and consequential damages, less expenses saved by the breach [UCC 2–713, 2A–519].

B. WHEN THE SELLER OR LESSOR DELIVERS NONCONFORMING GOODS

1. **The Right to Reject**
A buyer or lessee can reject the part of goods that fails to conform to the contract (and rescind the contract or obtain cover) [UCC 2–601, 2A–509].

a. **Notice Required**
Notice must be timely, and a buyer or lessee must tell the seller or lessor what the defect is [UCC 2–602(1), 2–605, 2A–509(2), 2A–514].

b. **Duties of a Merchant Buyer or Lessee**
Follow the seller or lessor's instructions about the goods [UCC 2–603, 2A–511]. Without instructions, perishable goods can be resold; otherwise they must be stored or returned.

c. **The Right to Retain and Enforce a Security Interest**
Buyers who rightfully reject or who justifiably revoke acceptance of goods in their possession have a security interest in the goods. A buyer can recover payments made for the goods and expenses to inspect, transport, and hold the goods, or can resell, withhold delivery, or stop delivery [UCC 2–711, 2–706].

2. **The Right to Revoke Acceptance**

a. **Substantial Impairment**
Any nonconformity must substantially impair the value of the goods *and* either not be seasonably cured or be difficult to discover [UCC 2–608, 2A–517].

b. **Notice of a Breach Must Be within a Reasonable Time**
Before the goods have undergone substantial change (not caused by their own defects, such as spoilage) [UCC 2–608(2), 2A–517(4)].

3. **The Right to Recover Damages for Accepted Goods**
Notice of a breach must be within a reasonable time. The measure of damages is the difference between value of goods as accepted and value if they had been as promised [UCC 2–714(2), 2A–519(4)].

VII. STATUTE OF LIMITATIONS

An action for breach of contract under the UCC must be brought within four years of the breach. In their contract, the parties can reduce this period to not less than one year [UCC 2–725(1), 2A–506(1)]. If goods are nonconforming but the buyer accepts them, notice of the breach must be within a reasonable time or all remedies are lost [UCC 2–607(3)(a), 2A–516(3)].

VIII. LIMITATION OF REMEDIES

Parties can provide for remedies in addition to or in lieu of those in the UCC, or they can change the measure of damages [UCC 2–719, 2A–503]. If a buyer or lessee is a consumer, limiting consequential damages for personal injuries on a breach of warranty is *prima facie* unconscionable.

TRUE-FALSE QUESTIONS

___ 1. Performance of a sales contract is controlled by the agreement between the seller and the buyer.

___ 2. If a particular carrier is unavailable through no fault of either party, a commercially reasonable substitute may be used.

___ **3.** If identified goods are destroyed through no fault of either party, and risk has not passed to the buyer, the parties are excused from performance.

___ **4.** Payment is always due at the time of delivery.

___ **5.** A buyer or lessee can always reject delivered goods on discovery of a defect, regardless of previous opportunities to inspect.

___ **6.** An award of damages is considered inappropriate if specific performance can be obtained.

___ **7.** If a seller delivers nonconforming goods, the buyer can accept the goods, notify the seller, and recover the difference between the value of the goods as accepted and the value they would have had as promised.

___ **8.** When a seller discovers that a buyer has received goods on credit while insolvent, the seller can reclaim the goods.

___ **9.** If a buyer or lessee is in breach, the seller or lessor can cancel the contract and sue for damages.

___ **10.** If a seller or lessor cancels a contract without justification, he or she is in breach, and the buyer or lessee can sue for damages.

FILL-IN QUESTIONS

A seller's obligations include holding ______________ (conforming/nonconforming) goods at a buyer's disposal ______________ (and/or) giving notice reasonably necessary for the buyer to take delivery. Unless the parties have agreed otherwise, the ______________ (seller/buyer) must provide facilities reasonably suited for ______________ (delivery/receipt) of the goods. Also, unless the parties have agreed otherwise, a buyer must pay at the time and place of receipt, ______________ (even if/unless) the place of shipment is the place of delivery.

MULTIPLE-CHOICE QUESTIONS

___ **1.** Silver Textiles, Inc., contracts to sell five hundred bolts of denim to Gold Clothing. Silver is to deliver the goods in Chicago. Gold is to specify the exact address before the delivery date. Gold fails to specify the address, causing Silver to fail to deliver on time. Which of the following is TRUE?

a. Gold can cancel the contract.
b. Silver is excused for the delay in delivery.
c. Gold is excused for failing to specify the address.
d. Silver is in breach of contract.

___ **2.** Smith Company in San Diego agrees to ship 500,000 plastic silver dollars to the Zenith Casino in Las Vegas. The goods are in a warehouse in Barstow. The agreement says that Zenith will pick up the goods, but says nothing about the place. The place of delivery is

a. San Diego.
b. Las Vegas.
c. Barstow.
d. none of the above.

____ **3.** Pep Paints agrees to sell to Monar Painters Grade A-1 latex outdoor paint to be delivered September 8. On September 7, Pep tenders Grade B-2 paint. Monar rejects the Grade B-2 paint. If, two days later, Pep tenders Grade C-3 paint with an offer of a price allowance, Pep will have

a. one day to cure.
b. a reasonable time to cure.
c. additional, unlimited time to cure.
d. none of the above.

____ **4.** World Globe Company agrees to sell to Tom's Map Shop fifty globes. World tenders delivery, but Tom refuses to accept or to pay for the globes. If World sues Tom for damages, World could recover the difference between the contract price and the market price at the time and place of

a. contracting.
b. tender.
c. rejection.
d. none of the above.

____ **5.** Roy's Game Town orders virtual reality helmets from VR, Inc. VR delivers, but Roy rejects the shipment without telling VR the reason. If VR had known the reason, it could have corrected the problem within hours. If Roy sues VR for damages, Roy will

a. win, because VR's tender did not conform to the contract.
b. win, because VR made no attempt to cure.
c. lose, because Roy's rejection was unjustified—VR could have cured.
d. lose, because a buyer cannot reject goods *and* sue for damages.

____ **6.** Alto Corporation agrees to buy one hundred hard drives from Gopher Equipment. When Gopher fails to deliver, Alto is forced to cover. Alto sues Gopher. Alto can recover from Gopher

a. the cover price, less the contract price.
b. incidental and consequential damages.
c. both a and b.
d. none of the above.

____ **7.** AdamCo agrees to sell the latest version of the Go! CD-ROMs to Cutter Computers. AdamCo delivers an outdated version of Go! (nonconforming goods). Cutter's possible remedies may include

a. recovering damages.
b. revoking acceptance.
c. rejecting part or all of the goods.
d. all of the above.

____ **8.** Office Equip, Inc., agrees to lease fifty computers to Pine Company. When Office tries to deliver, Pine refuses to accept. There is nothing wrong with the computers. Office sues Pine, seeking damages. Office is entitled to the difference between

a. the contract price and the market price.
b. the market price and Office's lost profits.
c. Office's lost profits and the contract price.
d. none of the above.

___ 9. Phil Parts, Inc., agrees to sell clock parts to Time Clocks. Phil does not deliver. Time's normal remedies include

a. damages.
b. a forced discount.
c. specific performance.
d. all of the above.

___ 10. Max Products agrees to sell sports equipment to Geo Sports. Before the time for performance, Max tells Geo that it will not deliver. Geo may

a. treat this as a breach and pursue a remedy.
b. wait to see whether Max will perform.
c. either a or b.
d. none of the above.

SHORT ESSAY QUESTIONS

1. What is a seller's right to cure and how does it affect a buyer's right to reject?

2. What is a buyer's right of cover?

ISSUE SPOTTERS

1. Mike agrees to sell 1,000 espresso makers to Jenny to be delivered on May 1. Due to a strike in the last week of April, there is a temporary shortage of delivery vehicles. Mike can deliver the espresso makers 200 at a time over a period of ten days, with the first delivery on May 1. Does Mike have the right to deliver the goods in five lots?

2. Country Fruit Stand orders eighty cases of peaches from Citrus Farms. For no good reason, Citrus delivers thirty cases instead of eighty, and the delivery is late. Does Country have the right to reject the shipment?

3. Parade Instruments agrees to sell to American Carnivals fifteen electronic calliopes, to be delivered in five installments. The first installment consists of two electronic calliopes and a manual one. Can American cancel the whole contract?

4. Pic Post-Stars agrees to sell Ace Novelty 5,000 posters of celebrities, to be delivered on April 1. On March 1, Pic tells Ace, "The deal's off." Ace says, "I expect you to deliver. I'll be waiting." Can Ace sue Pic without waiting until April 1?

5. Pizza King agrees to buy tomatoes from Mac Farms. When Mac tenders the goods, the owner of Pizza King says, "I changed my mind. I don't want the tomatoes." Mac quickly sells the tomatoes to another buyer, for a lower price. Can Mac recover from Pizza King even though the tomatoes are sold? If so, what's the measure of recovery?

QUICKEN CD-ROM BUSINESS LAW PARTNER APPLICATIONS

Open **Quicken Business Law Partner**. Click on the *New Documents* icon. Select the *Equipment Lease*. Respond to the *Interview* questions with actual facts or hypothetical ones. For example, imagine that Litco Corporation agrees to lease computers from Desktop, Inc. As you complete the *Interview*, answer the following questions.

____ **1.** Unless the parties provide otherwise, in this lease, the risk of loss is with

a. Desktop (the lessor).
b. Litco (the lessee).
c. both parties, in equal measure.
d. none of the above.

____ **2.** The parties can provide in this lease that Litco (the lessee) may change or alter the leased equipment

a. *only* with the permission of Desktop (the lessor).
b. *only* if the value of the equipment is not decreased.
c. with Desktop's permission *or* if the value is not decreased.
d. none of the above.

____ **3.** The parties can provide in this lease that Litco (the lessee) has an option

a. to renew the lease only.
b. to buy the equipment only.
c. to renew the lease or to buy the equipment.
d. none of the above.

____ **4.** The parties can provide in this lease that Desktop (the lessor)

a. disclaims all warranties.
b. is not liable for any injuries arising from use of the equipment.
c. both a and b.
d. none of the above.

____ **5.** Default can occur, under this lease, if

a. the lessee fails to make a payment when it is due.
b. either party fails to enforce any provision of the lease.
c. both a and b.
d. none of the above.

 **Learning Objectives**

The learning objectives in this chapter include:

1. Warranties that arise in a sales or lease transaction.
2. Warranty disclaimers.
3. How negligence and misrepresentation provide a basis for product liability.
4. The requirements for an action in strict liability.
5. Possible defenses against product liability claims.

Chapter 16: Warranties and Product Liability

WHAT THIS CHAPTER IS ABOUT

Most goods are covered by some type of warranty that imposes a duty on the seller. A breach of the warranty is a breach of the seller's promise. Manufacturers, processors, and sellers may also be liable to consumers, users, and bystanders for physical harm or property damage caused by defective goods. This is product liability.

CHAPTER OUTLINE

I. WARRANTIES

A. WARRANTIES OF TITLE

1. **Good Title**
   Sellers warrant that they have good and valid title and that the transfer of title is rightful [UCC 2–312(1)(a)].

2. **No Liens**
   Sellers warrant that goods are free of a security interest of which the buyer has no knowledge [UCC 2–312(1)(b)]. Lessors warrant no third party will interfere with the lessee's use of the goods [UCC 2A–211(1)].

3. **No Infringements**
   Sellers warrant that the goods are free of any third person's patent, trademark, or copyright claims [UCC 2–312(3)].

   a. **Sales Contract—If the Warranty Is Breached and the Buyer Is Sued**
      The buyer must notify the seller. If the seller agrees in writing to defend and bear all costs, the buyer must let the seller do it (or lose all rights against the seller) [UCC 2–607(3)(b), (5)(b)].

b. **Lease—If the Warranty Is Breached and the Lessee Is Sued**
Same as above, except that a consumer who fails to notify the lessor within a reasonable time does not lose any rights against the lessor [UCC 2A–516(3)(b), (4)(b)].

4. **Disclaimer of Title Warranty**
In a sales contract, a disclaimer can be made only by specific contractual language [UCC 2–312(2)]). In a lease, the disclaimer must be specific, in writing, and conspicuous [UCC 2A–214(4)].

B. EXPRESS WARRANTIES

1. **When Express Warranties Arise**
A seller or lessor warrants that goods will conform to affirmations or promises of fact, descriptions, samples or models [UCC 2–313, 2A–210].

2. **Basis of the Bargain**
An affirmation, promise, description, or sample must be part of the basis of the bargain: it must come at such a time that the buyer could have relied on it when agreeing to the contract [UCC 2–313, 2A–210].

3. **Statements of Opinion**

a. **Opinions**
A statement relating to the value of goods or a statement of opinion or recommendation about goods is not an express warranty [UCC 2–313(2), 2A–210(2)], unless the seller or lessor who makes it is an expert and gives an opinion as an expert.

b. **Puffing**
Whether a statement is an express warranty or puffing is not easy to determine. Factors include the reasonableness of the buyer's reliance on the statement and the specificity of the statement.

C. IMPLIED WARRANTIES

An **implied warranty** is derived by implication or inference from the nature of a transaction or the relative situations or circumstances of the parties.

1. **Implied Warranty of Merchantability**
A warranty automatically arises in every sale or lease of goods by a merchant who deals in such goods that the goods are merchantable [UCC 2–314, 2A–212].

a. **Reasonably Fit for Ordinary Purposes**
Goods that are merchantable are "reasonably fit for the ordinary purposes for which such goods are used."

b. **Characteristics of Merchantable Goods**
Average, fair, or medium-grade quality; pass without objection in the market for goods of the same description; adequate package and label, as provided by the agreement; and conform to the promises or affirmations of fact made on the container or label.

2. **Implied Warranty of Fitness for a Particular Purpose**
Arises when seller or lessor (merchant or nonmerchant) knows or has reason to know the purpose for which buyer or lessee will use goods and knows he or she is relying on seller to select suitable goods [UCC 2–315, 2A–213]. Goods can be merchantable but unfit for a particular purpose.

3. **Implied Warranty from Dealing, Performance, or Trade Usage**
When the parties know a well-recognized trade custom, it is inferred that they intended it to apply to their contract [UCC 2–314, 2A–212].

D. OVERLAPPING WARRANTIES

1. **When Warranties Are Consistent, They Are Cumulative**

2. **When Warranties Are Inconsistent—**

   a. Express warranties displace inconsistent implied warranties (except fitness for a particular purpose).

   b. Samples take precedence over inconsistent general descriptions.

   c. Technical specs displace inconsistent samples or descriptions.

E. THIRD PARTY BENEFICIARIES OF WARRANTIES

1. **The Common Law Requires Privity**
At common law, privity of contract must exist between a plaintiff and a defendant to bring any action based on a contract.

2. **The UCC Eliminates Privity**
The UCC includes three optional, alternative provisions eliminating privity with respect to certain types of injuries for certain beneficiaries. Each state may adopt one of the alternatives [UCC 2–318, 2A–216].

F. WARRANTY DISCLAIMERS

1. **Express Warranties**
A seller can avoid making express warranties by not promising or affirming anything, describing the goods, or using of a sample or model.

   a. **Oral Warranties**
   Oral warranties made during bargaining cannot be modified later.

   b. **Negating or Limiting Express Warranties**
   A written disclaimer—clear and conspicuous—can negate all warranties not in the written contract [UCC 2–316(1), 2A–214(1)].

2. **Implied Warranties**

   a. **General Language**
   Implied warranties can be disclaimed by the expression "as is" or a similar phrase [UCC 2–316(3)(a), 2A–214(3)(a)].

   b. **Specific Language**
   Implied warranty of fitness for a particular purpose: disclaimer must be in writing and be conspicuous (the word *fitness* is not required). Implied warranty of merchantability: disclaimer must mention merchantability; if it is in writing, it must be conspicuous.

3. **Buyer's Examination of the Goods**
If a buyer examines the goods before entering a contract, there is no implied warranty with respect to defects that a reasonable examination would reveal [UCC 2–316(3)(b), 2A–214(2)(b)]. The same is true if the buyer refuses to examine over the seller's or lessor's demand.

4. **Unconscionability**
Courts view disclaimers with disfavor, especially when consumers are involved, and have sometimes held disclaimers unconscionable [UCC 2–302, 2A–108].

G. MAGNUSON–MOSS WARRANTY ACT
No seller is required to give a written warranty for consumer goods, but if a seller chooses to do so and the cost of the goods is more than—

1. **$10**
The warranty must be clearly labeled full or limited. A full warranty requires free repair or replacement of defective parts (there is no time limit). A limited warranty is any warranty that is not full.

2. **$15**
The seller must state (fully and conspicuously in a single document in "readily understood language") the seller's name and address, what is warranted, procedures for enforcing the warranty, any limitations on relief, and that the buyer has legal rights.

II. LEMON LAWS
If a car under warranty has a defect that significantly affects the vehicle's value or use, and it is not remedied by the seller within a specified number of opportunities, the buyer is entitled to a new car, replacement of defective parts, or return of all consideration paid.

III. PRODUCT LIABILITY

A. NEGLIGENCE
If the failure to exercise reasonable care in the making or marketing of a product causes an injury, the basis of liability is negligence.

1. **Privity of Contract between Plaintiff and Defendant Is Not Required**

2. **Manufacturer's Duty of Care**
Due care must be exercised in designing, assembling, and testing a product; selecting materials; inspecting and testing products bought for use in the final product; and placing warnings on the label to inform users of dangers of which an ordinary person might not be aware.

B. MISREPRESENTATION
If a misrepresentation (such as intentionally concealing product defects) results in an injury, there may liability for fraud.

C. STRICT LIABILITY
Under the doctrine of strict liability, a defendant may be liable for the result of his or her act regardless of intention or exercise of reasonable care.

1. **Requirements of Strict Product Liability**
The requirements for strict product liability, under the *Restatement (Second) of Torts*, Section 402A, are—

   a. **Product Is in a Defective Condition when the Defendant Sells It**

   b. **The Defendant Is Normally in the Business of Selling the Product**

   c. **The Defect Makes the Product Unreasonably Dangerous**
   A product may be so defective if either—

1) **The Product Is Dangerous beyond the Consumer's Expectation**
There may have been a flaw in the manufacturing process that led to some defective products being marketed, or a perfectly made product may not have had adequate warning on the label.

2) **There Is a Less Dangerous, Economically Feasible Alter-native that the Manufacturer Failed to Use**
A manufacturer may have failed to design a safe product.

d. **The Plaintiff Incurs Harm to Self or Property by Use of the Product**

e. **The Defect Is the Proximate Cause of the Harm**

f. **The Product Was Not Substantially Changed after It Was Sold**

2. **Market-Share Liability**
Some courts hold that all firms that manufactured and distributed DES (diethylstilbestrol) during a certain period are liable for injuries in proportion to the firms' respective shares of the market.

3. **Other Applications of Strict Liability**
Defendants may be liable to injured bystanders. Suppliers of component parts and lessors may be liable for injuries caused by defective products.

D. DEFENSES TO PRODUCT LIABILITY

1. **Assumption of Risk**
In some states, this is a defense if (1) plaintiff knew and appreciated the risk created by the defect and (2) plaintiff voluntarily engaged in the risk, event though it was unreasonable to do so.

2. **Product Misuse**
The use must not be the one for which the product was designed, and the misuse must not be reasonably foreseeable.

3. **Comparative Negligence**
Most states consider a plaintiff's actions in apportioning liability.

4. **Commonly Known Dangers**
Failing to warn against such a danger is not ground for liability.

TRUE-FALSE QUESTIONS

___ 1. If a seller makes a specific representation concerning the condition of a product, an express warranty arises.

___ 2. A contract cannot involve both an implied warranty of merchantability and an implied warranty of fitness for a particular purpose.

___ 3. A trade custom does not apply to a contract unless it is in writing.

___ 4. A seller's best protection from being held accountable for promises is not to make them in the first place.

___ 5. Privity of contract is required to hold a manufacturer liable in a product liability action based on negligence.

___ **6.** In an action based on strict liability, a plaintiff must prove that there was a failure to exercise due care.

___ **7.** In a defense of comparative negligence, an injured party's failure to take care against a known defect will be considered in apportioning liability.

___ **8.** A clear, conspicuous, written statement brought to a buyer's attention when a contract is formed can disclaim all warranties not in a written contract.

___ **9.** Under the doctrine of strict liability, a defendant is liable for the results of his or her acts only if he or she intended those results.

___ **10.** No seller is required to give a written warranty for consumer goods.

FILL-IN QUESTIONS

An express warranty ______________ (can/cannot) be disclaimed in writing if it is called to the buyer's attention. An implied warranty of fitness for a particular purpose ____________ (can/cannot) be disclaimed in writing. An implied warranty of merchantability __________ (can/cannot) be disclaimed in writing. A disclaimer of the implied warranty of fitness for a particular purpose ______________ (must/need not) use the word "fitness." A disclaimer of the implied warranty of merchantability ____________ (must/need not) include the word merchantability.

MULTIPLE-CHOICE QUESTIONS

___ **1.** Noel's Ski Shop sells a pair of skis to Fred. When he first uses the skis, they snap in two. The cause is something that Noel did not know about and could not have discovered. If Fred sues Noel, he will likely

a. win, because Noel breached the merchant's implied duty of inspection.
b. win, because Noel breached the implied warranty of merchantability.
c. lose, because Noel knew nothing about the defect that made the skis unsafe.
d. lose, because consumers should reasonably expect to find on occasion that a product will not work as warranted.

___ **2.** As a hobby, Dick converts old Volkswagens into off-road vehicles and sells them. During one sale, the buyer tells Dick that she knows nothing about off-road vehicles and wants Dick to pick a "good one" for her. On her first off-road drive, she is injured when the car's front axle snaps in two and the car rolls over. The axle would not have broken in ordinary driving. Dick is

a. liable, because he breached the implied warranty of fitness.
b. liable, because he is not a merchant.
c. not liable, because the axle would not have snapped in ordinary driving.
d. not liable, because he is not a merchant.

___ **3.** Tyler Desk Corporation writes in its contracts, in large red letters, "THERE ARE NO WARRANTIES THAT EXTEND BEYOND THE DESCRIPTION ON THE FACE HEREOF." The disclaimer negates the implied warranty of

a. merchantability.
b. fitness for a particular purpose.
c. title.
d. all of the above.

___ **4.** While using a grain auger made by Silo Implements, Bob fell into an opening on the top of the machine, injuring his legs. At the opening were several warning labels. Jane, Bob's employer, later welded a grid over the top to prevent future similar events. The grid did not interfere with the auger. If Bob sues Silo, on the ground of strict liability, Silo will likely be

a. liable, because Silo did not disclaim its warranties.
b. liable, because a less dangerous alternative (than the unguarded opening) was economically feasible, but Silo failed to use it.
c. not liable, because warning labels were around the opening.
d. not liable, because a less dangerous alternative (than the unguarded opening) was economically feasible, but Bob and Jane failed to use it.

___ **5.** Kate is standing in line at a convenience store. A bottle of Bolt Cola is on the floor about six inches from where she is standing. The bottle explodes, and Kate's legs are severely injured. If Kate sues Bolt Cola Company on the ground of strict liability, Bolt will likely be held

a. liable, because it was reasonably foreseeable that a bystander would be injured by the defective bottle of Bolt.
b. liable, if Kate can prove that the company failed to exercise due care.
c. not liable, because Kate assumed the risk that the Bolt might explode—she was voluntarily standing in line.
d. not liable, because there was no privity between Kate and Bolt.

___ **6.** Sam is injured in an accident involving a defective tractor. Sam sues the maker of the tractor. For the defendant to successfully claim assumption of risk as a defense, it must show all of the following EXCEPT

a. Sam voluntarily engaged in the risk while realizing the potential danger.
b. Sam knew and appreciated the risk created by the defect.
c. Sam's decision to undertake the known risk was unreasonable.
d. Sam used the product for something for which it was not designed.

___ **7.** Sport Supplies sells a treadmill to John without warning him of the fact, known to Sport, that the safety shut-off device does not work. In using the treadmill, John discovers the defect. Later, while running on the treadmill, John's shoelace is caught in the gears, which do not shut off, and his foot is injured. If John sues Sport on the ground of strict liability in a jurisdiction that recognizes comparative negligence, Sport may be

a. entirely liable, because Sport was comparatively negligent.
b. partially liable, because Sport was comparatively negligent.
c. entirely liable, because John was comparatively negligent.
d. not liable, because John was comparatively negligent.

___ **8.** Linn Manufacturing, Inc., sells a watch to Ted. Their contract states, "The manufacturer warrants that this watch will not lose more than one second for one year from the date of purchase." Under the Magnuson-Moss Warranty Act, making this express warranty means that Linn

a. cannot disclaim or modify the implied warranty of merchantability or the implied warranty of fitness for a particular purpose.
b. can impose a time limit of one year on any implied warranty.
c. both a and b.
d. none of the above.

___ **9.** A merchant seller warrants all of the following EXCEPT

a. the seller has good title and the transfer of title is rightful.
b. goods are free of security interest of which the buyer has no knowledge.
c. goods are free of any third person's patent, trademark, or copyright claim.
d. goods are the best that money can buy at the contract price.

___ **10.** An express warranty does NOT arise when

a. a brochure states, "This drill bit will penetrate steel without dulling."
b. a label on a crate reads, "Crate contains one 150-horsepower diesel engine."
c. a salesperson claims, "This is the finest automobile ever manufactured."
d. a seller's representative asserts, "The upholstery will match this sample."

SHORT ESSAY QUESTIONS

1. Discuss the UCC's implied warranty of merchantability and implied warranty of fitness for a particular purpose—how each arises and the difference(s) between them.

2. What sort of product defect will support a cause of action in strict liability? What factors indicate whether a less dangerous alternative was economically feasible?

ISSUE SPOTTERS

1. Barb sells a car to Stan. Two months later, Ace Credit Company comes to Stan to repossess the car. Ace shows Stan papers proving that it has a security interest in the car and that Barb has missed five payments. Stan says, "I know nothing about any of this. You have to get your money from Barb. You can't take the car." Is Stan right?

2. Dan loves Sunny Foods, which are cholesterol-rich. When Dan is diagnosed as suffering from heart disease, he sues the Sunny Company, on the ground that its foods are not fit to eat. He claims they breach the implied warranty of merchantability. Is it likely that the court will agree with Dan?

3. Bailey Vehicles sells to Greg, a farmer, a used pick-up truck. The contract, in large type, states, "THE SALE OF THIS TRUCK IS 'AS IS.'" When the truck is delivered, it has no wheels. Can Bailey use the statement in the contract to avoid liability for delivering a truck with no wheels? Could the statement be used to hold Bailey liable?

4. RollCo makes automobile wheels, which it sells to the Mac Motor Corporation to put on its cars. One set of wheels is made of defective materials, which an inspection, before putting them on a car, would reveal. Mac does not inspect the wheels. The car is sold to Love's Auto Sales. Keith buys the car. The wheels collapse while he is driving the car, causing an accident in which he and his passengers are injured. Is Mac liable?

5. Powell Candies manufactures a box of candy, which it sells to Jingle Concessions, a distributor of candy to theaters. Jingle sells it to Sky Cinemas. Judy buys the candy from Sky and gives it to Marie. Eating the candy, Marie breaks a tooth on a stone that is the same size, shape, and color of a piece of the candy. If they were not negligent, can Powell, Jingle, or Sky be held liable for the injury?

 **Learning Objectives**

The learning objectives in this chapter include:

1. The requirements for an instrument to be negotiable.
2. Requirements for HDC status.
3. The liability of parties who sign negotiable instruments.
4. Defenses to avoid payment on negotiable instruments.
5. How liability on a negotiable instrument is discharged.

Chapter 17: Negotiability, Transferability, and Liability

WHAT THIS CHAPTER IS ABOUT

A **negotiable instrument** is a written promise or order to pay a sum of money. It is transferred more readily than an ordinary contract, and a person who acquires it is subject to less risk than the assignee of a contract right. This chapter discusses those instruments, which include checks and promissory notes.

CHAPTER OUTLINE

I. ARTICLE 3 OF THE UCC

UCC Article 3 applies to transactions involving negotiable instruments. Since 1990, most states have adopted revised versions of these articles.

II. TYPES OF INSTRUMENTS

A. ORDERS TO PAY

A person who signs or makes an order to pay is a **drawer**. Person to whom an order is made is a **drawee**. A person to whom payment is ordered is a **payee**.

1. **Draft**
An unconditional written order by one person to another to pay money. The drawee must be obligated to the drawer either by an agreement or through a debtor-creditor relationship to honor the order.

a. **Time Draft**
Payable at a definite future time.

b. **Sight Draft (Demand Draft)**
Payable on sight (when presented for payment). A draft payable at a stated time after sight is both a time and a sight draft.

c. **Trade Acceptance**
Draft in which seller is both drawer and payee. Orders buyer to pay specific sum of money to seller, at a stated time in the future.

2. **Check**
A draft drawn on a bank and payable on demand. A **cashier's check** is a draft in which the bank is both the drawer and drawee.

B. PROMISES TO PAY

A person who promises to pay is a **maker**. A person to whom the promise is made is a **payee**.

1. **Promissory Note**
A written promise by one party to pay money to another party.

2. **Certificate of Deposit**
A note made by a bank promising to repay a deposit of funds with interest on a certain date [UCC 3–104(j)].

III. REQUIREMENTS FOR NEGOTIABILITY

A. FORM AND LOCATION OF SIGNATURE

A signature can be any place on an instrument and in any form (a mark or rubber stamp) that purports to be a signature and authenticates the writing [UCC 1–201(39), 3–401(b)].

B. REQUIREMENTS

To be negotiable, an instrument must [UCC 3–104(a)]—

1. Be in writing.
2. Be signed by the maker or drawer.
3. Be an unconditional promise or order to pay—A promise must be more than a mere acknowledgment of a debt (an I.O.U. does not qualify; use of the words "I promise" or "Pay" qualifies) [UCC 3–103(a)(9)].
4. State a fixed amount of money—Variable interest rate notes can be negotiable [UCC 3–104].
5. Be payable on demand or at a definite time.
6. Be payable to order ("to the order of an identified person" or to "an identified person or order") or bearer (does not designate a specific payee), unless it is a check [UCC 3–109].

IV. TRANSFER OF INSTRUMENTS

A. TRANSFER BY ASSIGNMENT

A transfer by assignment (see Chapter 11) gives the assignee only those rights the assignor possessed. Defenses that can be raised against an assignor can normally be raised against an assignee.

B. TRANSFER BY NEGOTIATION

On negotiation, the transferee becomes a holder and receives the rights of the previous possessor (possibly more) [UCC 3–201(a), 3–202(b), 3–203(b), 3–305, 3–306]. An order instrument is negotiated by delivery with indorsement; a bearer instrument is negotiated by delivery only [UCC 3–201(b)].

V. INDORSEMENTS

An **indorsement** is a signature required to negotiate an order instrument.

A. BLANK INDORSEMENT

Specifies no particular indorsee and can consist of a mere signature [UCC 3–205(b)]. Converts an order instrument to a bearer instrument.

B. SPECIAL INDORSEMENT

Names the indorsee [UCC 3–205(a)]. No special words are needed. Converts a bearer instrument to an order instrument.

C. QUALIFIED INDORSEMENT

Disclaims or limits contract liability (see below) (the notation "without recourse" is commonly used) [UCC 3–415(b)]. A blank qualified indorsement requires only delivery for further negotiation. A special qualified indorsement requires indorsement and delivery for further negotiation.

D. RESTRICTIVE INDORSEMENTS

1. Conditional Indorsement

Requires indorsement and delivery for further negotiation. A person paying or taking for value can disregard the condition [UCC 3–206(b)].

2. Prohibitive Indorsement

Need indorsement and delivery for further negotiation [UCC 3–206(a)].

3. For Deposit or Collection Indorsement

Locks the instrument into the bank collection process [UCC 3–206(c)].

4. Trust Indorsement

An indorsement by one who is to hold or use the funds for the benefit of the indorser or a third party [UCC 3–206(d), (e)]. Requires indorsement and delivery for further negotiation.

VI. HOLDER IN DUE COURSE (HDC)

A. HOLDER

A **holder** is a person in possession of an instrument drawn, issued, or indorsed to him or her, to his or her order, or to bearer or in blank [UCC 1–201(20)]. A holder is subject to the same defenses that could be asserted against the transferor (the party from whom the holder obtained the instrument).

B. HOLDER IN DUE COURSE

A holder who meets certain requirements becomes a **holder in due course (HDC)**, and takes an instrument free of all claims to it and most defenses against payment that could be successfully asserted against the transferor.

C. REQUIREMENTS FOR HDC STATUS

To become an HDC, a person must be a holder and take an instrument (1) for value; (2) in good faith; and (3) without notice that it is overdue, that it has been dishonored, that any person has a defense against it or a claim to it, or that it contains unauthorized signatures, alterations, or is so irregular or incomplete as to call into question its authenticity [UCC 3–302].

VII. HOLDER THROUGH AN HDC

A. SHELTER PRINCIPLE

A person who does not qualify as an HDC but who acquires an instrument from an HDC or from someone with HDC rights receives the rights and privileges of an HDC [UCC 3–203(b)].

B. LIMITATIONS TO THE SHELTER PRINCIPLE

A holder who was a party to fraud or illegality affecting an instrument or who, as a prior holder, had notice of a claim or defense cannot improve his or her status by repurchasing it from a later HDC [UCC 3–203(b)].

VIII. SIGNATURE LIABILITY

Every party (except a qualified indorser) who signs an instrument is primarily or secondarily liable to pay it when it is due.

A. PRIMARY LIABILITY

Only makers and **acceptors** (a drawee who promises to pay an instrument when it is presented later for payment) are primarily liable—they are absolutely required to pay (subject to certain defenses) [UCC 3–305].

B. SECONDARY LIABILITY

Drawers and unqualified indorsers are secondarily liable. Drawer pays if drawee does not; indorser pays if maker defaults. Secondary liability is triggered by proper presentment, dishonor, and notice of dishonor.

1. Proper Presentment

a. To the Proper Person

A note or CD is presented to the maker; a draft to the drawee for acceptance, payment, or both (whatever is required); a check to the drawee [UCC 3–501(a), 3–502(b)].

b. In the Proper Manner

Depending on the type of instrument [UCC 3–501(b)]: (1) any commercially reasonable means (oral, written, or electronic; but it is not effective until the demand is received); (2) a clearinghouse procedure used by banks; or (3) at the place specified in the instrument.

c. Timely

Failure to present on time is the most common reason for improper presentment [UCC 3–414(f), 3–415(e), 3–501(b)(4)].

2. Dishonor

Occurs when payment or acceptance is refused or cannot be obtained within the prescribed time, or when required presentment is excused and the instrument is not accepted or paid [UCC 3–502(e), 3–504].

3. Proper Notice

On dishonor, to hold secondary parties liable, notice must be given within thirty days following the day on which a person receives notice of the dishonor (except a bank, which must give notice before midnight of the next banking day after receipt) [UCC 3–503].

C. UNAUTHORIZED SIGNATURES

An unauthorized signature does not bind a person whose name is forged unless the person (1) ratifies the signature [UCC 3–403(a)] or (2) was negligent [UCC 3–115, 3–406, 4–401(d)(2)]. An unauthorized signature does bind the *signer* in favor of an HDC [UCC 3–403(a)].

D. SPECIAL RULES FOR UNAUTHORIZED INDORSEMENTS

Generally, the loss falls on the first party to take the instrument. The loss falls on the maker or drawer in cases involving—

1. **Imposters**
Indorsement of an **imposter** (one who induces a maker or drawer to issue an instrument in name of an impersonated payee) can be effective against the drawer [UCC 3–404(a)].

2. **Fictitious Payees**
Indorsement of a **fictitious payee** (one to whom an instrument is payable but who has no right to receive payment—often, dishonest employees issue such instruments or deceive employers into doing so) can hold employer liable to an innocent holder [UCC 3–404(b)(2)].

IX. WARRANTY LIABILITY

A. TRANSFER WARRANTIES

1. **The Warranties**
Any person who transfers an instrument for consideration warrants to the transferee and, if the transfer is by indorsement, to all later transferees and holders who take the instrument in good faith [UCC 3–416]—

   a. The transferor is entitled to enforce the instrument.

   b. All signatures are authentic and authorized.

   c. The instrument has not been altered.

   d. The instrument is not subject to a defense or claim that can be asserted against the transferor.

   e. The transferor has no knowledge of any insolvency proceedings against the maker, the acceptor, or the drawer of the instrument.

2. **To Whom the Warranties Run**
Order paper: to any subsequent holder who takes the instrument in good faith. Bearer paper: only to the immediate transferee [UCC 3–416(a)].

B. PRESENTMENT WARRANTIES

Any person who obtains payment or acceptance of an instrument warrants to any other person who in good faith pays or accepts it [UCC 3–417(a), (d)]—

1. The person obtaining payment or acceptance is entitled or authorized to enforce the instrument (no missing or unauthorized indorsements).

2. The instrument has not been altered.

3. The person obtaining payment or acceptance has no knowledge that the signature of the issuer of the instrument is unauthorized.

X. DEFENSES TO LIABILITY

A. UNIVERSAL DEFENSES

Valid against all holders, including HDCs and holders who take by HDCs [UCC 3–305, 3–401, 3–403, 3–407].

1. Forgery.

2. Fraud in the execution (when a person is deceived into signing an instrument, believing that it is something else).

3. Material alteration (an alteration that changes the terms between any two parties in any way).

4. Discharge in bankruptcy.
5. Minority (if the contract is voidable).
6. Illegality, mental incapacity, or extreme duress (if contract is void).

B. PERSONAL DEFENSES

Personal defenses avoid payment to an ordinary holder (but not an HDC).

1. Breach of contract or breach of warranty.
2. Lack or failure of consideration [UCC 3–303(b), 3–305(a)(2)]
3. Fraud in the inducement (ordinary fraud).
4. Illegality or mental incapacity (if contract is voidable).
5. Discharge by payment or cancellation.
6. Unauthorized completion of an incomplete instrument.
7. Nondelivery of an instrument.
8. Ordinary duress or undue influence (if the contract is voidable).

XI. DISCHARGE FROM LIABILITY

A. PAYMENT OR TENDER OF PAYMENT

All parties are discharged if the party primarily liable pays to a holder the amount due in full [UCC 3–602, 3–603]. Payment by any other party discharges only that party and subsequent parties.

B. CANCELLATION

A holder can discharge any party by intentionally destroying, mutilating, or canceling an instrument, canceling or striking out a party's signature, or adding words (such as "Paid") to the instrument indicating discharge [UCC 3–604].

C. IMPAIRMENT OF RIGHT OF RECOURSE

If a holder adversely affects an indorser's right to recover payment from prior parties, the indorser is discharged [UCC 3–605].

TRUE-FALSE QUESTIONS

___ 1. A negotiable instrument can be transferred only by negotiation.

___ 2. A bearer instrument is payable to whoever possesses it.

___ 3. To be negotiable, an instrument must be in writing.

___ 4. An instrument that does not designate a specific payee is an order instrument.

___ 5. Indorsements are required to negotiate bearer instruments.

___ 6. Anyone who takes an instrument for value, in good faith, and without notice is a holder in due course (HDC).

___ 7. Generally, no one is liable on an instrument unless his or her signature appears on it.

___ **8.** Every party who signs an instrument is primarily liable for payment of it when it comes due.

___ **9.** Universal defenses can be raised to avoid payment to an HDC.

___ **10.** Warranty liability is subject to the same conditions of proper presentment, dishonor, and notice of dishonor as signature liability.

FILL-IN QUESTIONS

A person who does not qualify as an HDC ______________ (can/cannot) acquire the rights of an HDC if a person who does not qualify as an HDC acquires an instrument from an HDC. A holder who was a party to fraud or illegality affecting an instrument ______________ (can/cannot) improve his or her status by repurchasing the instrument from a later HDC. A holder who, as a prior holder, had notice of a claim or defense against the instrument ______________ (can/cannot) improve his or her status by repurchasing it from a later HDC.

MULTIPLE-CHOICE QUESTIONS

___ **1.** Alex makes out a check "Pay to the order of Mel." Mel indorses the check on the back by signing his name. Before Mel signed his name, the check was

a. bearer paper.
b. order paper.
c. both a and b.
d. none of the above.

___ **2.** Jules owes money to Vern. Vern owes money to Chris. Vern signs an instrument that orders Jules to pay to Chris the money that Jules owes to Vern. This instrument is a

a. note.
b. check.
c. certificate of deposit.
d. draft.

___ **3.** Jasmine writes out a check payable to the order of Nancy. Nancy receives the check but wants to negotiate it further to her friend Max. Nancy can negotiate the check further by

a. indorsing it.
b. delivering it to the transferee.
c. both a and b.
d. none of the above.

___ **4.** Kurt receives from Lee a check that is made out "Pay to the order of Kurt." Kurt turns it over and writes on the back, "Pay to Adam. [Signed] Kurt." Kurt's indorsement is a

a. blank indorsement.
b. special indorsement.
c. restrictive indorsement.
d. qualified indorsement.

____ **5.** Alex opens an account at the First National Bank with a $4,000 check drawn on another bank and payable to himself. He indorses the check in blank. The bank credits his account and allows him to draw on the $4,000 immediately. The bank knows of no defense to the check. The bank is

a. an HDC to the extent that Alex draws against the $4,000 balance.
b. an HDC for the full amount of the check.
c. an HDC to the extent of any amount that is collected on the check.
d. not an HDC.

____ **6.** Sam issues a $5,000 note to Mike due six months from the date issued. One month later, Mike negotiates the note to Julie for $2,500 in cash and a negotiable check for $2,500. Julie is an HDC of the note to the extent of

a. $2,500.
b. $5,000.
c. $7,500.
d. none of the above.

____ **7.** Don signs a note that states, "Payable in thirty days." The note is dated March 2, which means it is due April 1. Jo buys the note on April 12. She is

a. an HDC to the extent that she paid for the note.
b. an HDC to the extent that the note is not yet paid.
c. not an HDC.
d. none of the above.

____ **8.** Able Company issues a draft for $1,000 on July 1, payable to the order of the Baker Corporation. The draft is drawn on the First National Bank. Before the bank accepts the draft, who has primary liability for payment?

a. Able Company
b. Baker Corporation
c. First National Bank
d. No one

____ **9.** Tony writes a check payable to the order of Gina. The check is stolen, and John forges Gina's name on the back. He cashes the check at the First State Bank, which presents it for payment to City Bank, the drawee. In presenting the check to City Bank, State Bank breaches the warranty that

a. State Bank did not know the signature of the drawer was unauthorized.
b. the instrument had not been materially altered.
c. State Bank had good title to the instrument.
d. none of the above.

____ **10.** Bill issues a check for $4,000, dated June 1, to Ed. The check is drawn on the First National Bank. Ed indorses the check and transfers it to Jane. Which of the following will trigger the liability of Bill and Ed on the check, based on their signatures?

a. Presentment only
b. Dishonor only
c. Both presentment and dishonor
d. Neither presentment nor dishonor

SHORT ESSAY QUESTIONS

1. How are instruments negotiated?
2. What are the defenses that may be raised to avoid payment on an instrument?

ISSUE SPOTTERS

1. If Louis makes out a check "Pay to the order of Maria," and Maria indorses the check on the back by signing her name, is the check order paper or bearer paper?

2. Lisa writes out a check payable to the order of Jeff. Negotiation occurs when Jeff receives the check. How does Jeff subsequently negotiate the check?

3. Phil issues a check for $100. Andy steals it and alters the amount to $10,000. He negotiates the check to Lily, who takes it in good faith, for value, and without notice of the alteration. When Lily attempts to recover on the check, Phil refuses to pay more than the check's original tenor—$100. If Lily sues Phil, will she recover more?

4. Jay signs corporate checks for the Clef Corporation. Jay's assistant Lena usually enters the amounts and payees' names before Jay signs the checks. Lena makes a check payable to the Cole Company, to whom Clef actually owes no money. Jay signs the check. Lena forges Cole's indorsement and cashes the check at the First National Bank, the drawee. Does Clef have any recourse against the bank for the payment?

5. Alan transfers a note, for consideration, to George by blank indorsement and delivery. George transfers the note to Brenda, who takes it in good faith. What does Alan warrant to Brenda?

QUICKEN CD-ROM
BUSINESS LAW PARTNER APPLICATIONS

Open **Quicken Business Law Partner**. Click on the *New Documents* icon. Select the *Promissory Note*. Respond to the *Interview* questions with actual facts or hypothetical ones. For example, imagine that Daly agrees to lend $5,000 to Taylor. As you complete the *Interview*, answer the following questions.

___ **1.** In this form, the parties can provide that the note will be

a. due on demand only.
b. paid in full on a specific date only.
c. paid in installments only.
d. due on demand, paid in full on a certain date, or paid in installments.

___ **2.** According to this note, the payments of Taylor (the promisor, or maker) to Daly (the payee) are applied first to

a. accrued interest.
b. principal.
c. administrative costs.
d. taxes.

____ **3.** To be negotiable, this note must be in writing and be signed by Taylor (the maker). It must also include a statement of

a. the principal, in a fixed amount.
b. the interest, in a fixed amount.
c. both a and b.
d. none of the above.

____ **4.** The parties can provide in this note that if payment is overdue, Daly can

a. assess late charges.
b. be reimbursed for collection costs.
c. both a and b.
d. none of the above.

____ **5.** Default can occur, under this note, if

a. the promisor fails to make a payment when it is due.
b. either party fails to enforce any provision of the note.
c. both a and b.
d. none of the above.

Chapter 18: Checks and the Banking System

Learning Objectives

The learning objectives in this chapter include:

1. Types of checks.
2. When a bank may dishonor a customer's check without liability.
3. A bank's responsibilities for stale checks, stop-payment orders, and forged or altered checks.
4. How banks collect payment on checks.
5. The laws governing electronic fund transfers.

WHAT THIS CHAPTER IS ABOUT

This chapter outlines the duties and liabilities that arise when a check is issued and paid. Checks are governed by UCC Articles 3 and 4. If there is a conflict between the articles, Article 4 controls. This outline also covers electronic fund transfers.

CHAPTER OUTLINE

I. CHECKS

A **check** is a draft drawn on a bank, ordering the bank to pay a fixed amount of money on demand [UCC 3–104(f)]. If a bank wrongfully dishonors any of the following special types of checks, the holder can recover expenses, interest, and consequential damages [UCC 3–411].

A. CASHIER'S CHECK

A check drawn by a bank on itself; negotiable on issue [UCC 3–104(g)].

B. TELLER'S CHECK

A draft drawn by a bank on another bank, or if drawn on a nonbank, payable at or through a bank [UCC 3–104(h)].

C. TRAVELER'S CHECK

A check on which a financial institution is both drawer and drawee. The buyer must sign it twice (buying it and using it) [UCC 3–104(i)].

D. CERTIFIED CHECK

A check accepted by the bank on which it is drawn [UCC 3–409(d)]. When a bank certifies a check, it immediately charges the drawer's account and transfers those funds to its own account. The effect of certification is to discharge the drawer and prior indorsers [UCC 3–414(c), 3–415(d)].

II. THE BANK-CUSTOMER RELATIONSHIP

A. WHAT A BANK IS

A "person engaged in the business of banking, including a savings bank, savings and loan association, credit union or trust company" [UCC 4–105(1)]. Rights and duties of bank and customer are contractual.

B. WHAT A CUSTOMER IS

A customer is a creditor of the bank (and the bank, a debtor of the customer) when the customer deposits funds in his or her account. A bank acts as an agent for the customer when he or she writes a check drawn on the bank or deposits a check in his or her account for the bank to collect [UCC 4–201(a)].

III. BANK'S DUTY TO HONOR CHECKS

If a bank dishonors a check for insufficient funds, it has no liability. The customer is liable to the payee or holder of the check in a civil suit. If intent to defraud is proved, the customer is also subject to criminal prosecution. If a bank wrongfully dishonors a check, however, it is liable to the customer [UCC 4–402].

A. OVERDRAFTS

If there are insufficient funds in a customer's account, the bank can pay an item drawn on it or dishonor it. If the bank pays, it can charge the customer's account (if the customer has authorized payment) [UCC 4–401(a)]. If a check "bounces," a holder can resubmit it but must notify any indorsers of the first dishonor (or they are discharged).

B. POSTDATED CHECKS

A bank can charge a postdated check against a customer's account if the customer does not give the bank enough notice. If the bank has notice but charges the check anyway, the bank is liable [UCC 4–401(c)].

C. STALE CHECKS

A bank is not obliged to pay an uncertified check presented for payment more than six months after its date [UCC 4–404]. If a bank pays in good faith, it can charge the customer's account for the amount.

D. STOP-PAYMENT ORDERS

1. Who Can Order a Stop-Payment and When It Must Be Received

Only a customer or person authorized to draw on the account. Must be received in a reasonable time and manner [UCC 4–403(a), 4–405].

2. How It Can Be Given and How Long It Is Effective

In most states, it can be given orally, but it is binding for only fourteen calendar days unless confirmed in writing. In writing, it is effective for six months, when it may be renewed [UCC 4–403(b)].

3. If the Bank Pays over an Order

It must recredit the customer's account for any loss, including damages for the dishonor of subsequent items [UCC 4–403(c)].

4. The Customer's Risks

Possible liability to payee for the amount of the item (and damages). Defense against payment to a payee may not prevent payment to a subsequent HDC [UCC 3–305, 3–306].

E. DEATH OR INCOMPETENCE OF A CUSTOMER

Until a bank knows of the situation and has time to act, it is not liable for paying items [UCC 4–405]. If a bank knows of a death, for ten days after the date of death it can pay items drawn on or before the date of death (unless a person claiming an interest in the account orders a stop payment).

F. FORGED DRAWERS' SIGNATURES

1. The General Rule

A forged signature on a check has no legal effect as the signature of a drawer [UCC 3–403(a)]. If the bank pays, it must recredit the account.

2. Customer Negligence

If the customer's negligence substantially contributed to the forgery, the bank is not obligated to recredit the account [UCC 3–406(a)].

a. Reducing a Customer's Liability

A customer's liability may be reduced by a bank's negligence (if it substantially contributed to the loss) [UCC 3–406(b)].

b. Timely Examination of Bank Statements Required

The customer must examine the bank statement and canceled checks promptly and report any forged signatures [UCC 4–406(c)].

1) When There's a Series of Forgeries by the Same Wrongdoer

To recover for all items, a customer must report the first forgery to the bank within *thirty* calendar days of receiving the statement and canceled checks [UCC 4–406(d)(2)].

2) When the Bank Is Also Negligent

If the bank fails to exercise ordinary care ("reasonable commercial standards"), it may have to recredit the customer's account for a portion of the loss (on the basis of comparative negligence) [UCC 4–406(e)].

c. Absolute Time Limit

A customer must report a forged signature within one year of the date the statement and canceled checks were available [UCC 4–406].

G. FORGED INDORSEMENTS

1. The General Rule

If the bank pays a check with a forged indorsement, it must recredit the account (or be held liable for breach of contract) [UCC 4–401(a)].

2. Timely Examination of Bank Statements Required

The customer must examine the bank statement and canceled checks and report forged indorsements promptly. Failure to do so within three years relieves the bank of liability [UCC 4–111].

3. Parties from Whom the Bank May Recover

The bank can recover for breach of warranty from the bank that cashed the check [UCC 4–207(a)(2)]. Ultimately, the loss usually falls on the first party to take the instrument.

H. ALTERED CHECKS

If the bank fails to detect an alteration, it is liable to its customer for the loss [UCC 4–401(d)(1)].

1. The Customer's Negligence

If a bank traces its loss to the customer's negligence or, on successive altered checks, to the customer's failure to discover the first alteration, its liability is reduced (unless it was negligent) [UCC 4–401, 4–406].

2. Parties from Whom the Bank May Recover

The bank can recover from the transferor, for breach of warranty. Exceptions involve cashier's, teller's, and certified checks [UCC 3–417(a)(2), 4–208(a)(2), 4–207(a)(2)].

IV. BANK'S DUTY TO ACCEPT DEPOSITS

A. AVAILABILITY SCHEDULE FOR DEPOSITED CHECKS

Under the Expedited Funds Availability Act of 1987 and Regulation CC—

1. Funds That Must Be Available the Next Business Day after Deposit

a. The First $100 of Any Deposit and the Next $400 of a Local Check

The first $100 must be available for withdrawal on the opening of the next business day. The next $400 of a local check must be available by no later than 5:00 P.M. the next business day.

b. Cash Deposits, Wire Transfers, and Certain Checks

Funds must be available on the next business day for cash deposits, wire transfers, government checks, the first $100 of a day's check deposits, cashier's checks, certified checks, and checks for which the depositary and payor banks are the same institution.

2. Funds That Must Be Available within Five Business Days

All nonlocal checks and nonproprietary ATM deposits, including cash.

3. Funds That Can Be Held for Eight Days or an Extra Four Days

Eight days: funds in new accounts (open less than thirty days). Four days: deposits over $5,000 (except government and cashier's checks), accounts with many overdrafts, checks of questionable collectibility (the bank must tell the depositor it suspects fraud or insolvency).

B. TRUTH-IN-SAVINGS ACT OF 1991

1. When a Bank Must Pay Interest

Interest must be paid on the full balance of an account each day.

2. What a Bank Must Tell Customers

New customers must be told, in writing, the minimum to open an interest-bearing account, the interest in terms of the annual percentage yield, whether interest is calculated daily, and fees and other charges.

C. THE COLLECTION PROCESS

1. Banks Involved in the Collection Process

Depositary bank: first bank to receive a check for payment. **Payor bank**: bank on which a check is drawn. **Collecting bank**: bank (except payor bank) that handles a check for collection. **Intermediary bank**: any bank (except payor and depositary banks) involved in the collection process.

2. **Check Collection between Customers of the Same Bank**
An item payable by a depositary bank that is also the payor bank is an "on-us item." If the bank does not dishonor it by the second banking day, it is considered paid [UCC 4–215(e)(2)].

3. **Check Collection between Customers of Different Banks**
A depositary bank must arrange to present a check either directly or through intermediary banks to the appropriate payor bank.

a. **Midnight Deadline**
Each bank in the collection chain must pass a check on before midnight of the next banking day following receipt [UCC 4–202(b)].

b. **Deferred Posting and the Midnight Deadline**
Posting of checks received after a certain time can be deferred until the next day [UCC 4–108].

c. **Electronic Check Presentment**
Can be done the same day a check is deposited. The check may be kept at the place of deposit with only information about the check presented for payment under a Federal Reserve agreement, clearinghouse rule, or truncation agreement [UCC 4–110].

V. ELECTRONIC FUND TRANSFERS

A. CONSUMER FUND TRANSFERS

Governed by Electronic Fund Transfer Act (EFTA) of 1978 and Regulation E.

1. **Who Is Subject to the EFTA**
Financial institutions that offer electronic fund transfers (EFTs) involving customer asset accounts established for personal, family, or household purposes. Telephone transfers are covered only if they are made pursuant to a prearranged plan involving periodic transfers.

2. **Financial Institutions' Responsibilities**
Financial institutions must provide customers with—

a. **Receipts**
At the time a transaction is made through an electronic terminal.

b. **Periodic Statements**

1) **What They Must Include**
The amounts and dates of transfers, the fees, identification of the terminals, names of third parties involved, and an address and phone number for inquiries and error notices.

2) **How Often They Must Be Provided**
Monthly statements are required for every month in which there is an electronic transfer of funds.

3. **Unauthorized Electronic Fund Transfers**

a. **What an Unauthorized Transfer Is**
(1) A transfer is initiated by a person who has no actual authority to initiate the transfer; (2) the consumer receives no benefit from it; and (3) the consumer did not furnish the person "with the card, code, or other means of access" to his or her account.

b. **Customer Liability**
If a debit card is lost or stolen, and misused, a customer is liable for (1) $50—if he or she notifies the bank within two business days of learning of the loss; (2) $500—if he or she does not tell the bank until after the second day; or (3) unlimited amounts—if notice does not occur within sixty days after the transfer appears on the customer's statement.

4. **Error Resolution and Damages**
The bank must investigate and give the customer a report or be liable for actual damages, court costs, attorneys' fees, punitive damages.

B. **COMMERCIAL TRANSFERS**
In most states, UCC Article 4A clarifies the rights and liabilities of parties involved in fund transfers not subject to the EFTA or other federal or state statutes. In those states that have not adopted Article 4A, commercial fund transfers are governed by contract law and tort law.

TRUE-FALSE QUESTIONS

___ 1. A check is a draft drawn on a bank and payable on demand.

___ 2. If a bank pays a stale check in good faith without consulting the customer, the bank cannot charge the customer's account.

___ 3. If a bank receives an item payable from a customer's account in which there are insufficient funds, the bank cannot pay the item.

___ 4. A bank in the collection chain must normally pass a check on before midnight of the next banking day following receipt.

___ 5. The Electronic Fund Transfer Act (EFTA) requires financial institutions to provide a receipt of an electronic transfer at the time of the transfer.

___ 6. A customer must examine the statements provided by the institution handling his or her account and notify it of any errors within sixty days.

___ 7. The rights and duties of a bank and its customers are partially contractual.

___ 8. All funds deposited in all bank accounts must be available for withdrawal no later than the next business day.

___ 9. If a bank pays a customer's check that has a forged indorsement, and the customer's negligence did not contribute to the forgery, the bank must recredit the customer's account.

___ 10. A forged drawer's signature on a check is effective as the signature of the person whose name is signed.

FILL-IN QUESTIONS

A depositor is the ________________ (drawee/drawer) of a check. The depositor is the bank's ________________ (creditor/debtor) as to the amount on deposit in the depositor's account. The depositor is the bank's ________________ (agent/principal) in the deposit contract. The bank is the ________________ (drawee/drawer) of a check. The bank is the depositor's ________________ (creditor debtor) as to the amount on deposit in the depositor's account. The bank is the depositor's __________________ (agent/principal) in the handling of the account and in the collection process.

MULTIPLE-CHOICE QUESTIONS

___ **1.** On July 1, Liz steals two blank checks from her employer, Dave's Market. On July 3, Liz forges Dave's signature and cashes the first check. The check is returned with Dave's monthly statement from the First National Bank on August 1. Dave does not examine the statement or the checks. On August 24, Liz forges Dave's signature and cashes the second check. This check is returned with Dave's monthly statement on September 1. Dave examines both statements, discovers the forgeries, and insists that the bank recredit the account for both checks. Assuming that the bank was not negligent in paying the checks, the bank must recredit Dave's account for

a. both checks.
b. the first check only.
c. the second check only.
d. neither of the checks.

___ **2.** Tom is paid with a check drawn on Pete's account at the First State Bank. The check has a forged drawer's signature. Tom indorses the check to Eve, who takes it in good faith and for value, and cashes it at the bank. When Pete discovers the forgery, he notifies the bank, which recredits his account. The bank can recover the amount of its loss from Eve

a. only if she has a bank account at any bank.
b. only if she has an account at the First State Bank.
c. under any circumstances.
d. under no circumstances.

___ **3.** Ann buys three $300 television sets from Gail, paying with a check. That night, one of the sets explodes. Ann phones the City Bank, the drawee, and orders a stop payment. The next day, Gail presents the check to the bank for payment. If the bank honors the check, it must recredit Ann's account for

a. $300.
b. $900.
c. nothing, because the stop-payment order was oral.
d. nothing, because Gail did not present the check until the next day.

___ **4.** On May 1, Pat steals from Frank two checks drawn payable to the order of Beth. On May 3, Pat forges Beth's signature and cashes the checks. The checks are returned with Frank's monthly statement from his bank on June 1. Frank discovers the forgery and demands that the bank recredit his account. The bank must recredit Frank's account for

a. both checks.
b. the first check only.
c. the second check only.
d. neither of the checks.

___ **5.** Colin draws a check for $500 payable to the order of Mary. Mary indorses the check in blank and transfers it to Sam. Sam presents the check to the First National Bank, the drawee, for payment. If the bank does not pay the check, the bank is liable to

a. Sam.
b. Colin.
c. Mary.
d. none of the above.

___ **6.** Delta Company uses its computer system to issue payroll checks. Ed, a Delta employee, uses the system without authorization to issue himself a check for $5,000. City Bank, Delta's bank, cashes the check. The bank need not recredit Delta's account for the entire $5,000 if

a. Delta owed Ed $5,000 in unpaid wages.
b. the bank did not take reasonable care to determine whether the check was good.
c. Delta did not take reasonable care to limit access to its payroll system.
d. none of the above.

___ **7.** Roy writes a check for $300 payable to the order of Gene. Pam steals the check, alters the amount to $3,000, and forges Gene's indorsement. She presents the check to State Bank, the drawee, which cashes it. Roy demands that the bank recredit his account. The bank must recredit the account for

a. $3,000.
b. $2,300.
c. $300.
d. nothing.

___ **8.** Jay arranges with the First National Bank to make automatic monthly payments on his student loan. More than three days before a scheduled payment, Jay can stop the automatic payments by notifying the bank

a. orally.
b. in writing.
c. in person.
d. any of the above.

___ **9.** On January 1, Dick discovers that his debit card to City Bank's ATMs is missing. On January 7, Tim uses the card to make a $200 withdrawal from Dick's account. On January 14, Dick tells the bank that the card is missing. For Tim's unauthorized use of the access card, Dick is liable for

a. $0.
b. $50.
c. $200.
d. $10,000.

___ **10.** Jennifer receives a check from Mary for $300. The check is drawn on a local bank. If Jennifer deposits it in her bank, the $300 will be available to her

a. immediately.
b. the next business day.
c. within four days.
d. within eight days.

SHORT ESSAY QUESTIONS

1. Describe the circumstances in which a customer might be unable to recover from a bank that pays on a forged check drawn on the customer's account.

2. What are the principal features of the Electronic Fund Transfer Act (EFTA)?

ISSUE SPOTTERS

1. Lynn draws a check for $900 payable to the order of Jan. Jan indorses the check in blank and transfers it to Owen. Owen presents the check to the First National Bank, the drawee bank, for payment. If the bank does not honor the check, is Lynn liable to Owen? Could Lynn also be subject to criminal prosecution?

2. Herb steals a check from Kay's checkbook, forges Kay's signature, and transfers the check to Will for value. Unaware that the signature is not Kay's, Will presents the check to the First State Bank, the drawee. The bank cashes the check. Kay discovers the forgery and insists that the bank recredit her account. Can the bank refuse to recredit Kay's account? If not, can the bank recover the amount paid to Will?

3. Rose draws a check for $70 payable to the order of Serena. Serena indorses the check in blank and transfers it to Val. Val alters the check to read $700 and presents it to City Bank, the drawee, for payment. The bank cashes it. Rose discovers the alteration and sues the bank. How much can Rose recover? From whom can the bank recover?

4. First National Bank mistakenly transfers $1,000 from a customer's account in its bank to another account in the First State Bank. The transfer is done electronically. When First National learns of the mistake, it credits its customer's account and asks First State to "return" the $1,000. First State refuses. First National sues, claiming that First State violated First National's rights under the EFTA. First State argues that the EFTA does not apply, because First National and First State are financial institutions, not consumers. Will the court agree?

5. Carla authorizes City Bank to make transfers from her account to make her automobile payments. After three payments, the dealership repossesses the car and refuses to return it. Carla phones the bank to stop the payments and follows up with a confirming letter. The bank fails to stop the fourth and fifth payments, and the dealership refuses to refund anything. Can Carla get her money from the bank?

QUICKEN CD-ROM BUSINESS LAW PARTNER APPLICATIONS

Open **Quicken Business Law Partner**. Click on the *New Documents* icon. Choose the *Stop Payment on Check*. Respond to the *Interview* questions with actual facts or hypothetical ones. For example, imagine that Paula (the drawer) issues a check drawn on First National Bank (the drawee) for $500 payable to the order of Mario (the payee). As you complete the *Interview*, answer the following questions.

___ 1. A stop payment letter is used to

a. provide written notice that a check has not been cashed.
b. respond to a demand for payment.
c. notify a bank to refuse to cash a check.
d. none of the above.

____ **2.** Using this form, the party writing the letter can include

a. information identifying the check.
b. an explanation for the stop payment.
c. an agreement to pay a service charge.
d. all of the above.

____ **3.** Using this form, the party writing the letter can agree to

a. assume liability if the check information is wrong.
b. give the recipient a reasonable time to act.
c. both a and b.
d. none of the above.

____ **4.** Using this form, the party writing the letter can promise, in regard to the recipient's costs of compliance,

a. to assume liability for those costs.
b. not to assume liability for those costs.
c. either a or b.
d. none of the above.

____ **5.** If the recipient does not comply with the terms of the letter,

a. the drawee must recredit the drawer's account.
b. the drawer must give the payee cash for the amount of the check.
c. the payee must exchange a cashier's check for the drawer's original check .
d. none of the above.

Learning Objectives

The learning objectives in this chapter include:

1. The terms used in secured transactions.
2. The elements of an enforceable security interest.
3. How and why security interests are perfected.
4. How priority disputes among creditors are decided.
5. A secured creditor's remedies when a debtor defaults.

Chapter 19: Secured Transactions

WHAT THIS CHAPTER IS ABOUT

This chapter covers transactions in which the payment of a debt is secured (guaranteed) by personal property owned by the debtor or in which the debtor has a legal interest. The importance of being a secured creditor cannot be overemphasized—secured transactions are as basic to modern business as credit.

CHAPTER OUTLINE

I. THE TERMINOLOGY OF SECURED TRANSACTIONS

UCC Article 9 applies to secured transactions.

A. SECURED TRANSACTION

Transaction in which payment of a debt is guaranteed by personal property owned by the debtor or in which the debtor has a legal interest.

B. SECURITY INTEREST, SECURED PARTY, COLLATERAL, AND DEBTOR

A **security interest** is any interest "in personal property or fixtures which secures payment or performance of an obligation" [UCC 1–201(37)]. A **secured party** is any person in whose favor there is a security interest [UCC 9–105(1)(m)]. **Collateral** is the property subject to a security interest [UCC 9–105(1)(c)]. **Debtor** is the party who owes the payment [UCC 9–105(1)(d)].

II. CREATING AND PERFECTING A SECURITY INTEREST

A creditor's two main concerns are, if a debtor fails to pay, (1) satisfaction of the debt through possession or sale of the collateral and (2) priority over other creditors to the collateral.

A. CREATING A SECURITY INTEREST

A creditor's rights attach to collateral, creating an enforceable security interest against a debtor if the following requirements are met [UCC 9–203].

1. Written Security Agreement

(1) It must be signed by the debtor and (2) contain a description of the collateral, (3) which the description must reasonably identify [UCC 9–203(1), 9–110]. Or the secured party must possess the collateral.

2. Secured Party Must Give Value

Value is any consideration that supports a contract [UCC 1–201(44)]).

3. Debtor Must Have Rights in the Collateral

The debtor must have an ownership interest or right (current or future legal interest) to obtain possession of the collateral.

B. PERFECTING A SECURITY INTEREST

Perfection is the process by which secured parties protect themselves against the claims of others who wish to satisfy their debts out of the same collateral.

1. Perfection by Filing

Filing is the most common means of perfecting a security interest.

a. What a Financing Statement Must Contain

It must contain (1) the signature of the debtor, (2) the names and addresses of both the debtor and the creditor, and (3) a description of the collateral by type or item [UCC 9–402(1)].

b. Where to File a Financing Statement

Depending on how the collateral is classified, filing is with the county clerk (consumer goods), the secretary of state (other collateral), or both [UCC 9–401].

2. Perfection Without Filing

a. Perfection by Possession

A creditor can possess collateral and return it when the debt is paid [UCC 9–203(1)(a)]. For some securities, negotiable instruments, and nonnegotiable transferable instruments, this is the only way to perfect.

b. Automatic Perfection

1) Purchase-Money Security Interest (PMSI)

A PMSI is (1) retained in, or taken by the seller of, goods to secure part or all of the price, or (2) taken by a lender, such as a bank, as part of a loan to enable a debtor to buy the collateral [UCC 9–107].

2) Perfection of a PMSI

A PMSI in consumer goods (and, in some states, farm equipment under a certain value) is perfected automatically when it is created. The seller need do nothing more [UCC 9–302(1)(d)].

3. Perfection of a Security Interest in a Motor Vehicle

The above methods do not apply. A security interest in a motor vehicle is perfected by noting the interest on the certificate of title.

4. **Collateral Moved to Another Jurisdiction**

a. **Continues to Be Perfected for Up to Four Months**
From the date it is moved or for the period remaining in the perfection in the original jurisdiction, whichever expires first [UCC 9–103(1)(d), (3)(e)]. Collateral moved from county to county within a state (if local filing is required) may not have a four-month limit [UCC 9–403(3)].

b. **Automobiles**
If the original state does not require a certificate of title, perfection automatically ends four months after the move. If the original state requires title registration, and the security interest is noted on the certificate, perfection continues after the car is moved to another state requiring a certificate until the car is registered there [UCC 9–103(2)].

5. **Effective Time of Perfection**
A financing statement is effective for five years [UCC 9–403(2)]. A continuation statement filed within six months before the expiration date continues the effectiveness for five more years (and so on) [UCC 9–403(3)].

III. THE SCOPE OF A SECURITY INTEREST

A. PROCEEDS

Proceeds include whatever is received when collateral is sold or otherwise disposed of. A secured party has an interest in proceeds that perfects automatically on perfection of the security interest and remains perfected for at least ten days after the debtor receives the proceeds. The interest remains perfected for more than ten days if—

1. A filed financing statement covers the original collateral and the proceeds are property (or cash used to acquire property) in which a security interest may be perfected by filing in the same office [UCC 9–306(3)(a)].

2. There is a filed statement that covers the original collateral and the proceeds are identifiable cash proceeds [UCC 9–306(3)(b)].

3. The security interest in the proceeds is perfected before the expiration of the ten-day period [UCC 9–306(3)(c)].

B. AFTER-ACQUIRED PROPERTY

A security agreement may provide for coverage of **after-acquired property** [UCC 9–204(1)]—collateral acquired by a debtor after execution of a security agreement. May consist of any property except consumer goods.

C. FUTURE ADVANCES

A security agreement may provide that future advances against a line of credit are subject to a security interest in the collateral [UCC 9–204(3)].

D. THE FLOATING-LIEN CONCEPT

A **floating lien** is a security agreement that provides for the creation of a security interest in any (or all) of the above. The concept can apply to a shifting stock of goods—the lien can start with raw materials and follow them as they become finished goods and inventories and as they are sold, turning into accounts receivable, chattel paper, or cash [UCC 9–205].

IV. PRIORITIES AMONG SECURITY INTERESTS

When several creditors claim a security interest in the same collateral of a debtor, which interest has priority?

A. SECURED PARTIES V. UNSECURED PARTIES

Secured parties (perfected or not) prevail over unsecured creditors and creditors who have obtained judgments against the debtor but who have not begun the legal process to collect on those judgments [UCC 9–301].

B. SECURED PARTIES V. OTHER SECURED PARTIES

1. The General Rule

The first interest to be filed or perfected has priority over other filed or perfected security interests. If none of the interests has been perfected, the first to attach has priority [UCC 9-312(5)].

2. Exception—Purchase-Money Security Interest (PMSI)

When the first in time to file or perfect is a PMSI, the PMSI is first in priority rights to the collateral. Also—

a. Inventory

A perfected PMSI prevails over a previously perfected security interest if the holder of the PMSI perfects and gives the holder of the other interest written notice of the PMSI before the debtor takes possession of the new inventory [UCC 9–312(3)].

b. Other Collateral

A PMSI has priority over a previously perfected security interest if the PMSI is perfected either before or within ten days after the debtor takes possession. No notice is required [UCC 9–312(4)].

C. SECURED PARTIES V. BUYERS

1. The General Rule

A security interest in collateral continues even after the collateral has been sold unless the secured party authorized the sale [UCC 9-306(2)].

2. Exception—Buyer in the Ordinary Course of Business

Takes goods free of any security interest (unless the buyer knows that the purchase violates a third party's rights) [UCC 1–201(9), 9-307(1)].

3. Exception—Buyers of Consumer Goods from Consumers

The consumer must not know of the original interest; the purchase must occur before the secured party files a statement [UCC 9–307(2)].

V. RIGHTS AND DUTIES OF DEBTORS AND CREDITORS

A. INFORMATION REQUESTS

When filing, creditors can ask the filing officer to note the file number, the date, and the hour on a copy of the statement and send it to the creditor [UCC 9–407(1)]. Others (such as prospective creditors) can ask the filing officer to provide a certificate that gives information on possible perfected financing statements [UCC 9–407(2)].

B. ASSIGNMENT, AMENDMENT, AND RELEASE

A secured party can release part or all of the collateral [UCC 9–406], or assign part or all of the security interest [UCC 9–405(2)]. A filed financing statement can be amended, if both parties sign [UCC 9–402].

C. THE STATUS OF THE DEBT

When the debtor asks, the secured party must tell the debtor the amount of the unpaid debt (within two weeks of the debtor's request) [UCC 9–208].

D. TERMINATION STATEMENT

When a debt is paid, the secured party can send a termination statement to the debtor or file it with the original financing statement.

1. If the Collateral Is Consumer Goods

The statement must be filed within one month after the debt is paid, or—if the debtor requests the statement in writing—within ten days of receipt of the request, whichever is earlier [UCC 9–404(1)].

2. If the Collateral Is Other Goods

The statement must be filed or furnished to the debtor within ten days after a written request is made by the debtor.

VI. DEFAULT

Default is whatever the parties stipulate in their agreement [UCC 9–501(1)]. It occurs most often when the debtor fails to make payments or goes bankrupt.

A. BASIC REMEDIES

1. Execution and Levy

A secured party give up the security interest and proceed to judgment on the debt (this is done if the value of the collateral is less than the debt and the debtor has other assets) [UCC 9–501(1)].

2. Take Possession of the Collateral

A secured party can take possession of the collateral [UCC 9–503] and retain it for satisfaction of the debt [UCC 9–505(2)] or resell it and apply the proceeds toward the debt [UCC 9–504] (see below).

B. SECURED PARTY'S RIGHT TO TAKE POSSESSION OF THE COLLATERAL

A secured party can take possession of the collateral without a court order, if it can be done without a breach of the peace [UCC 9–503]. Generally, this means not going onto the debtor's property, which could be trespass.

C. DISPOSITION OF COLLATERAL

1. Retention of Collateral by the Secured Party

a. Notice

A secured party must give written notice to the debtor. In all cases except consumer goods, notice must also be sent to any other secured party from whom the secured party has received notice of a claim.

b. If Debtor or Other Secured Party Objects within Twenty-One Days

The secured party must sell or otherwise dispose of the collateral [UCC 9–505(2)].

2. **Consumer Goods**
If the collateral is consumer goods with a PMSI and the debtor has paid 60 percent or more on the price or loan, the secured party must sell within ninety days [UCC 9–505(1), 9–507(1)].

3. **Disposition Procedures**
(1) A sale must be in a commercially reasonable manner and (2) the debtor must be notified of the sale [UCC 9–504].

   a. **What Qualifies as a Commercially Reasonable Sale?**
   When collateral is sold in the usual manner in the usual market for selling such goods or in conformity with reasonable commercial practices among dealers in the type of property sold [UCC 9–507].

   b. **The Secured Party Must Give Written Notice to the Debtor**
   In all cases except consumer goods, notice must also be sent to any other secured party from whom the secured party has received notice of a claim [UCC 9–504(3)], unless the collateral is perishable or is customarily sold in a recognized market.

4. **Proceeds from Disposition**
Must be applied to (1) expenses stemming from the retaking, holding, or preparing for sale, (2) satisfaction of the debt, (3) creditors with subordinate security interests [UCC 9–504(1)], and (4) surplus to the debtor.

5. **Deficiency Judgment**
In most cases, if a sale of collateral does not repay the debt, the debtor is liable for any deficiency. A creditor can obtain a judgment to collect.

6. **Redemption Rights**
Before the secured party retains or disposes of the collateral, the debtor or any other secured party can take the collateral by tendering performance of all secured obligations and paying the secured party's expenses [UCC 9–506].

TRUE-FALSE QUESTIONS

___ 1. Perfection is the process by which a secured party protects his or her interest against some claims of third parties who may wish to have their debts satisfied out of the same collateral.

___ 2. A secured party needs to file copies of a financing statement only in his or her own office to protect all of his or her rights.

___ 3. A security interest in proceeds does not perfect automatically.

___ 4. The descriptions of collateral in a security agreement and a financing statement must be different.

___ 5. Generally, a security interest in collateral terminates when the debt is paid.

___ 6. A security agreement determines most of the parties' rights and duties concerning the security interest.

___ 7. When a debt is paid, the secured party can send a termination statement to the debtor or file one with the officer to whom the financing statement was given.

___ 8. Default occurs most commonly when a debtor fails to repay the loan for which his or her property served as collateral.

___ 9. After a debtor has defaulted and the secured party has taken possession of the property that was the collateral, the debtor can never get it back.

___ 10. When several secured parties claim a security interest in the same collateral of a debtor, the last to have been perfected takes priority.

FILL-IN QUESTIONS

1. Generally, in a secured transaction, the ______________________ (creditor/debtor) files a financing statement with the appropriate state office. When the debt is paid, the ______________________ (creditor/debtor) may also send a termination statement to the officer with whom the financing statement was filed.

2. When two or more secured parties have perfected security interests in the same collateral, generally the __________ (first/last) to perfect has priority. When two conflicting security interests are unperfected, the __________ (first/last) to attach has priority.

MULTIPLE-CHOICE QUESTIONS

___ 1. A document reads, "Debtor (Michael's Sports, 711 Fifth Avenue, St. Paul, MN) grants to secured party (Ace Finance Company, 115 First Street, St. Paul, MN) a security interest in debtor's inventory." For this document to qualify as a *financing statement*, which of the following is NOT necessary?

a. The debtor's signature
b. The creditor 's signature
c. Both parties' addresses
d. The description of the collateral ("debtor's inventory")

___ 2. Eve and Rick sign an agreement that states, "Debtor (Eve) grants to secured party (Rick) a security interest in debtor's 1997 Miata." Rick gives Eve a check for $5,000. For Rick to have an enforceable security interest, which of the following is NOT necessary?

a. Eve's giving of rights in her car
b. The written agreement
c. Rick's signature on the agreement
d. The check that Rick gave to Eve

___ 3. Paul owns a Veggies Too restaurant. Paul wants to borrow $60,000 from the First National Bank to open another Veggies Too, using his first restaurant as collateral. The bank asks Paul to sign a *security agreement*. Besides Paul's signature, to be effective the agreement must

a. contain a description that reasonably identifies the collateral.
b. include the addresses of the debtor and the creditor.
c. both a and b.
d. none of the above.

____ **4.** In which of the following situations is a PMSI created?

a. To buy a computer, Dan signs an agreement with Cell Electronics, the seller, to pay $100 down and $50 per month until the price and interest are paid.
b. B&B Financing Agency advances Doug money to buy a computer from Cell Electronics, and Doug uses the money for that purpose.
c. Both a and b
d. None of the above

____ **5.** A security agreement for a loan from First State Bank to C.C. Computers provides for the coverage of inventory, proceeds, future advances, and after-acquired property. C.C. sells its inventory for trade-ins plus cash and buys new inventory with funds from the bank. The bank has a perfected interest in

a. the trade-ins under the *proceeds* clause.
b. the funds to buy the new inventory under the *proceeds* clause.
c. the new inventory under the *inventory* clause.
d. none of the above.

____ **6.** Friendly Loan Company loans $15,000 to Steve to buy a new car. Their agreement provides that Steve will repay the loan over a five-year period and that he is in default if he misses a single payment. One year later, Steve fails to make two payments, and the lender declares him to be in default. The lender may take possession of the car and

a. keep it.
b. sell it to anyone after giving Steve an opportunity to fully comply with the security agreement.
c. sell it to Steve on Steve's full compliance with the security agreement.
d. any of the above.

____ **7.** Amigo Credit Agency loans $10,000 to Al's Hardware. The loan is secured by Al's inventory, which includes tools and supplies that Al sells to some customers on installment payment plans. Eventually, Al defaults on the loan. Amigo is entitled to

a. all of the inventory sold to customers.
b. any remaining installment payments.
c. both a and b.
d. none of the above.

____ **8.** Amy buys a car with money borrowed from Bob, who takes a security interest in the car. The transaction occurs in a state that requires title registration and Bob's interest is noted on the certificate of title. If Amy moves to another state requiring a certificate, Bob's interest is

a. no longer effective.
b. effective for five years from the date the car is moved.
c. effective for four months from the date the car is moved.
d. effective until the car is registered in the new state.

___ 9. On May 1, First State Bank lends $10,000 to Diane. On May 10, the bank files a financing statement. Before that statement is filed, however, Diane uses the same collateral to borrow $5,000 from City Bank, which files a statement on May 4. In a dispute between the banks over the collateral

a. First State Bank wins because it lent money first.
b. First State Bank wins because its interest attached first.
c. City Bank wins because it perfected first.
d. City Bank wins because its interest attached first.

___ 10. Chris defaults on a loan from EZ Loan Company. EZ takes possession of the collateral and would like to keep it. Ace Capital, which also has an interest in the collateral, sends EZ notice of its claim. EZ may

a. not retain the collateral because it would violate Ace's interest.
b. retain the collateral if it sends notice to Ace.
c. be forced to sell the collateral if Ace objects to the retention.
d. be forced to sell the collateral and be forced to pay Ace.

SHORT ESSAY QUESTIONS

1. Define the floating lien concept.

2. What are a secured party's rights on a debtor's default?

ISSUE SPOTTERS

1. Stan needs $300 to buy textbooks, notebooks, and other supplies. Duane says, "I'll lend you $300 if you'll agree that if you don't pay it back, I get your laptop." Stan agrees, they put their agreement in writing, and Duane gives Stan $300. How does Duane let other creditors know of his interest in the laptop?

2. The Money Shop loans $25,000 to Wolf's Photo, secured by the store's inventory. Wolf sells cameras and other equipment from inventory to consumers on installment payment plans. Wolf defaults on the loan, but all of the inventory has been sold. Many installment payments remain, however. How can the Money Shop recover its funds?

3. Assume that in the previous question Wolf's business was more complicated: Wolf sold inventory for trade-ins plus cash and bought new inventory with additional funds advanced from the Money Shop. How can the lender be sure that its interest isn't lost in all the transactions?

4. Imagine that in the previous question Wolf sold to Mann a camcorder covered by the Money Shop's agreement with Wolf. Before Mann's check cleared, Wolf defaulted on the loan to the Money Shop. Is the lender entitled to the camcorder or the check?

5. Avco Finance loans $5,000 to Brad to buy a computer. The loan is secured by the computer. Brad defaults on the loan. Avco can repossess and keep the computer, but Avco does not want it. What are the alternatives?

 **Learning Objectives**

The learning objectives in this chapter include:

1. Remedies available to a creditor on a debtor's default.
2. Suretyship and guaranty arrangements.
3. The steps in a bankruptcy proceeding.
4. What property constitutes a debtor's estate in bankruptcy.
5. Relief available under Chapter 7, Chapter 11, Chapter 12, and Chapter 13.

Chapter 20: Creditors' Rights and Bankruptcy

WHAT THIS CHAPTER IS ABOUT

This chapter sets out the rights and remedies available to a creditor, when a debtor defaults, under laws other than UCC Article 9. This chapter also covers the federal bankruptcy laws.

CHAPTER OUTLINE

I. LAWS ASSISTING CREDITORS

A. LIENS

A lien is an encumbrance on property to satisfy a debt or protect a claim for payment of a debt.

1. **Mechanic's Lien**

Can be placed by a creditor on real property when a person contracts for labor, services, or materials to improve the property but does not pay.

a. **When a Creditor Must File a Mechanic's Lien**

Within a specific period, measured from the last date on which materials or labor were provided (usually within 60 to 120 days).

b. **If the Owner Does Not Pay**

The property can be sold to satisfy the debt. Notice of the foreclosure and sale must be given to the debtor in advance.

2. **Artisan's Lien**

A security device by which a creditor can recover from a debtor for labor and materials furnished in the repair of personal property.

a. **The Creditor Must Possess the Property**
Lien terminates if possession is voluntarily surrendered, unless the lienholder records notice of the lien in accord with state statutes.

b. **If the Owner Does Not Pay**
The property can be sold to satisfy the debt. Notice of the foreclosure and sale must be given to the debtor in advance.

3. **Innkeeper's Lien**
A security device placed on the baggage of guests for hotel charges that are not paid. The lien terminates when the charges are paid, or the baggage is returned or sold to satisfy the debt.

4. **Judicial Liens**

a. **Attachment**
Attachment is a court-ordered seizure and taking into custody of property before the securing of a judgment for a past-due debt. A sheriff or other officer seizes nonexempt property. If the creditor prevails at trial, the property can be sold to satisfy the judgment.

b. **Writ of Execution**
A **writ of execution** is an order, usually issued by the clerk of court, directing the sheriff to seize and sell any of the debtor's nonexempt property within the court's geographical jurisdiction. Proceeds of the sale pay the debt.

B. GARNISHMENT
Garnishment is when a creditor collects a debt by seizing property of the debtor (such as wages or money in a bank account) that is being held by a third party (such as an employer or a bank). The creditor obtains a judgment against the debtor and serves it on the third party.

C. CREDITORS' COMPOSITION AGREEMENTS
A **creditors' composition agreement** is a contract between a debtor and his or her creditors for discharge of the debtor's liquidated debts on payment of a sum less than that owed.

D. MORTGAGE FORECLOSURE
A mortgagor can foreclose on the mortgaged property if the debtor defaults. The usual method is a judicial sale. The proceeds are applied to the debt. If they do not cover the costs and the debt, the mortgagee can recover the difference from the mortgagor by obtaining a deficiency judgment.

E. SURETYSHIP AND GUARANTY

1. **Suretyship**
A promise by a third person to be responsible for a debtor's obligation. Does not have to be in writing. A surety is *primarily* liable—a creditor can demand payment from the surety the moment the debt is due.

2. **Guaranty**
A promise to be *secondarily* liable for the debt or default of another. A guarantor pays only after the debtor defaults and the creditor has made an attempt to collect from the debtor. A guaranty must be in writing unless the main-purpose exception applies (see Chapter 10).

3. **Defenses of the Surety and the Guarantor**
To avoid payment, a surety (guarantor) may use the following defenses.

a. **Material Change to the Contract between Debtor and Creditor**
Without obtaining the consent of the surety (guarantor), a surety is discharged completely or to the extent the surety suffers a loss.

b. **The Principal Obligation Is Paid or Valid Tender Is Made**
The surety (guarantor) is discharged from the obligation.

c. **Most of the Defenses of the Principal Debtor**
Defenses that cannot be used: the debtor's incapacity, bankruptcy, and the statute of limitations.

d. **A Surety or Guarantor's Own Defenses**

e. **A Creditor's Surrender or Impairment of the Collateral**
Without the surety's (guarantor's) consent, releases the surety to the extent of any loss suffered from the creditor's actions.

4. **Rights of the Surety and the Guarantor**
If the surety (guarantor) pays the debt—

a. **Right of Subrogation**
The surety (guarantor) has available any remedies that were available to the creditor against the debtor.

b. **Right of Reimbursement**
The surety (guarantor) is entitled to receive from the debtor all outlays made on behalf of the suretyship arrangement.

c. **Co-Sureties' Right of Contribution**
A surety who pays more than his or her proportionate share on a debtor's default is entitled to recover from co-sureties.

II. LAWS ASSISTING DEBTORS

A. HOMESTEAD EXEMPTION
Each state allows a debtor to keep the family home (in some states only if the debtor has a family) in its entirety or up to a specified amount.

B. EXEMPT PERSONAL PROPERTY
Household furniture up to a specified dollar amount; clothing and other possessions; a vehicle (or vehicles); certain animals; and equipment that the debtor uses in a business or trade.

III. BANKRUPTCY AND REORGANIZATION
Bankruptcy law (1) protects a debtor by giving him or her a fresh start and (2) ensures equitable treatment to creditors competing for a debtor's assets. Bankruptcy proceedings are held in federal bankruptcy courts. Current law is based on the Bankruptcy Reform Act of 1978 (the Bankruptcy Code). Relief can be granted under the Code's Chapter 7, Chapter 11, Chapter 12, or Chapter 13.

IV. BANKRUPTCY—CHAPTER 7 LIQUIDATION
This is the most familiar type of bankruptcy proceeding. A debtor declares his or her debts and gives all assets to a trustee, who sells the nonexempt assets and distributes the proceeds to creditors.

A. WHO CAN FILE FOR A LIQUIDATION

Any "person"—individuals, partnerships, and corporations (spouses can file jointly)—except railroads, insurance companies, banks, savings and loan associations, certain investment companies, and credit unions.

B. FILING THE PETITION

1. Voluntary Bankruptcy

a. The Debtor Files a Petition with the Court
Includes a list of (1) creditors and debts, (2) debtor's financial affairs, (3) debtor's property, (4) current income and expenses.

b. Filing of the Petition Constitutes an Order for Relief
The clerk of the court must give the trustee and creditors notice of the order within not more than twenty days.

c. Substantial Abuse
A court can dismiss a petition if granting it would constitute "substantial abuse" [11 U.S.C. Section 707(b)].

2. Involuntary Bankruptcy

A debtor's creditors can force the debtor into bankruptcy proceedings.

a. Who Can Be Forced into Involuntary Proceedings
A debtor with twelve or more creditors, three or more of whom (with unsecured claims of at least $10,775) file a petition. A debtor with fewer than twelve creditors, one or more of whom (with a claim of $10,775) files. Not a farmer or a charitable institution.

b. When an Order for Relief Will Be Entered
If the debtor does not challenge the petition, the debtor is generally not paying debts as they come due, or a receiver, assignee, or custodian took possession of the debtor's property within 120 days before the petition was filed.

C. AUTOMATIC STAY

When a petition is filed, an **automatic stay** suspends all action by creditors against the debtor. A court may grant some relief. The stay does not apply to paternity, alimony, or family maintenance and support claims.

D. CREDITORS' MEETING AND CLAIMS

Within "not less than ten days or more than thirty days," the court calls a meeting of creditors, at which the debtor answers questions. Within ninety days of the meeting, a creditor must file a proof of claim. The proof lists the creditor's name and address, as well as the amount of the debt.

E. PROPERTY OF THE ESTATE

1. What Property Is Included in the Debtor's Estate

Interests in property presently held; jointly owned property; property transferred in transactions voidable by the trustee; proceeds and profits; after-acquired property; interests in gifts, inheritances, property settlements, and life insurance death proceeds to which the debtor becomes entitled within 180 days after filing.

2. What Property Is Not Included

Property acquired after the filing of the petition, except as noted.

F. EXEMPTED PROPERTY

1. Federal Law

Exempts such property as interests in a residence to $16,150, a motor vehicle to $2,575, household goods to $8,000, and tools of a trade to $1,625, and the rights to receive Social Security and other benefits.

2. State Law

Most states preclude the use of federal exemptions; others allow a debtor to choose between state and federal. State exemptions may include different value limitations and exempt different property.

G. THE TRUSTEE'S ROLE

After the order for relief, an interim trustee is appointed to administer the debtor's property until the first meeting of creditors, when a permanent trustee is elected. A trustee's duty is to collect and reduce to money the property of the estate and distribute the proceeds.

1. Trustee's Powers

A trustee can require persons holding the debtor's property to turn it over to the trustee. A trustee also has the same rights as, for example, a lien creditor with priority over an unperfected secured party.

2. Voidable Rights

Any reason that a debtor can use to obtain the return of his or her property can be used by the trustee (fraud, duress, etc.)

3. Preferences

A trustee can recover payments made by a debtor (1) within ninety days before the petition and (2) for a preexisting debt.

a. Insiders or Fraud

If a creditor is an insider (partner, corporate officer, relative) or a transfer is fraudulent, a trustee may recover transfers made within one year before filing.

b. Transfers That Are Not Preferences

Property sold to an innocent third party.

H. DISTRIBUTION OF PROPERTY

1. Secured Creditors

Within thirty days of the petition or before the first creditors' meeting (whichever is first), a debtor must state whether he or she will retain secured collateral (or claim it as exempt, etc.).

2. Unsecured Creditors

Paid in the order of priority. The order of priority is—

a. Administrative expenses (court costs, trustee and attorney fees).
b. In an involuntary bankruptcy, expenses incurred by the debtor in the ordinary course of business from the filing of the petition to the appointment of the trustee or the issuance of an order for relief.
c. Unpaid wages, salaries, and commissions earned within ninety days of the petition, to $4,300 per claimant. A claim in excess is a claim of a general creditor (no. i below).

d. Unsecured claims for contributions to employee benefit plans, limited to services performed within 180 days before the petition and $4,300 per employee.
e. Claims by farmers and fishers, to $4,300, against storage or processing facilities.
f. Consumer deposits to $1,950 given to the debtor before the petition to buy, lease, or rent property or services that were not received.
g. Claims for paternity, alimony, maintenance, and support.
h. Taxes and penalties due to the government.
i. Claims of general creditors.

I. DISCHARGE

A discharge voids any judgment on a discharged debt and prohibits any action to collect a discharged debt. A co-debtor's liability is not affected.

1. **Exceptions—Debts That May Not Be Discharged**
   Claims for back taxes, amounts borrowed to pay back taxes, goods obtained by fraud, debts that were not listed in the petition, alimony, child support, student loans, certain cash advances, and others.

2. **Objections—Debtors Who May Not Receive a Discharge**
   Those who conceal property with the intent to hinder, delay, or defraud a creditor; who fail to explain a loss of assets; or who have been granted a discharge within six years of the filing of the petition.

3. **Revocation of Discharge**
   A discharge may be revoked within one year if the debtor was fraudulent or dishonest during the bankruptcy proceedings.

4. **Reaffirmation of Debt**
   A reaffirmation of debt is a debtor's agreement to pay an otherwise dischargeable debt. The agreement must be made before a discharge is granted and must be approved by the court. Can be rescinded within sixty days or before the discharge is granted.

V. BANKRUPTCY—CHAPTER 11 REORGANIZATION

In a Chapter 11 reorganization, the creditors and the debtor formulate a plan under which the debtor pays a portion of the debts, is discharged of the rest, and continues in business.

A. WHO IS ELIGIBLE FOR RELIEF UNDER CHAPTER 11

Any debtor (except a stockbroker or a commodities broker) who is eligible for Chapter 7 relief. Used most commonly by corporate debtors. The same principles apply that govern liquidation (automatic stay, etc.).

B. DEBTOR IN POSSESSION

On entry of an order for relief, the debtor continues to operate his or her business as a debtor in possession (DIP).

1. **If Gross Mismanagement Is Shown**
   The court may appoint a trustee (or receiver) to operate the business. This may also be done if it is in the best interests of the estate.

2. **DIP's Role Is Similar to That of a Trustee in a Liquidation**
   The DIP can avoid pre-petition preferential payments and fraudulent transfers and decide whether to cancel pre-petition executory contracts.

C. CREDITORS' COMMITTEES

A committee of unsecured creditors is appointed to consult with the trustee or DIP. Certain small businesses can avoid creditors' committees.

D. THE REORGANIZATION PLAN

1. What the Plan Must Do

Administer the debtor's assets in the hope of a return to solvency; designate classes of claims and interests; specify the treatment to be afforded the classes; and provide an adequate means for execution.

2. Who Can File a Plan

Only the debtor within the first 120 days (100 days in some cases) after the date of the order for relief. Any other party, if the debtor does not meet the deadline or fails to obtain creditor consent within 180 days.

3. The Plan Is Submitted to Creditors for Acceptance

Each class adversely affected by a plan must accept it (two-thirds of the total claims must approve). If only one class accepts, the court may confirm it if it "does not discriminate unfairly" against any creditors. The debtor is given a discharge from all claims not within the plan (except those that would be denied in a liquidation).

VI. BANKRUPTCY—CHAPTER 13 REPAYMENT PLAN

A. WHO IS ELIGIBLE

Individuals (not partnerships or corporations) with regular income and unsecured debts of less than $269,250 or secured debts of less than $807,750.

B. VOLUNTARY FILING ONLY

A Chapter 13 case can be initiated by the filing of a voluntary petition only. A trustee is appointed. The automatic stay takes effect (on consumer debts, not business debts).

C. THE REPAYMENT PLAN

The plan must provide for turnover to the trustee of the debtor's future income.

1. Filing and Confirming the Plan

Only the debtor can file a plan, which the court will confirm if (1) the secured creditors accept it, (2) it provides that creditors retain their liens and the value of the property to be distributed to them is not less than the secured portion of their claims, or (3) the debtor surrenders the property securing the claim to the creditors.

2. Payments under the Plan

The time for payment must be less than three years (five years, with court approval). The payments must be timely, or the court can convert the case to a liquidation or dismiss the petition. Before completion of payments, the plan may be modified at the request of the debtor, the trustee, or an unsecured creditor.

3. Objection to the Plan

Over the objection of the trustee or an unsecured creditor, the court may approve a plan only if (1) the value of the property to be distributed is equal to the amount of the claims, or (2) all the debtor's disposable income during the plan will be used to make payments.

D. **DISCHARGE**

After completion of all payments, all debts provided for by the plan are discharged. A discharge obtained by fraud can be revoked within one year.

VII. BANKRUPTCY—CHAPTER 12 FAMILY FARMER PLAN

Chapter 12 is nearly identical to Chapter 13. Eligible debtors include a family farmer whose gross income is at least 50 percent farm dependent and whose debts are at least 80 percent farm related (total debt must not exceed $1 million), and a partnership or closely held corporation (at least 50 percent owned by a farm family).

TRUE-FALSE QUESTIONS

___ **1.** A mechanic's lien always involves real property, and an artisan's lien always involves personal property.

___ **2.** Federal and state laws limit the amount that can be garnished from wages, but they cannot be applied together to determine how much is exempt.

___ **3.** A creditors' composition agreement discharges only the debtor's debts owed to those creditors who agree.

___ **4.** An innkeeper's lien is placed on the baggage of guests for agreed-on hotel charges that remain unpaid.

___ **5.** Generally, to avoid liability, a surety or a guarantor cannot use any defenses available to the principal debtor.

___ **6.** A debtor must be insolvent to file a voluntary petition under Chapter 7.

___ **7.** Debtors are protected from losing the value of their property as a result of the automatic stay.

___ **8.** In a bankruptcy proceeding, any creditor's claim is allowed automatically unless contested by the trustee, the debtor, or another creditor.

___ **9.** If a debtor surrenders collateral to a secured party and the secured party forecloses on it, the secured party has priority to it over other creditors.

___ **10.** The same principles cover the filing of a Chapter 7 petition and a Chapter 11 proceeding.

FILL-IN QUESTIONS

Liquidation is the purpose of Chapter ______ (7/11/13). Reorganization is the purpose of Chapter ______ (7/11/13). Adjustment is the purpose of Chapter ______ (7/11/13). Under Chapter ______ (7/11/13), nonexempt property is sold, with proceeds distributed in a certain priority to classes of creditors, and dischargeable debts are terminated. Under Chapter ______ (7/11/13), a plan for reorganization is submitted, and if it is approved and followed, debts are discharged. Under Chapter ______ (7/11/13), a plan must be approved if the debtor turns over all disposable income for a three-year period, after which debts are discharged. The advantages of Chapter ______ (7/11/13) include the debtor's opportunity for a fresh start. The advantages of Chapter ______ (7/11/13) include the debtor's continuation in business under a plan that allows for reorganization of debts. The advantages of Chapter ____ (7/11/13) include the debtor's continuation in business and discharge of most debts.

MULTIPLE-CHOICE QUESTIONS

____ 1. Melita leaves her necklace with Berman Jewelers to be repaired. When Melita returns to pick up the necklace, she says, "I don't have the money right now, but I'll pay you for the repairs later." Berman

a. can keep the necklace until Melita pays for the repairs.
b. can keep the necklace for a reasonable time but must then return it to Melita even if she does not pay for the repairs.
c. cannot keep the necklace.
d. none of the above.

____ 2. Sam's $6,000 debt to the Ace Credit Company is past due, and Ace files suit. Before the judge hears the case, Ace learns that Sam has hidden some of her property from her creditors. Ace believes that Sam is about to hide the rest of her property. To ensure there will be some assets to satisfy the debt if Ace wins the suit, Ace can use

a. garnishment.
b. a mechanic's lien.
c. an artisan's lien.
d. attachment.

____ 3. Ed's $2,500 debt to Owen is past due. Ed does not own a house and has very little personal property, but he has a checking account, a savings account, and a job. To reach these assets to satisfy the debt, Owen can use

a. garnishment.
b. a mechanic's lien.
c. an artisan's lien.
d. attachment.

____ 4. Bob obtains a judgment for $30,000 and a writ of execution against Mary. To enforce the writ, Mary's home is sold for $60,000. The homestead exemption is $35,000. All of Mary's personal property is exempt, except two motorcycles that are sold for $5,000. After applying the appropriate amounts to payment of the debt, how much of the debt will be unpaid?

a. $25,000
b. $10,000
c. $5,000
d. $0

____ 5. L&R Hardware, Inc., wants to borrow money from the First National Bank. The bank refuses to lend L&R the money unless Lee, the sole stockholder, agrees to assume liability if L&R does not pay off the loan. Lee agrees. L&R makes the first four payments. When the fifth payment is due, the bank can seek payment from L&R

a. but not Lee, because Lee is a guarantor.
b. but not Lee, because L&R is a surety.
c. or Lee, because Lee is a surety.
d. or Lee, because Lee is a guarantor.

___ **6.** Trim Loan Company lends $90,000 to Patty's Balloons. Carl, Lynn, and Floyd are co-sureties. The maximum liability of each is: Carl $18,000, Lynn $27,000, and Floyd $45,000. Patty's defaults. The balance due is $60,000. Floyd pays $45,000 and Patty's pays $15,000. Floyd can recover

a. $18,000 from Carl and $27,000 from Lynn.
b. $13,500 from Carl and $20,250 from Lynn.
c. $9,000 from Carl and $13,500 from Lynn.
d. $0 from Carl and $0 from Lynn.

___ **7.** Ted is the sole proprietor of Duncan's Restaurant, which owes secured debts of $225,000 and unsecured debts of $75,000. The amount is more than Ted believes he and the restaurant can reasonably repay. Most of Duncan's creditors agree that liquidating Ted and the restaurant would not be in their best interests. To stay in business, Ted could file for bankruptcy under

a. Chapter 7.
b. Chapter 11.
c. Chapter 13.
d. both b and c.

___ **8.** Jerry's monthly income is $2,500, his monthly expenses are $2,100, and his debts are nearly $15,000. If he applied the difference between his income and expenses to pay off the debts, they could be eliminated within three years. The provision in the Bankruptcy Code that covers this sort of plan is

a. Chapter 7.
b. Chapter 11.
c. Chapter 13.
d. none of the above.

___ **9.** A bankruptcy trustee has the power to avoid

a. preferences.
b. fraudulent transfers.
c. transactions that the debtor could rightfully avoid, or cancel.
d. all of the above.

___ **10.** Dick pays for college by taking out student loans. After graduation, he marries, has a child, and works briefly before divorcing and filing for Chapter 7 bankruptcy. Dick's only debts are student loans, taxes accruing within the three previous years, and alimony and child support. The debts that can be discharged in the bankruptcy are

a. the student loans.
b. the taxes.
c. the alimony and child support.
d. none of the above.

SHORT ESSAY QUESTIONS

1. Define a lien, list four ways in which a lien can arise, and state a lienholder's priority.

2. State the differences between contracts of suretyship and guaranty contracts.

ISSUE SPOTTERS

1. Joe contracts with Larry of Midwest Roofing to fix Joe's roof. Joe pays half of the contract price in advance. Larry and Midwest complete the job, but Joe refuses to pay the rest of the price. What can Larry and Midwest do?

2. Laura wants to borrow $10,000 from the Ace Finance Company to buy a new car, but Ace refuses to lend the money unless Bob cosigns the note. Bob cosigns the note and makes three of the payments to Ace when Laura fails to do so. Can Bob get the money for these three payments from Laura?

3. Northwest Company's creditors include First National Savings & Loan with a perfected security interest in Northwest's building and equipment, Trager Construction with a mechanic's lien on the building that predates First National's security interest, and Universal Supplies, Inc., with an unperfected security interest. Northwest files a petition for Chapter 7 liquidation. In what order are the creditors entitled to be paid?

4. Adam is a vice president for Para Company. On May 1, Adam loans Para $10,000. On June 1, the company repays the loan. On July 1, Para files for bankruptcy. Len is appointed trustee. Can Len recover the $10,000 paid to Adam on June 1?

5. Jan is a farmer. Her debts are 90 percent farm-related. They total more than $1 million, and Jan believes that bankruptcy is the only viable alternative for discharging them. Jan does not want to lose the farm, however, and most of her creditors agree that liquidation would not serve their best interests. Is there a proceeding under the bankruptcy laws through which she can retain the farm and the creditors can have some of the debt repaid?

QUICKEN CD-ROM BUSINESS LAW PARTNER APPLICATIONS

Open **Quicken Business Law Partner**. Click on the *New Documents* icon. Choose the *Guaranty Agreement*. Respond to the *Interview* questions with actual facts or hypothetical ones. For example, imagine that Ace Credit Company loans money to Mike, and Nora signs the guaranty agreement. As you complete the *Interview*, answer the following questions.

___ **1.** A guaranty agreement may be used to

a. prevent a creditor from collecting a debt from the debtor.
b. provide an incentive for a loan to a third party.
c. induce a creditor to enter into a contract with a third party.
d. all of the above.

___ **2.** A guaranty agreement may require the guarantor to

a. give up defenses the guarantor may have against payment of the debt.
b. pay the debt even if it is unenforceable against the debtor.
c. both a and b.
d. none of the above.

____ **3.** Under a guaranty agreement, without notice to the guarantor and without affecting the guarantor's liability, a creditor may have the authority to

a. lend more money to the debtor.
b. alter the debtor's obligation.
c. both a and b.
d. none of the above.

____ **4.** To whose advantage is it to require the guarantor's written consent if the creditor makes, alters, or renews a contract or agreement with the debtor?

a. The creditor's
b. The debtor's
c. The guarantor's
d. None of the above

____ **5.** Unless the guaranty agreement provides otherwise, the guarantor's obligation is discharged by

a. the guarantor's death.
b. the creditor's assignment of the agreement.
c. the creditor's release of the security for the debt.
d. none of the above.

 **Learning Objectives**

The learning objectives in this chapter include:

1. The difference between employees and independent contractors.
2. How an agency relationship can arise.
3. The duties that agents and principals owe to each other.
4. The liability of the principal and the agent to third parties.
5. How an agency relationship can terminate.

Chapter 21: Agency Relationships

WHAT THIS CHAPTER IS ABOUT

This chapter covers agency relationships, including how they are formed and the duties involved. An agency relationship involves two parties: the principal and the agent. Agency relationships are essential to a corporation, which can function and enter into contracts only through its agents.

CHAPTER OUTLINE

I. AGENCY RELATIONSHIPS

In an agency relationship, the parties agree that the agent will act on behalf and instead of the principal in negotiating and transacting business with third persons.

A. EMPLOYER-EMPLOYEE RELATIONSHIPS

Normally, all employees who deal with third parties are deemed to be agents. Statutes covering workers' compensation and so on apply only to employer-employee relationships.

B. EMPLOYER–INDEPENDENT CONTRACTOR RELATIONSHIPS

Those who hire independent contractors have no control over the details of their physical performance. Independent contractors can be agents.

C. CRITERIA FOR DETERMINING EMPLOYEE STATUS

The greater an employer's control over the work, the more likely it is that the worker is an employee. Another key factor is whether the employer withholds taxes from payments to the worker and pays unemployment and Social Security taxes covering the worker.

II. AGENCY FORMATION

Consideration is not required. A principal must have capacity to contract; anyone can be an agent. An agency can be created for any legal purpose.

A. AGENCY BY AGREEMENT

Normally, an agency must be based on an agreement that the agent will act for the principal. Such an agreement can be an express written contract, can be implied by conduct, or can be oral. Exceptions to oral agency agreements—

1. Equal Dignity Rule

In most states, if the contract being executed is or must be in writing, the agent's authority must also be in writing.

2. Power of Attorney

A power of attorney can be special or general. An ordinary power terminates on the incapacity or death of the person giving it. A durable power is not affected by the principal's incapacity.

B. AGENCY BY RATIFICATION

A person who is not an agent (or who is an agent acting outside the scope of his or her authority) may make a contract on behalf of another (a principal). If the principal approves or affirms that contract by word or by action, an agency relationship is created by ratification.

C. AGENCY BY ESTOPPEL

1. The Principal's Actions

When a principal causes a third person to believe that another person is his or her agent, and the third person deals with the supposed agent, the principal is estopped to deny the agency relationship.

2. The Third Party's Reasonable Belief

The third person must prove that he or she reasonably believed that an agency relationship existed and that the agent had authority—that an ordinary, prudent person familiar with business practice and custom would have been justified in concluding that the agent had authority.

D. AGENCY BY OPERATION OF LAW

An agency relationship in the absence of a formal agreement may occur in family relationships or in an emergency, if the agent's failure to act outside the scope of his or her authority would cause the principal substantial loss.

III. DUTIES OF AGENTS AND PRINCIPALS

The principal-agent relationship is fiduciary.

A. AGENT'S DUTIES TO THE PRINCIPAL

1. Performance

An agent must perform with reasonable diligence and skill.

2. Notification

An agent must notify the principal of all matters concerning the agency.

3. Loyalty

An agent must act solely for the benefit of the principal.

4. Obedience

An agent must follow all lawful instructions of the principal.

5. **Accounting**
An agent must keep and make available to the principal an account of everything received and paid out on behalf of the principal.

B. PRINCIPAL'S DUTIES TO THE AGENT

1. **Compensation**
A principal must pay the agent for services rendered.

2. **Reimbursement and Indemnification**
A principal must (1) reimburse the agent for money paid at the principal's request or for necessary expenses and (2) indemnify an agent for liability incurred because of authorized acts.

3. **Cooperation**
A principal must cooperate with his or her agent.

4. **Safe Working Conditions**
A principal must provide safe working conditions.

IV. SCOPE OF AN AGENT'S AUTHORITY

A. ACTUAL AUTHORITY

Express authority may be oral or in writing. Implied authority may be conferred by custom, can be inferred from the position an agent occupies, or is implied as reasonably necessary to carry out express authority.

B. APPARENT AUTHORITY

An agent has apparent authority when a principal, by word or action, causes a third party reasonably to believe that an agent has authority, though the agent has no authority. The principal may be estopped from denying it if the third party changes position in reliance.

C. RATIFICATION

A principal can ratify an unauthorized contract or act, if he or she is aware of all material facts. Ratification can be done expressly or impliedly (by accepting the benefits of a transaction). An entire transaction must be ratified; a principal cannot affirm only part.

V. LIABILITY IN AGENCY RELATIONSHIPS

A. LIABILITY FOR CONTRACTS

Who is liable to third parties for contracts formed by an agent?

1. If an Agent Acts within the Scope of His or Her Authority

a. **Disclosed Principal**
If a principal's identity is known to a third party when an agent makes a contract, the principal is liable. The agent is not liable.

b. **Partially Disclosed Principal**
If a principal's identity is not known to a third party when an agent makes a contract but the third party knows the agent is acting for a principal, the principal is liable. In most states, the agent is also liable.

c. **Undisclosed Principal**
If the principal's identity is not known to a third party when an agent makes a contract, the principal *and* the agent are liable. Exceptions—

1) The principal is expressly excluded as a party in the contract.

2) The contract is a negotiable instrument (check or note).

3) The performance of the agent is personal to the contract.

2. **If the Agent Has No Authority**
The principal is not liable in contract to a third party. The agent is liable, unless the third party knew the agent did not have authority.

B. **LIABILITY FOR TORTS AND CRIMES**
An agent is liable to third parties for his or her torts and crimes. Is the principal also liable?

1. **Liability for Agent's Torts**

a. **The Doctrine of *Respondeat Superior***
An employer is liable for harm caused (negligently or intentionally) to a third party by an employee acting within the scope of employment, without regard to the fault of the employer.

b. **Scope of Employment**
Factors for determining whether an act is within the scope of employment are—

1) the time, place, and purpose of the act.

2) whether the act was authorized by the employer.

3) whether the act is one commonly performed by employees on behalf of their employers.

4) whether the employer's interest was advanced by the act.

5) whether the private interests of the employee were involved.

6) whether the employer furnished the means by which an injury was inflicted.

7) whether the employer had reason to know that the employee would do the act in question.

8) whether the act involved the commission of a serious crime.

c. **Misrepresentation**
A principal is responsible for an agent's misrepresentation made within the scope of the agent's authority.

2. **Liability for Independent Contractor's Torts**
An employer is not liable for physical harm caused to a third person by an independent contractor's tort (except in for hazardous activities—blasting operations, transportation of highly volatile chemicals, and use of poisonous gases—in which strict liability is imposed).

3. **Liability for Agent's Crimes**
A principal is not liable for an agent's crime, unless the principal participated. In some states, a principal may be liable for an agent's violating, in the course and scope of employment, such regulations as those governing sanitation, prices, weights, and the sale of liquor.

VI. AGENCY TERMINATION

A. **TERMINATION BY ACT OF THE PARTIES**
An agency ends when the time specified in the agreement expires, its purpose is achieved, a specified event occurs, or by mutual agreement. Both parties have the *power* to terminate an agency, but they may not have the *right* and may therefore be liable for breach of contract.

B. **TERMINATION BY OPERATION OF LAW**
Circumstances under which an agency terminates by operation of law include death or insanity of either party, destruction of the subject matter of the agency, changed circumstances, bankruptcy of either party, and war between the principal's and agent's countries.

C. **NOTICE OF TERMINATION**
If an agency terminates by operation of law because of death, insanity, or some other unforeseen circumstance, there is no duty to notify third persons, unless the agent's authority is coupled with an interest. If the parties themselves terminate the agency, the principal must inform any third parties who know of the agency that it has ended.

TRUE-FALSE QUESTIONS

___ 1. An agent can perform legal acts that bind the principal.

___ 2. An agency relationship must be based on an affirmative indication that the agent agrees to act for the principal and the principal agrees to have the agent act for him or her.

___ 3. A disclosed or partially disclosed principal is liable to a third party for a contract made by an agent acting within the scope of authority.

___ 4. Generally, a principal whose agent commits a tort in the scope of his or her employment is not liable to persons injured.

___ 5. An employer is generally not expected to bear responsibility for an independent contractor's torts unless exceptionally hazardous activities are involved.

___ 6. An agent may always be held liable for a contract he or she enters into on behalf of an undisclosed principal.

___ 7. In an ordinary agency relationship, the agency terminates automatically on the death of the principal.

___ 8. An agency relationship is fiduciary.

___ 9. An employer is liable for any harm caused to a third party by an employee acting within the scope of employment.

___ **10.** Both parties to an agency have the power and the right to terminate the agency at any time.

FILL-IN QUESTIONS

An agent's use of reasonable diligence and skill is part of the agent's duty of ______________ (obedience/performance). Informing a principal of all material matters that come to the agent's attention concerning the subject matter of the agency is an aspect of the agent's duty of ______________ (accounting/notification). Acting solely for the benefit of the principal and not in the interest of the agent or a third party is part of the agent's duty of ______________ (loyalty/performance). Following all lawful and clearly stated instructions of the principal is an aspect of the agent's duty of ______________ (loyalty/obedience). If an agent is required to keep and make available to the principal a record of all property and money received and paid out on behalf of the principal, this is part of the agent's duty of ______________ (accounting/notification).

MULTIPLE-CHOICE QUESTIONS

___ **1.** Ryan agrees to buy a certain amount of goods from Desktop Suppliers, Inc. Ryan will pay for and sell the goods at prices set by Desktop, deposit 90 percent of the proceeds in an account for Desktop, and return unsold goods. Desktop will pay half of Ryan's expenses. Ryan is

a. an agent.
b. a principal.
c. both a and b
d. none of the above

___ **2.** Bass Corporation hires Ellen to manage one of its stores. Bass does not specify the extent, if any, of Ellen's authority to contract with third parties. The express authority that Bass gives Ellen to manage the store implies authority to do whatever

a. is customary to operate the business.
b. can be inferred from the manager's position.
c. both a and b.
d. none of the above.

___ **3.** Baron Interiors, Inc., tells Jan, whose business is purchasing for others, to select and buy $200 worth of certain goods and ship them to Baron. Jan buys the goods from Adam's Store and ships them as directed, keeping an account for the expense in Baron's name. Baron and Jan

a. have an agency relationship.
b. do not have an agency relationship, because their agreement is not in writing.
c. do not have an agency relationship, because Jan's business is buying for others.
d. do not have an agency relationship, because Jan did not indicate that she was acting for Baron.

___ **4.** Mandy asks Bob, a real estate broker, to sell her land. Bob learns that the K.T. Mall Corporation is willing to pay a high price for the land. Without telling Mandy about K.T. Mall, Bob says that he will buy the land himself. Instead, Mandy sells the land to Ken. If Bob sues Mandy,

a. Bob will win, because Mandy breached her duty to Bob.
b. Bob will win, because he was never Mandy's agent.
c. Mandy will win, because Bob breached his duty to Mandy.
d. Mandy will win, because she was not Bob's principal.

___ **5.** Farrah, owner of Fancy Fixtures, Inc., often sends Jerry, Fancy Fixtures' production manager, to the First National Bank to borrow money in amounts of $1,000 to $10,000. One morning, Farrah sends Jerry to borrow $3,000, but he borrows $6,000. Farrah is obligated to repay

a. $6,000, because Jerry had apparent authority to borrow $6,000.
b. $6,000, because Jerry had actual authority to borrow $6,000.
c. $3,000, because Jerry had actual authority to borrow only $3,000.
d. $3,000, because Jerry had apparent authority to borrow only $3,000.

___ **6.** Security Guns & Ammo, Inc., directs its salespersons never to load a gun during a sale. Bert, a salesperson, loads a gun during a sale. The gun fires, negligently injuring Kathy, who is in the store. Security is

a. not liable, because Bert was not acting within the scope of employment.
b. not liable, because employers are not responsible for their employees' torts.
c. liable under the doctrine of *respondeat superior.*
d. liable under the doctrine of *res ipsa loquitur.*

___ **7.** Ron orally engages Diane to act as his agent. During the agency, Ron knows that Diane deals with Mary. Ron also knows that Pete and Brad are aware of the agency but have not dealt with Diane. Ron decides to terminate the agency. Regarding notice of termination,

a. Diane need not be notified in writing.
b. Diane's actual authority terminates without notice to her of Ron's decision.
c. Diane's apparent authority terminates without notice to Mary.
d. Pete and Brad must be directly notified.

___ **8.** Smith Petroleum, Inc., contracts to sell oil to Jones Petrochemicals, telling Jones that it is acting on behalf of "a rich Saudi Arabian who doesn't want his identity known." Smith signs the contract, "Smith, as agent only." In fact, Smith is acting on its own. If the contract is breached, Smith may

a. not be liable, because Smith signed the contract as an agent.
b. not be liable, unless Jones knew Smith did not have authority to act.
c. be liable, unless Jones knew Smith did not have authority to act.
d. be liable, because Smith signed the contract as an agent.

___ **9.** Al is Eve's agent for the purpose of buying a certain parcel of land. Al learns that an adjacent parcel is for sale at a favorable price. Unable to contact Eve, Al buys the adjacent property on Eve's behalf. Eve can be liable if she contacts the property owner to

a. ratify the contract.
b. disapprove of the contract.
c. disaffirm the contract.
d. all of the above.

___ 10. In which of the following situations is the agency relationship terminated?

a. Sam engages Taylor to sell Sam's car. Two years pass, during which Sam and Taylor do not communicate and the car is not sold.
b. Tom, the owner of Home & Yard, Inc., decides to close the business and engages Ace Liquidators to sell the remaining inventory. Ace sells the inventory, after which Tom decides to go into a different business.
c. Lee, the owner of Exotic Imports, engages Don to buy carvings to be imported from the Far East. Lee dies, effectively putting Exotic Imports out of business, but Don is not aware of the death.
d. All of the above

SHORT ESSAY QUESTIONS

1. What are the essential differences among the relationships of principal and agent, employer and employee, and employer and independent contractor? What are the factors that indicate whether an individual is an employee or an independent contractor?

2. Identify and describe situations in which a principal is liable for an agent's torts.

ISSUE SPOTTERS

1. Kurt contracts with Dee to buy a certain horse for Dee, who asks Kurt not to reveal her identity. Kurt makes a deal with Country Stables, the owner of the horse, and gives Country a down payment. Dee fails to pay the rest of the price. Country sues Kurt for breach of contract. Can Dee be liable for whatever damages Kurt may have to pay?

2. The Young Corporation wants to build a new mall on a specific tract of land. Young contracts with Sheila to buy the property. When Sheila learns of the difference between the price that Young is willing to pay and the price at which the owner is willing to sell, she wants to buy the land and sell it to Young herself. Can she do this?

3. Marie, owner of the Consumer Goods Company, employs Rachel as an administrative assistant. In Marie's absence, and without authority, Rachel represents herself as Marie and signs a promissory note in Marie's name. Under what circumstance could Marie be liable on the note?

4. The First Union Bank encourages its depositors to ask its advice concerning their investments. Ian, one of the bank's investment counselors, advises Bond to invest in Spectre Corporation, although Ian knows that Spectre's financial situation is precarious. If Bond loses money on the deal, can the bank be held liable?

5. The United Delivery Service employs Otis as a driver. One afternoon, United tells Otis to deliver a certain package within the hour. While making the delivery, to bypass a traffic jam, Otis recklessly drives onto the sidewalk, injuring Bea. Is United liable to Bea? Is Otis liable to Bea?

QUICKEN CD-ROM
BUSINESS LAW PARTNER APPLICATIONS

Open **Quicken Business Law Partner**. Click on the *New Documents* icon. Choose the *Work for Hire Agreement*. Respond to the *Interview* questions with actual facts or hypothetical ones. For example, imagine that National Suppliers, Inc., hires Smith to develop a software program for National's inventory control system. As you complete the *Interview*, answer the following questions.

___ **1.** Using this form, National (the employer) and Smith (the hired worker) *must* provide that Smith's "work product" is the property of

a. National only.
b. Smith only.
c. a third party.
d. none of the above.

___ **2.** Unless the parties state otherwise in this form, Smith is National's

a. employee only.
b. independent contractor only.
c. either employee or independent contractor, depending on the circumstances.
d. none of the above.

___ **3.** In this form, the clause that the parties could use to expressly designate Smith to be an independent contractor is

a. Relationship of Parties.
b. Work Product Ownership.
c. Confidentiality.
d. Non-Compete Agreement.

___ **4.** To develop the software, Smith is given National's pricing information. Smith's disclosure of this information to National's competitor would violate which clause in this agreement?

a. Relationship of Parties
b. Work Product Ownership
c. Confidentiality
d. Non-Compete Agreement

___ **5.** In this form, the clause that the parties could use to limit Smith's future employment by other employers is

a. Relationship of Parties.
b. Work Product Ownership.
c. Confidentiality.
d. Non-Compete Agreement.

★ **Learning Objectives**

The learning objectives in this chapter include:

1. The employment-at-will doctrine.
2. Federal statutes governing wages and working hours.
3. Major laws relating to health and safety in the workplace.
4. The major federal statutes that prohibit employment discrimination.
5. Defenses against claims of employment discrimination.

Chapter 22: Employment Law

WHAT THIS CHAPTER IS ABOUT

This chapter outlines the most significant laws regulating employment relationships, including those prohibiting employment discrimination.

CHAPTER OUTLINE

I. WAGE-HOUR LAWS

Fair Labor Standards Act of 1938 (FLSA) covers all employees and regulates—

A. CHILD LABOR

Children under fourteen can deliver newspapers, work for their parents, and work in entertainment and agriculture. Children fourteen and older cannot work in hazardous occupations.

B. MAXIMUM HOURS

Employees who work more than forty hours per week must be paid no less than one and a half times their regular pay for all hours over forty. Executives, administrators, professionals, outside salespersons are exempt.

C. MINIMUM WAGE

A specified amount (periodically revised) must be paid to employees in covered industries. Wages include the reasonable cost to furnish employees with board, lodging, and other facilities.

II. LABOR UNIONS

A. NORRIS-LAGUARDIA ACT

Enacted in 1932. Restricts federal courts' power to issue injunctions against unions engaged in peaceful strikes, picketing, and boycotts.

B. NATIONAL LABOR RELATIONS ACT (NLRA) OF 1935

Established rights to bargain collectively and to strike, and—

1. **Unfair Employer Practices**
   Prohibits interfering with union activities, discriminating against union employees, refusing to bargain with union, other practices.

2. **National Labor Relations Board (NLRB)**
   Created to oversee union elections, prevent employers from engaging in unfair practices, investigate employers in response to employee charges of unfair labor practices, issue cease-and-desist orders.

C. LABOR-MANAGEMENT RELATIONS ACT (LMRA) OF 1947

Prohibits unions from refusing to bargain with employers, engaging in certain types of picketing, featherbedding, and other unfair practices. Preserves union shops, but allows states to pass right-to-work laws, which make it illegal to require union membership for employment.

D. LABOR-MANAGEMENT REPORTING AND DISCLOSURE ACT OF 1959

1. **Union Business**
   Requires elections of union officers under secret ballot; prohibits ex-convicts and Communists from holding union office; makes officials accountable for union property; allows members to participate in union meetings, nominate officers, vote in proceedings.

2. **Hot-Cargo Agreements**
   Outlaws **hot-cargo agreements** (in which employers agree not to handle, use, or deal in non-union goods of other employers).

III. WORKER HEALTH AND SAFETY

A. OCCUPATIONAL SAFETY AND HEALTH ACT OF 1970

Attempts to ensure safe and healthful work conditions for most employees.

1. **Enforcement Agencies**

   a. **Occupational Safety and Health Administration (OSHA)**
      Inspects workplaces and issues safety standards, including standards covering employee exposure to harmful substances.

   b. **National Institute for Occupational Safety and Health**
      Researches safety and health problems and recommends standards for OSHA to adopt.

   c. **Occupational Safety and Health Review Commission**
      Hears appeals from actions taken by OSHA administrators.

2. **Procedures and Violations**
   Employees file complaints of OSHA violations (employers cannot retaliate); employers must keep injury and illness records; employers must file accident reports directly to OSHA. Penalties are limited.

B. WORKERS' COMPENSATION

State laws establish procedure for compensating workers injured on the job.

1. **Requirements for Recovery**
   There must be an employment relationship, and the injury must be accidental and occur on the job or in the course of employment.

2. **Filing a Claim**
An employee must notify the employer of an injury (usually within thirty days), and file a claim with a state agency within a certain period (sixty days to two years) from the time the injury is first noticed.

3. **Acceptance of Workers' Compensation Benefits Bars Suits**
An employee's acceptance of benefits bars the employee from suing for injuries caused by the employer's negligence.

IV. INCOME SECURITY

A. SOCIAL SECURITY AND MEDICARE

1. **Social Security**
The Social Security Act of 1935 provides for payments to persons who are retired, widowed, disabled, etc. Employers and employees must contribute under the Federal Insurance Contributions Act (FICA).

2. **Medicare**
A health insurance program administered by the Social Security Administration for people sixty-five years of age and older and for some under sixty-five who are disabled.

B. PRIVATE PENSION PLANS

The Employee Retirement Income Security Act (ERISA) of 1974 empowers the Labor Management Services Administration of the Department of Labor to oversee those who operate private pension funds.

C. UNEMPLOYMENT COMPENSATION

The Federal Unemployment Tax Act of 1935 created a state system that provides unemployment compensation to eligible individuals.

V. COBRA

The Consolidated Omnibus Budget Reconciliation Act (COBRA) of 1985 prohibits the elimination of a worker's medical, optical, or dental insurance on the termination of most workers' employment. Coverage must continue for up to 18 months (29 months in some cases). A worker pays the premium plus 2 percent.

VI. FAMILY AND MEDICAL LEAVE ACT (FMLA) OF 1993

Employers with fifty or more employees must provide them with up to twelve weeks of family or medical leave during any twelve-month period, continue health-care coverage during the leave, and guarantee employment in the same, or a comparable, position when the employee returns to work.

VII. WRONGFUL DISCHARGE

Under the employment at-will doctrine, either the employer or the employee may terminate an employment relationship at any time and for any reason (unless a contract or the law provides to the contrary).

A. EXCEPTIONS BASED ON CONTRACT THEORY

Some courts have held that an implied contract exists between an employer and an employee (if, for example, a personnel manual states that no employee will be fired without good cause). A few states have held that all employment contracts contain an implied covenant of good faith.

B. EXCEPTIONS BASED ON TORT THEORY

Discharge may give rise to a tort action for wrongful discharge.

C. EXCEPTIONS BASED ON PUBLIC-POLICY

An employer may not fire a worker for reasons that violate a public policy of the jurisdiction (for example, for refusing to violate the law).

VIII. WHISTLEBLOWER STATUTES

An employer cannot fire an employee in violation of a federal or state statute. If so, the employee may bring an action for wrongful discharge. Some state and federal statutes protect whistleblowers from retaliation. The False Claims Act of 1986 gives a whistleblower 15 to 25 percent of proceeds recovered from fraud.

IX. EMPLOYMENT DISCRIMINATION

Discrimination on the basis of race, color, religion, national origin, gender, age, or disability is prohibited. A class of persons defined by one or more of these criteria is known as a **protected class**.

A. TITLE VII OF THE CIVIL RIGHTS ACT OF 1964

Prohibits discrimination against employees, applicants, and union members on the basis of race, color, national origin, religion, and gender.

1. Who Is Subject to Title VII?

Employers with fifteen or more employees, labor unions with fifteen or more members, labor unions that operate hiring halls, employment agencies, and federal, state, and local agencies.

2. Procedures under Title VII

(1) Victim files a claim with the Equal Employment Opportunity Commission (EEOC); (2) EEOC investigates and seeks a voluntary settlement; (3) if no settlement is reached, EEOC may sue the employer; (4) if EEOC chooses not to sue, victim may file a lawsuit.

3. Types of Discrimination

Title VII prohibits both intentional and unintentional discrimination.

a. Disparate-Treatment Discrimination

Intentional discrimination by an employer against an employee.

1) *Prima Facie* Case—Plaintiff's Side of the Case

Plaintiff must show (1) he or she is member of a protected class, (2) he or she applied and was qualified for the job, (3) he or she was rejected by the employer, (4) employer continued to seek applicants or filled position with person not in protected class.

2) Defense—Employer's Side of the Case

Employer must articulate a legal reason for not hiring plaintiff. To prevail, plaintiff must show that employer's reason is a pretext and that discriminatory intent motivated the decision.

b. Disparate-Impact Discrimination

1) Types of Disparate-Impact Discrimination

Because of a requirement or hiring practice, (1) an employer's work force does not reflect the percentage of members of protected classes that characterizes qualified individuals in the local labor market, or (2) members of a protected class are excluded from the employer's work force at a substantially higher rate than nonmembers.

2) ***Prima Facie* Case—Plaintiff's Side of the Case**
Plaintiff must show connection between requirement or practice and disparity; no evidence of discriminatory intent is needed.

4. **Discrimination Based on Religion**
Title VII prohibits employers and unions from discriminating against persons because of their religions.

5. **Discrimination Based on Gender**
Employers cannot discriminate against employees on the basis of gender (unless the gender of the applicant can be proved essential to the job, etc.). The Pregnancy Discrimination Act of 1978 amended Title VII: Employees affected by pregnancy or related conditions must be treated the same as persons not so affected but similar in ability to work.

6. **Sexual Harassment**

a. **Forms of Harassment**
(1) *Quid pro quo* harassment: when promotions, etc., are doled out on the basis of sexual favors; (2) hostile-environment harassment: when an employee is subjected to offensive sexual comments, etc. (Courts are split as to whether plaintiffs can sue for same-gender harassment.)

b. **Harassment by Supervisors or Co-Workers**
If someone harasses an employee, and the employer knew, or should have known, and failed to take immediate corrective action, the employer is liable.

7. **Remedies under Title VII**
Reinstatement, back pay, retroactive promotions, damages.

a. **Compensatory Damages**
Available only in cases of intentional discrimination. Do not include back pay, interest on back pay, or other Title VII relief.

b. **Punitive Damages**
Only if an employer acted with malice or reckless indifference.

c. **Limitations**
Total damages are limited to specific amounts against specific employers (from $50,000 against those with one hundred or fewer employees to $300,000 against those with more than five hundred employees).

B. DISCRIMINATION BASED ON AGE

1. **Age Discrimination in Employment Act (ADEA) of 1967**
Prohibits employment discrimination on the basis of age (including mandatory retirement), by employers with twenty or more employees, against individuals forty years of age or older.

2. **Principles Are Similar to Title VII**
Requires the establishment of a *prima facie* case: plaintiff must show that he or she was (1) forty or older, (2) qualified for a position, and (3) rejected in circumstances that infer discrimination. The employer must articulate a legal reason; the plaintiff may show it is a pretext.

C. DISCRIMINATION BASED ON DISABILITY

Under the Americans with Disabilities Act (ADA) of 1990, an employer cannot refuse to hire a person who is qualified but disabled.

1. Procedures under the ADA

A plaintiff must show he or she (1) has a disability, (2) is otherwise qualified for a job and (3) was excluded solely because of the disability. A suit may be filed only after a claim is pursued through the EEOC.

2. Remedies under the ADA

Reinstatement, back pay, some compensatory and punitive damages (for intentional discrimination), and certain other relief. Repeat violators may be fined up to $100,000.

3. What is a Disability?

"(1) [A] physical or mental impairment that substantially limits one or more of the major life activities . . . ; (2) a record of such impairment; or (3) being regarded as having such an impairment." Includes AIDS, morbid obesity, etc.; not homosexuality or kleptomania.

4. Reasonable Accommodation

For person with a disability, employer may have to make a reasonable accommodation (more flexible hours, new job assignment, different training materials or procedures)—but not an accommodation that will cause **undue hardship** (impose "significant difficulty or expense").

D. DEFENSES TO EMPLOYMENT DISCRIMINATION

The first defense is to assert that plaintiff did not prove discrimination. If discrimination is proved, an employer may attempt to justify it as—

1. Business Necessity

An employer may show that there is a legitimate connection between a job requirement that discriminates and job performance.

2. Bona Fide Occupational Qualification (BFOQ)

Another defense applies when discrimination against a protected class is essential to a job—that is, when a particular trait is a BFOQ. Generally restricted to cases in which gender is essential. Race can never be a BFOQ.

3. Seniority Systems

An employer with a history of discrimination may have no members of protected classes in upper-level positions. If no present intent to discriminate is shown, and promotions, etc., are distributed according to a fair seniority system, the employer has a good defense.

E. AFFIRMATIVE ACTION

An affirmative action program attempts to make up for past discrimination by giving members of protected classes preferential treatment in hiring or promotion. Such a program cannot use quotas or preferences for unqualified persons, and once a program has succeeded, it must be changed or dropped.

F. STATE STATUTES

Most states have statutes that prohibit the kinds of discrimination prohibited under federal legislation. State statutes also often protect individuals, such as homosexuals, who are not protected under Title VII.

TRUE-FALSE QUESTIONS

___ 1. Employers can agree with unions not to handle, use, or deal in non-union-produced goods.

___ 2. Employment considered to be "at will" means that employers cannot fire employees without good cause.

___ 3. Employers are required by federal statute to establish health insurance and pension plans.

___ 4. Children fourteen and older can work in hazardous occupations.

___ 5. Under the FLSA, all nonexempt employees who work more than forty hours per week must be paid at least one and a half times their regular pay for all hours over forty.

___ 6. In a sexual harassment case, an employer cannot be held liable if an employee did the harassing.

___ 7. Employment discrimination against persons with a physical or mental impairment that substantially limits their everyday activities is prohibited.

___ 8. All employers are subject to Title VII of the Civil Rights Act of 1964 regardless of the number of their employees.

___ 9. Disparate-treatment discrimination occurs when an employer intentionally discriminates against an employee.

___ 10. Title VII prohibits employers and unions from discriminating against persons because of their religions.

FILL-IN QUESTIONS

Under the employment-at-will doctrine, ________________ (either/neither) party may terminate an employment relationship at any time and for any reason ________________ (unless/even if) a contract provides to the contrary. An employee who is fired in violation of a federal or state statute __________ (may/may not) bring an action for wrongful discharge. ____________ (Some/No) courts have held that an implied contract exists between an employer and an employee. ________________ (All/A few states) have held that all employment contracts contain an implied covenant of good faith. An employer _____________ (may/may not) fire a worker for reasons that violate a public policy of the jurisdiction.

MULTIPLE-CHOICE QUESTIONS

___ 1. Fast Jack is a fast-food restaurant that employs minors. Fast Jack is subject to the federal child-labor, minimum-wage, and maximum-hour laws in

a. the National Labor Relations Act.
b. the Labor-Management Relations Act.
c. the Fair Labor Standards Act.
d. none of the above.

___ **2.** Erin, an employee of CamCorp, is injured. For Erin to receive *workers' compensation*, the injury must be

a. accidental and arise out of a preexisting disease or condition.
b. accidental and occur on the job or in the course of employment.
c. intentional and arise out of a preexisting disease or condition.
d. intentional and occur on the job or in the course of employment.

___ **3.** Webb Corporation provides health insurance for its employees. When Webb closes one of its offices and terminates the employees, the employees

a. can continue their heath insurance at their expense.
b. can continue their heath insurance at Webb's expense.
c. lose their heath insurance immediately on termination of employment.
d. are entitled to "severance pay" equal to twelve weeks' of health insurance coverage.

___ **4.** Rim, Inc., provides health insurance for its one hundred employees, including Diana. When Diana takes twelve weeks' leave to care for her new baby, she

a. can continue her heath insurance at her expense.
b. can continue her heath insurance at Rim's expense.
c. loses her heath insurance immediately on taking leave.
d. is entitled to "leave pay" equal to twelve weeks' of health insurance coverage.

___ **5.** Ron is an employee of the Lang Company. Both Ron and Lang make contributions to the federal social security system under

a. the Federal Unemployment Tax Act.
b. the Federal Insurance Contributions Act.
c. the Employment Retirement Income Security Act.
d. none of the above.

___ **6.** Dan and Mary work for Quint Software, Inc. Dan is Mary's supervisor. During a review of her work, Dan makes comments and touches her in a way that she perceives as sexually offensive. She says nothing to the company, but suffers anxiety, quits less than a year later, and sues Quint. Mary will

a. win, because Dan's conduct constituted sexual harassment.
b. win, because Quint failed to take corrective action.
c. lose, because Mary overreacted—a few comments and a little touching never hurt anyone.
d. lose, because Mary said nothing to Quint.

___ **7.** Alpha Corporation requires all employees over forty-five years old to take and pass a physical exam that is not imposed on younger employees. If an employee does not pass the test, he or she is discharged. Alpha can avoid liability under the Age Discrimination in Employment Act only if it

a. changes the requirement to have all employees over forty take the exam.
b. changes the requirement to condition only promotions on the exam.
c. can show a legitimate business reason for the exam.
d. has between twenty and thirty employees.

___ 8. Janet, who is hearing impaired, applies for a position with Beta Company. Janet is qualified but is refused the job because, she is told, "We can't afford to accommodate you with an interpreter." If Janet sues Beta, she will

a. win, if Beta has installed ramps for disabled persons.
b. win, if an interpreter would be a "reasonable accommodation."
c. lose, because an interpreter would not be a "reasonable accommodation."
d. lose, if Beta has never done anything to accommodate any disabled person.

___ 9. Nash Company requires that all its secretaries be able to type. Alice, a member of a minority, applies to Nash for a secretarial job. Alice cannot type but tells the company that she is willing to learn. When Nash does not hire her, she sues. She will

a. win, if Nash's work force does not reflect the same percentage of members of a protected class that characterizes qualified individuals in the local labor market.
b. win, because Alice said that she was willing to learn, and an employer has an obligation to hire and train unqualified minority employees.
c. lose, because in this case being a member of the majority is a BFOQ.
d. lose, because Nash has a valid business necessity defense.

___ 10. Quarry Company requires job applicants to pass certain physical tests. Only a few women who apply to work for Quarry can pass the tests, but it they pass, they are hired. Quarry's best defense in a suit charging that the tests discriminate against women would be that

a. gender is a BFOQ.
b. some men cannot pass the tests.
c. any discrimination is not intentional.
d. passing the tests is a business necessity.

SHORT ESSAY QUESTIONS

1. What is the employment-at-will doctrine, and what are its exceptions?
2. What does the Americans with Disabilities Act require of employers?

ISSUE SPOTTERS

1. Falls Company issues an employee handbook that states employees will be discharged only for good cause. One day, Greg, a Falls supervisor, says to Larry, "I don't like your looks. You're fired." May Falls be held liable for breach of contract?

2. Workers' compensation laws establish a procedure for compensating workers who are injured on the job. Instead of suing, the worker files a claim with the appropriate state agency. Does the injury have to have been caused by the employer's negligence?

3. Lani, a member of a minority, learns of a job opening at Belco Engineering for which she is well-qualified. She applies for the job but is rejected. Belco continues to seek applicants for the position and eventually fills the position with a person who is not a member of a minority. Could Lani succeed in a suit against Belco for discrimination?

4. Grant is a supervisor for Subs & Suds, a restaurant. Judy is a Subs employee. When the owner announces that sales are down and some employees will be discharged, Grant tells Judy that if she has sex with him, she can keep her job. Is this sexual harassment?

5. Dick, a disabled person, learns of a job opening at the Bond Company for which he is well-qualified. He applies for the job but is rejected. Bond continues to seek applicants for the position and eventually fills the position with a person who is not disabled. Could Dick succeed in a suit against Belco for discrimination?

QUICKEN CD-ROM BUSINESS LAW PARTNER APPLICATIONS

Open **Quicken Business Law Partner**. Click on the *New Documents* icon. Choose the *Employment Agreement*. Respond to the *Interview* questions with actual facts or hypothetical ones. For example, imagine that Eagle Equipment Company hires Paulson as a management trainee. As you complete the *Interview*, answer the following questions.

___ **1.** In this form, the clause that limits the authority of Paulson (the employee) to act as an agent for Eagle (the employer) is

a. Reimbursement for Expenses in Accordance with Employer Policy.
b. Employee's Inability to Contract for Employer.
c. Compliance with Employer's Rules.
d. none of the above.

___ **2.** Which of the following clauses *may* be part of this employment agreement?

a. Reimbursement for Expenses in Accordance with Employer Policy.
b. Employee's Inability to Contract for Employer.
c. Compliance with Employer's Rules.
d. all of the above.

___ **3.** According to this form, the employee's salary or wages *must* be paid

a. monthly.
b. twice a month.
c. every two weeks.
d. none of the above.

___ **4.** In this form, Eagle *must* promise to reimburse Paulson for

a. travel and meals.
b. professional dues and job-related education.
c. both a and b.
d. none of the above.

___ **5.** In this agreement, Paulson can be required to keep certain information confidential

a. only during employment.
b. only after employment.
c. during or after employment.
d. none of the above.

 **Learning Objectives**

The learning objectives in this chapter include:

1. The advantages and disadvantages of a sole proprietorship, a partnership, and other forms of business organizations.
2. How a limited liability company differs from other business organizations.
3. The elements of a partnership.
4. How agency prinicples apply to partnerships.
5. The rights, duties, and powers of partners.

Chapter 23: Sole Proprietorships, Partnerships, and Limited Liability Companies

WHAT THIS CHAPTER IS ABOUT

This chapter sets out features of two of the major traditional business forms—sole proprietorships and partnerships—and other forms for doing business.

CHAPTER OUTLINE

I. SOLE PROPRIETORSHIPS

The simplest form of business—the owner is the business.

A. ADVANTAGES

The proprietor takes all the profits. Easier to start than other kinds of businesses (few legal forms involved); has more flexibility (proprietor is free to make all decisions); owner pays only personal income tax on profits.

B. DISADVANTAGES

The proprietor has all the risk (unlimited liability for all debts); limited opportunity to raise capital; the business dissolves when the owner dies.

II. PARTNERSHIPS

A partnerships arises from an agreement between two or more persons to carry on a business for profit. Partnership law is based on agency law (see Chapter 21). Partnerships are governed by the Uniform Partnership Act (UPA) or the Revised Uniform Partnership Act (RUPA).

III. DEFINITION OF A PARTNERSHIP

"[A]n association of two or more persons to carry on as co-owners a business for profit" [UPA 6(1)].

A. PARTNERSHIP STATUS

There are three essential elements to a partnership:

1. A sharing of profits or losses.
2. A joint ownership of the business.
3. An equal right in the management of the business.

B. ENTITY VERSUS AGGREGATE

1. **Partnership as an Entity**
   A partnership is treated as an entity for certain purposes. For example, generally a partnership can sue and be sued in the firm name. A partnership can own property as an entity.

2. **Aggregate Theory of Partnership**
   If a partnership is not regarded as a separate entity, it is treated as an aggregate of the individual partners. For example, a partnership is not a tax-paying entity.

IV. PARTNERSHIP FORMATION

A partnership agreement states the intention to create a partnership, contribute capital, share profits and losses, and participate in management.

A. THE PARTNERSHIP AGREEMENT

The agreement can be oral, written, or implied by conduct. Some must be in writing under the Statute of Frauds (see Chapter 10). Partners can agree to any terms that are not illegal or contrary to public policy.

B. PARTNERSHIP DURATION

1. **Partnership for a Term**
   The agreement can specify the duration of the partnership in terms of a date or completion of a particular project. Dissolution without all partners' consent before expiration is a breach of the agreement.

2. **Partnership at Will**
   No duration is set; any partner can dissolve a partnership any time.

C. THE CORPORATION AS PARTNER

Many states have restrictions on corporations becoming partners. The Revised Model Business Corporation Act allows corporations to contract and to incur liabilities; the UPA permits a corporation to be a partner [UPA 2].

D. PARTNERSHIP BY ESTOPPEL

When parties who are not partners hold themselves out as partners and make representations that third persons rely on in dealing with them, liability is imposed. A partner who misrepresents a nonpartner is also liable (and the nonpartner's acts may bind the partnership).

V. RIGHTS AMONG PARTNERS

A. INTEREST IN THE PARTNERSHIP

Unless partners agree otherwise, profits and losses are shared equally [UPA 18(a)]. A partner's interest can be assigned, and creditors can attach it by obtaining a charging order [UPA 28].

B. MANAGEMENT RIGHTS

1. Ordinarily, the Majority Rules

"All partners have equal rights in the management and conduct of partnership business" [UPA 18(e)]. Each partner has one vote.

2. When Unanimous Consent Is Required

(1) Alter the essential nature of the firm's business or capital structure; (2) admit new partners or enter a new business [UPA 18(g), (h)]; (3) assign firm property into a trust for the benefit of creditors; (4) dispose of the firm's goodwill; (5) confess judgment against the firm or submit firm claims to arbitration; (6) undertake any act that would make conduct of partnership business impossible [UPA 9(3)]; or (7) amend the partnership articles.

C. COMPENSATION

Doing partnership business is a partner's duty and not compensable. On the death of a partner, a surviving partner is entitled to compensation to wind up partnership affairs [UPA 18(f)].

D. INSPECTION OF BOOKS

A partner has a right to full information concerning the conduct of partnership business [UPA 20]. Partnership books must be kept at the firm's principal business office [UPA 19].

E. ACCOUNTING OF ASSETS

A partner has a right to a formal accounting—

1. When the partnership agreement provides for it.
2. When a partner is wrongfully excluded from the business or the books.
3. When a partner withholds profits or benefits belonging to the partnership.
4. When circumstances "render it just and reasonable."
5. On dissolution.

F. PROPERTY RIGHTS

1. Right to Share in the Partnership Profits

A partner has a right to share in the profits.

2. Right to Partnership Property

A partner is co-owner with his or her partners of partnership property, holding it as a tenant in partnership [UPA 25(1)].

a. Each Partner Has Equal Rights

Each partner can possess partnership property for business purposes or in satisfaction of firm debts, but cannot sell, assign, or deal with the property other than for partnership purposes without the consent of all of the partners.

b. If a Partner Dies

Surviving partners, not the heirs of the deceased, have a right of survivorship to the property (they must account to the decedent's estate for the value [UPA 25(2)]).

VI. DUTIES AND LIABILITIES OF PARTNERS

A. FIDUCIARY DUTIES

Partners (1) must act in good faith for the benefit of the partnership, (2) must subordinate his or her personal interests to the interests of the firm if a conflict arises, and (3) must account to the partnership for profits or benefits derived in a partnership transaction.

B. AUTHORITY OF PARTNERS

Agency concepts apply to partners' authority. Implied authority is determined by the character and scope of the partnership business and the customary nature of the business. Normally, partners exercise all implied powers reasonably necessary to carry on the business [UPA 11].

C. JOINT LIABILITY

In most states, partners are jointly liable for partnership debts and contracts [UPA 15(b)] (each partner is liable for the entire debt; if one pays, the partnership or the other partners must reimburse that partner [UPA 18(b)]). To bring a successful claim against the partnership, a plaintiff must name all the partners as defendants.

D. JOINT AND SEVERAL LIABILITY

In some states, partners are jointly and severally liable for partnership debts and contracts. In all states, partners are jointly and severally liable for torts and breaches of trust [UPA 15(a)] (a partner who commits a tort must reimburse the partnership for any damages it pays).

E. LIABILITY OF INCOMING PARTNER

Liable for partnership debts incurred before his or her admission only to the extent of his or her interest in the partnership [UPA 17].

VII. PARTNERSHIP TERMINATION

Caused by any change in the relations of the partners that shows unwillingness or inability to carry on partnership business [UPA 29]. To continue the business, a partner can organize a new partnership.

A. DISSOLUTION

Occurs when a partner ceases to associate with the carrying on of the business. Terminates the right of a partnership to exist as a going concern, but the partnership remains long enough to wind up its affairs.

1. Dissolution by Acts of Partners

a. Dissolution by Agreement

The partnership agreement can state events that will dissolve the firm. Partners can agree to dissolve the partnership early.

b. Partner's Power to Withdraw

No person can be compelled to be a partner. A partner's withdrawal dissolves the partnership.

c. Transfer of a Partner's Interest

Transfer of a partner's interest or sale of the interest for the benefit of creditors [UPA 28] leads to judicial dissolution.

2. Dissolution by Operation of Law

a. **Death**
Death of a partner dissolves the firm, even if the partnership agreement provides for carrying on the business.

b. **Bankruptcy**
Bankruptcy of a partner (or the firm) dissolves a partnership.

c. **Illegality**
Dissolution is caused by an event that makes it unlawful for either (1) the partnership to continue, unless the partners change the nature of the business and continue, or (2) any partner to continue.

3. **Dissolution by Judicial Decree**
A court can dissolve a partnership for a partner's mental incompetency, incapacity, or improper conduct; if the firm's business can be run only at a loss; or other circumstances [UPA 32].

4. **Notice of Dissolution**
Unless the other partners have notice, a withdrawing partner will continue to be bound to all contracts created for the firm. A third person who has extended credit to the partnership must receive actual notice. For others, constructive notice is sufficient.

B. WINDING UP

Involves collecting and preserving partnership assets, paying debts, and accounting to each partner for the value of his or her interest. No new obligations can be created on behalf of the partnership.

1. **Distribution of Assets**
Priorities for the distribution of a partnership's assets are [UPA 40(b)]: (1) payment to third party creditors; (2) refund of loans made to or for the firm by a partner; (3) return of capital contribution to a partner; and (4) the balance to partners proportionate to their shares in the profits.

2. **If the Partnership's Liabilities Are Greater Than Its Assets**
The partners bear the losses in the same proportion in which they shared the profits.

VIII. LIMITED PARTNERSHIPS

A limited partnership must include at least one general partner and one or more limited partners. General partners have management responsibility and liability for debts. The Revised Uniform Limited Partnership Act (RULPA) is the dominant law governing limited partnerships.

A. FORMATION

Partners sign a certificate of limited partnership, which is filed with the secretary of state.

B. RIGHTS AND LIABILITIES OF PARTNERS

1. **Rights of Limited Partners**
Essentially the same rights as general partners. Can assign their interests in the partnership [RULPA 702, 704]. Can sue on behalf of the firm if general partners refuse [RULPA 1001].

2. **Liabilities of Limited Partners**

a. **Limited Liability to Creditors of the Partnership**
Liable to the extent of any contribution that is promised to the firm or that was withdrawn [RULPA 502].

b. **Personal Liability for Defects in Formation**

1) **If a Firm Is Organized in an Improper Manner**
A limited partner who fails to withdraw on discovery of the defect can be personally liable to the firm's creditors.

2) **False Statements in the Partnership Certificate**
If a limited partner knows of a false statement, he or she may be liable to any person who relies on it [RULPA 207].

3. **Limited Partners and Management**
Participating in management results in liability for partnership debts, if the creditor knew of the participation [RULPA 303].

C. DISSOLUTION

1. **General Partners—Dissolution**
Retirement, death, incompetence or bankruptcy of a general partner dissolves a firm, unless continued by other general partners.

2. **Limited Partners—No Dissolution**
Death or assignment of interest of a limited partner does not dissolve a firm [RULPA 702, 704, 705], nor does personal bankruptcy.

3. **Court Decree**
A limited partnership can be dissolved by decree [RULPA 802].

4. **Priorities to Assets on Dissolution**
(1) Creditors, including partners who are creditors; (2) partners and former partners receive unpaid distributions of partnership assets and, except as otherwise agreed, a return on their contributions and amounts proportionate to their share of distributions [RULPA 804].

IX. LIMITED LIABILITY COMPANIES

A limited liability company (LLC) is a hybrid form of business enterprise that offers limited liability of a corporation with tax advantages of a partnership.

A. ADVANTAGES
Taxed as a partnership; liability of members is limited to the amount of their investment; members can participate in management; corporations, partnerships, and foreign investors can be members; no limit on the number of members.

B. DISADVANTAGES
Statutory restrictions on the transfer of ownership; because the LLC is a new form, little case law exists; until uniform statutes are adopted by most states, an LLC with multistate operations may face difficulties.

X. LIMITED LIABILITY PARTNERSHIPS

A. PROFESSIONAL LIMITED LIABILITY PARTNERSHIP (PLLP)
Professionals organized as LLP to gain the tax advantage of a partnership, while avoiding personal liability for the wrongdoing of other partners.

B. FAMILY LIMITED LIABILITY PARTNERSHIP (FLLP)
An LLP in which most of the partners are related. All partners must be natural persons or persons acting in a fiduciary capacity for natural persons. Family-owned farms may benefit from this form.

XI. LIMITED LIABILITY LIMITED PARTNERSHIPS

This form is similar to a limited partnership, except that the liability of all partners in a limited liability limited partnership (LLLP) is limited to the amount of their investment in the firm.

TRUE-FALSE QUESTIONS

____ 1. In a sole proprietorship, the owner is the business.

____ 2. A partnership is an association of two or more persons to carry on, as co-owners, a business for profit.

____ 3. A general partnership is entirely a creature of statute—if the statute is not followed exactly, a general partnership will not exist.

____ 4. The sharing of profits from joint ownership of property is usually enough to create a partnership.

____ 5. In forming a partnership, a writing is necessary only if the partnership would otherwise be in violation of the Statute of Frauds.

____ 6. Any partner can dissolve any partnership at any time without liability to the other partners for losses due to the termination.

____ 7. Unless the partnership agreement specifies otherwise, each partner has one vote in management matters, regardless of the size of his or her interest in the firm.

____ 8. A limited partnership must be formed publicly and formally.

____ 9. A general partnership must be formed publicly and formally.

____ 10. Professionals who are partners in a limited liability partnership pay the same taxes as partners in general partnerships and limited partnerships.

FILL-IN QUESTIONS

In most states, partners ________________ (are/are not) subject to joint liability on partnership debts, contracts, and torts. Joint liability means that if a third party sues a partner on a partnership ____________________________ (obligation/tort), the partner has the right to insist that the other partners be sued with him or her. If the third party does not sue all of the partners, those partners who are _______________ (not sued/sued) cannot be required to pay a judgment. In that circumstance, the assets of the partnership _____________________ (can/cannot) be used to satisfy the judgment. The third party's release of one partner ______________________________ (does not release/releases) the other partners. In most states, to bring a successful claim against a partnership on a debt or contract, a plaintiff ___________________ (may/must) name all the partners as defendants.

MULTIPLE-CHOICE QUESTIONS

___ **1.** To obtain a contract with Dick, Cindy misrepresents that she is a partner with Karl and Frank. Karl overhears Cindy's misrepresentation, but says nothing to Dick. Frank also overhears Cindy and says to Dick, "Cindy is our partner." Cindy breaches the contract. Who is liable to Dick?

a. Cindy only
b. Cindy and Karl only
c. Cindy and Frank only
d. Cindy, Karl, and Frank

___ **2.** Jaspar and Leigh are partners in an investment brokerage firm. Jaspar convinces Hazel, a customer, to invest heavily in a nonexistent mine in Colombia. Jaspar absconds with Hazel's money. If Hazel sues Leigh, Hazel will

a. win, because partners are jointly and severally liable for torts.
b. win, because partnership assets would be available to pay the judgment.
c. lose, because partners are not jointly and severally liable for torts.
d. lose, because only partnership assets would be available to pay the judgment.

___ **3.** Pam and Pete form a general partnership. Pam invests $40,000 and Pete invests $10,000. They agree to share profits in this proportion. Later, Pete loans the firm another $10,000. When they decide to dissolve the partnership, the firm owes Cal $60,000 and Clara $40,000. Partnership assets amount to $185,000. The order of priority for distribution of these assets is:

a. Pam $40,000 and Pete $10,000; Pam $20,000 and Pete $5,000; Cal $60,000 and Clara $40,000; Pete $10,000.
b. Kim $40,000 and Pete $10,000; Pam $20,000 and Pete $5,000; Pete $10,000; Cal $60,000 and Clara $40,000.
c. Cal $60,000 and Clara $40,000; Kim $40,000 and Pete $10,000; Pam $20,000 and Pete $5,000; Pete $10,000.
d. Cal $60,000 and Clara $40,000; Pete $10,000; Pam $40,000 and Pete $10,000; Pam $20,000 and Pete $5,000.

___ **4.** Which of the following statements concerning the rights and liabilities of a limited partner is FALSE?

a. A limited partner has greater managerial powers than a general partner.
b. A limited partner can sue on behalf of the firm if the general partner with authority refuses to do so.
c. A limited partner is liable only to the extent of the partner's promised or actual contribution to the firm, unlike a general partner.
d. A limited partner who participates in the management of the partnership risks having the liability of a general partner.

___ **5.** On dissolution, general partners have authority to do all of the following EXCEPT

a. enter new obligations on behalf of the partnership.
b. complete transactions begun but not yet finished at the time of dissolution.
c. collect and preserve partnership assets and discharge partnership liabilities.
d. account to each partner for the value of his or her interest in the partnership.

___ **6.** When resolving a dispute over whether a business arrangement is a partnership, a court will normally look for all of the following EXCEPT

a. sharing of profits or losses.
b. joint ownership of the business.
c. payment of wages to employees.
d. equal rights in the management of the business.

___ **7.** Lee and Jackson do business as a partnership under the name Southern Investments. Southern

a. cannot sue others in its own name.
b. cannot collect judgments in its own name.
c. is not a tax-paying entity for federal income tax purposes.
d. cannot hold title to real property.

___ **8.** Martin owns M Carpets, a home furnishings store. He hires Lois as a salesperson, agreeing to pay $6.50 per hour plus 10 percent of the amount of her sales. Martin and Lois are

a. partners, because Lois receives a share of the store's profits.
b. partners, because Lois is responsible for some of the store's sales.
c. not partners, because Lois does not have an ownership interest or management right in the store.
d. not partners, because Lois does not receive an equal share of the store's profits.

___ **9.** April, Brady, and Carol are partners in an accounting firm. April tells Brady and Carol that effective immediately, she is quitting the firm. Later the same day, at Brady's insistence, Brady and Carol sign a contract with a supplier. The contract is binding on

a. Brady only.
b. Brady and Carol only.
c. April, Brady, and Carol.
d. none of the partners.

___ **10.** Dr. Jones and Dr. Smith are partners in a medical clinic. Jones manages the clinic, which is organized as a limited liability partnership. A court holds Smith liable in a malpractice suit. Jones is

a. not liable.
b. liable only to the extent of her share of that year's profits.
c. liable only to the extent of her investment in the firm.
d. liable beyond her investment in the firm, because she managed the clinic.

SHORT ESSAY QUESTIONS

1. What are the three primary ways by which partnerships are dissolved?

2. Compare and contrast the following characteristics of general partnerships and limited partnerships: creation, sharing of profits and loses, liability, capital contribution, management, duration, assignment, and priorities on liquidation.

ISSUE SPOTTERS

1. Lonnie's Music leases space in the Mall of the Americas. As part of the rent, Lonnie pays the mall a percentage of its gross receipts. One of the elements of a partnership is the sharing of profits or losses from a business. Is the mall a partner in Lonnie's business? Is Lonnie a partner in the mall's business?

2. Logan and Murphy are partners in a computer peripherals operation. Logan dies. Logan's widow calls Murphy and says, "As Logan's heir, I'm entitled to take Logan's place as your partner." Murphy says, "No, you're not." Logan says, "Ok, then, as Logan's heir, I'm entitled to all the CD-ROM drives in the warehouse." Murphy says, "No, you're not. As Logan's heir, all you're entitled to is the *value* of Logan's interest in partnership property." Who's right?

3. Hans and Gretchen are partners in a delivery business. When business is slow, without Gretchen's knowledge, Hans leases out the delivery vehicles as moving vans. Because the vehicles would otherwise be sitting idle in a parking lot, can Hans keep the lease money or does Hans have to account to Gretchen?

4. Dave and Ira agree to become partners in an investment firm. Their written agreement states that the partnership dissolves on each being paid $1 million from partnership earnings. Ten years later, when the goal is reached, Dave and Ira decide that they want to continue the firm. Can they do so, despite what their agreement says?

5. Olga is a limited partner, and Anton is a general partner of the Platinum Fitness Club, a limited partnership. Anton manages the firm. Olga has some expertise in the area and believes that she could do a better job than Anton at managing, but she abstains from becoming actively involved. Why might she choose to keep away from management activities?

Learning Objectives

The learning objectives in this chapter include:

1. The basic characteristics of a corporate entity.
2. The express and implied powers of a corporation.
3. The ways in which corporations are classified.
4. The steps to form a corporation, and the effects of improper incorporation.
5. How corporations are financed, and the difference between stocks and bonds.

Chapter 24: Corporate Formation and Financing

WHAT THIS CHAPTER IS ABOUT

This chapter covers corporate rights, powers, classifications, formation, and financing. Most corporations are formed under state law, and a majority of states follow some version of the Revised Model Business Corporation Act (RMBCA).

CHAPTER OUTLINE

I. THE NATURE OF THE CORPORATION

A. CORPORATE PERSONNEL
Shareholders elect a board of directors, which is responsible for overall management and hires corporate officers to run daily operations.

B. CORPORATE TAXATION
Corporate profits are taxed twice: as income to the corporation and, when distributed as dividends, as income to the shareholders.

C. CONSTITUTIONAL RIGHTS OF CORPORATIONS
A corporation is recognized by the law as a "person" and, under the Bill of Rights, has the same rights as a natural person (see Chapter 1). Only officers and employees have the right against self-incrimination, however, and the privileges and immunities clause does not protect corporations.

D. TORTS AND CRIMINAL ACTS
A corporation is liable for the torts committed by its agents within the course and scope of employment. A corporation may be held liable for the crimes of its employees and agents if the punishment for the crimes can be applied to a corporation.

II. CORPORATE POWERS

A. EXPRESS AND IMPLIED POWERS

Express powers are in (in order of priority) the U.S. Constitution, state constitution, state statutes, articles of incorporation, bylaws, and board resolutions. A corporation has the *implied* power to perform all acts reasonably appropriate and necessary to accomplish its purposes.

B. *ULTRA VIRES* DOCTRINE

Ultra vires acts are beyond the purposes stated in the articles. Most such acts have involved contracts (which generally are enforced [RMBCA 3.04]). Courts usually allow any legal action a firm takes to profit shareholders.

III. CLASSIFICATION OF CORPORATIONS

A. DOMESTIC, FOREIGN, AND ALIEN CORPORATIONS

A corporation is a **domestic corporation** in the state in which it incorporated, a **foreign corporation** in other states, and an **alien corporation** in other countries. A foreign corporation normally must obtain a certificate of authority to do business in any state except its home state.

B. PUBLIC AND PRIVATE CORPORATIONS

A **public corporation** is formed by the government to meet a political or governmental purpose (the U.S. Postal Service, AMTRAK). A **private corporation** is created for private benefit and is owned by private persons.

C. NONPROFIT CORPORATIONS

Corporations formed without a profit-making purpose (private hospitals, educational institutions, charities, and religious organizations).

D. CLOSE CORPORATIONS

To qualify as a **close corporation**, a firm must have a limited number of shareholders, and restrict its issue and transfer of stock.

1. Advantage

Exempt from most of the nonessential formalities of corporate operation (bylaws, annual meetings, etc. [RMBCA 7.32]).

2. Management

Resembles that of a sole proprietorship or a partnership—one or a few shareholders usually hold the positions of directors and officers.

3. Transfer of Shares

Often restricted by stipulating that shareholders offer their shares to the corporation or other shareholders before offering them to outsiders.

E. S CORPORATIONS

1. Requirements

Must be a domestic corporation; must not be a member of an affiliated group of corporations; shareholders must be individuals, estates, or certain trusts; must have thirty-five or fewer shareholders; can have only one class of stock; no shareholder can be a nonresident alien.

2. Advantages

Shareholders can use corporate losses to offset other income; only a single tax on corporate income is imposed at individual income tax rates at the shareholder level (whether or not it is distributed).

F. PROFESSIONAL CORPORATIONS

Generally subject to the law governing ordinary corporations.

1. Limited Liability

A shareholder in a professional corporation is protected from liability for torts (except malpractice) committed by other members.

2. Unlimited Liability

A court might regard a professional corporation as a partnership, in which each partner may be liable for the malpractice of the others.

IV. CORPORATE FORMATION

A. PROMOTIONAL ACTIVITIES

Promoters take the first steps in organizing a corporation: issue a prospectus (see Chapter 27) and secure the corporate charter (see below).

1. Promoter's Liability

Personally liable on preincorporation contracts, unless the contracting party agrees otherwise. This liability continues after incorporation unless the third party releases the promoter or the corporation assumes the contract by novation (see Chapter 11).

2. Subscriptions

Subscribers (who agree to buy stock in a future corporation) become shareholders as soon as the corporation is formed or as soon as the corporation accepts their subscription agreement with the promoter.

a. Subscribers' Liability

A subscription is irrevocable for six months unless the parties agree otherwise [RMBCA 6.20]. In some states, a subscriber can, without liability, revoke an offer to buy before the corporation accepts.

b. Corporation's Liability

Preincorporation subscriptions are continuing offers to buy stock. On or after its formation, a corporation can choose to accept the offer.

B. INCORPORATION PROCEDURES

1. State Chartering

Some states offer more advantageous tax or incorporation provisions.

2. Articles of Incorporation

The articles include basic information about the corporation and serve as a primary source of authority for its organization and functions.

a. Corporate Name

Cannot be the same as, or deceptively similar to, the name of a corporation doing business in the state.

b. Duration

A corporation can have perpetual existence in most states.

c. Nature and Purpose

The intended business activities of the corporation must be specified. Stating a general corporate purpose is usually sufficient.

d. Capital Structure
The amount of stock authorized for issuance; its valuation; and other information as to equity, capital, and credit must be outlined.

e. Internal Organization
Management structure can be described in bylaws later.

f. Registered Office and Agent
Usually, the registered office is the principal office of the corporation; the agent is a person designated to receive legal documents on behalf of the corporation.

g. Incorporators
Incorporators (some states require only one) must sign the articles when they are submitted to the state; often this is their only duty, and they need have no other interest in the corporation.

3. Certificate of Incorporation (Corporate Charter)
The articles of incorporation are sent to the appropriate state official (usually the secretary of state). Many states issue a certificate of incorporation authorizing the corporation to conduct business.

4. First Organizational Meeting (After the Charter Is Granted)

a. Who Holds the Meeting
The incorporators or the board; the business conducted depends on state law, the nature of the corporation's business, the provisions of the articles, and the wishes of the promoters.

b. Adoption of the Bylaws
The most important function of the first organizational meeting.

V. CORPORATE STATUS

A. IMPROPER INCORPORATION
On the basis of improper incorporation—

1. Shareholders May Be Personally Liable for Corporate Obligations
A person attempting to enforce a contract or bring a tort suit against the corporation could seek to make the shareholders personally liable.

2. Third Parties May Avoid Liability to the Corporation
If a corporation seeks to enforce a contract, the defaulting party who learns of a defect in incorporation may be able to avoid liability.

B. *DE JURE* AND *DE FACTO* CORPORATIONS

1. *De Jure* Existence
Occurs if there is substantial compliance with all requirements for incorporation. In most states, the certificate of incorporation is evidence that all requirements have been met, and neither the state nor a third party can attack the corporation's existence.

2. *De Facto* Existence
The existence of a corporation cannot be challenged by third persons (except the state) if (1) there is a statute under which the firm can be incorporated, (2) the parties made a good faith attempt to comply with it, and (3) the firm has attempted to do business as a corporation.

C. CORPORATION BY ESTOPPEL

If an association that is neither an actual corporation nor a *de facto* or *de jure* corporation holds itself out as being a corporation, it will be estopped from denying corporate status in a lawsuit by a third party.

D. DISREGARDING THE CORPORATE ENTITY

A court may ignore the corporate structure (pierce the corporate veil), exposing the shareholders to personal liability, if—

1. A party is tricked or misled into dealing with the corporation rather than the individual.
2. The corporation is set up never to make a profit or always to be insolvent, or it is too thinly capitalized.
3. Statutory corporate formalities are not followed.
4. Personal and corporate interests are commingled to the extent that the corporation has no separate identity.

VI. CORPORATE FINANCING

A. BONDS

Bonds are issued as evidence of funds that business firms borrow from investors. A lending agreement called a **bond indenture** specifies the terms (maturity date, interest). A trustee ensures that the terms are met.

B. STOCKS

The most important characteristics of stocks are (1) they need not be paid back, (2) stockholders receive dividends only when voted by the directors, (3) stockholders are the last investors to be paid on dissolution, and (4) stockholders vote for management and on major issues.

TRUE-FALSE QUESTIONS

___ 1. A corporation is an artificial person.

___ 2. A corporation that is formed in a country other than the United States, but which does business in the United States, is a foreign corporation.

___ 3. Generally, a promoter is personally liable on a preincorporation contract until the corporation assumes it by novation or adopts it by performance.

___ 4. When conflicts arise among documents involving corporations, resolutions of the board of directors have the highest priority.

___ 5. Stocks are certificates that evidence corporate ownership.

___ 6. Bonds are certificates that evidence corporate debt.

___ 7. Unlike a sole proprietorship and many partnerships, a corporation is not a legal entity separate and distinct from its owners.

___ 8. A corporation enjoys many of the same rights and privileges that U.S. citizens enjoy.

___ 9. A corporation is liable for the torts of its employees committed within the scope of their employment.

___ 10. One disadvantage of an S corporation is that tax is imposed on income at the corporate and shareholder levels.

FILL-IN QUESTIONS

Those who, for themselves or others, take the preliminary steps in organizing a corporation are ____________________ (promoters/incorporators). These persons enter into contracts with professionals, whose services are needed in planning the corporation, and are personally liable on these contracts, ____________________ (unless/even if) the third party issues a release or the corporation assumes the contract. A person who applies to the state on behalf of the corporation to obtain its certificate of incorporation is ____________________ (a promoter/an incorporator). This person ______________ (must/need not) have any interest in the corporation.

MULTIPLE-CHOICE QUESTIONS

___ 1. All of a corporation's shareholders are the corporation's

a. owners.
b. managers.
c. incorporators.
d. promoters.

___ 2. When the American Press Corporation was organized, the directors were chosen by the organizers. During the first three years of business, however, American's shareholders become dissatisfied with the directors' management. The directors can be replaced by

a. organizing American into a new corporation.
b. a vote of the shareholders.
c. a vote of the organizers.
d. the board of directors.

___ 3. Natural Eats, Inc., is incorporated in Iowa, its only place of business. Its stock is owned by ten shareholders. Two are resident aliens. Three of the others are the directors and officers. The stock has never been sold to the public. If a shareholder wants to sell his or her shares, the other shareholders must be given the opportunity to buy them first. Natural is

a. a close corporation.
b. a foreign corporation.
c. an alien corporation.
d. none of the above.

___ 4. Which of the following statements concerning the implied powers of a corporation is FALSE?

a. Corporate officers have the authority to bind the corporation in matters of great significance to the corporate purpose.
b. Corporate officers have the authority to bind the corporation in matters directly connected to the ordinary business affairs of the corporation.
c. A corporation has the implied power to borrow money within certain limits.
d. A corporation has the implied power to extend credit to those with whom it has a legal or contractual relationship.

___ 5. Which of the following is NOT a step in forming a corporation?

a. Promoters make preincorporation contracts.
b. Incorporators execute articles of incorporation.
c. Shareholders approve or disapprove of corporate business matters at a shareholders' meeting.
d. Incorporators or a board of directors holds an organizational meeting to complete details of incorporation.

___ 6. Which of the following is TRUE?

a. Bonds need not be repaid, and their owners receive interest payments only when so voted by the directors of the corporation.
b. Common stock represents a proportionate interest in a corporation with regard to control, earning capacity, and net assets.
c. Bonds and preferred stock are identical from an investment standpoint.
d. A bondholder is the last investor to be paid on a corporation's dissolution.

___ 7. STV Corporation is a small audio and video equipment repair business owned and operated by Halle and Bert. Their prices are very competitive, and business is expanding. STV wants to open repair facilities in other cities but lacks the money to do so. To raise funds, STV may wish to issue

a. liabilities.
b. assets.
c. securities.
d. dividends.

___ 8. Corporate characteristics include all of the following EXCEPT

a. a corporation substitutes itself for its shareholders in conducting corporate business and in incurring liability.
b. responsibility for the overall management of a corporation rests with a board of directors, which is elected by the shareholders.
c. corporate officers, who are hired by the board of directors to run daily corporate operations, answer to the board rather than to the shareholders.
d. corporate profits may be passed to shareholders as tax-free dividends.

___ 9. A court will look behind the corporate structure, or "pierce the corporate veil," and hold a shareholder personally liable for a corporate debt when

a. a party is tricked or misled into dealing with the corporation rather than the individual.
b. the corporation is set up never to make a profit or always to be insolvent or is too thinly capitalized.
c. personal and corporate interests are commingled to the extent that the corporation has no separate identity.
d. all of the above.

___ 10. The Smith sisters form a computer equipment company. As a source of authority for their firm's organization and functions, their articles of incorporation are

a. not a reliable source.
b. a primary source.
c. a secondary source.
d. a source of final resort.

SHORT ESSAY QUESTIONS

1. Discuss the significance of the following items as they relate to a company's articles of incorporation: (1) corporate name, (2) nature and purpose, (3) duration, (4) capital structure, (5) internal organization, (6) registered office and agent, and (7) incorporators.

2. Describe the primary features of nonprofit, close, S, and professional corporations.

ISSUE SPOTTERS

1. The Kinata Corporation was formed in Iowa. Kinata does business through sales representatives in Illinois, but has no office or warehouse in Illinois. Can Illinois exercise jurisdiction over Kinata?

2. The PRK Corporation is a small business. Incorporated in Missouri, its one class of stock is owned by twelve members of a single family. Ordinarily, corporate income is taxed at the corporate and shareholder levels. Is there a way for PRK to avoid this double income taxation?

3. Ann, Greg, and Brian form the Coasters Corporation and elect its directors, Diane, Erin, and Frank. During the first year of business, Coaster shareholders become dissatisfied with Diane. How can Diane be replaced?

4. The incorporators of Consumer Investments, Inc., want their new corporation to have the authority to transact virtually all types of conceivable business. Can they grant this authority to their firm? How?

5. The Apple Corporation is convicted of conspiring with the Orange Corporation to violate a federal law that is punishable by a term of imprisonment and a fine. The prosecutor argues that the firms should be subject to both types of punishment. The attorneys for the defendants argue that a corporation cannot be imprisoned and thus should be subject only to a fine. How might the prosecutor's request be carried out?

QUICKEN CD-ROM
BUSINESS LAW PARTNER APPLICATIONS

Open **Quicken Business Law Partner**. Click on the *New Documents* icon. Select the *Articles of Incorporation, Corporate Bylaws,* and *Organizational Consent* documents. Respond to the *Interview* questions with actual facts or hypothetical ones. For example, imagine that Andrews, Carter, and Smith are the incorporators for ACS Corporation. As you complete the *Interview,* answer the following questions.

____ **1.** To begin ACS's corporate existence, Andrews, Carter, and Smith should file, with the appropriate secretary of state,

a. *Articles of Incorporation.*
b. *Corporate Bylaws.*
c. *Organizational Consent.*
d. any of the above.

___ **2.** ACS's registered agent must be listed in

a. *Articles of Incorporation.*
b. *Corporate Bylaws.*
c. *Organizational Consent.*
d. any of the above.

___ **3.** Andrews, Carter, and Smith want to provide that ACS's bylaws can be amended by a two-thirds majority (of a certain number of directors or shareholders). This provisions should be included in

a. *Articles of Incorporation.*
b. *Corporate Bylaws.*
c. *Organizational Consent.*
d. any of the above.

___ **4.** The document that will provide information concerning ACS's annual and special meetings is

a. *Articles of Incorporation.*
b. *Corporate Bylaws.*
c. *Organizational Consent.*
d. any of the above.

___ **5.** To state the end of ACS's fiscal year, and approve of its stock certificates and corporate seal (if any), Andrews, Carter, and Smith should use

a. *Articles of Incorporation.*
b. *Corporate Bylaws.*
c. *Organizational Consent.*
d. any of the above.

★ Learning Objectives

The learning objectives in this chapter include:

1. The role of corporate directors and officers.
2. The duties owed to the corporation by directors and officers.
3. The effect of the business judgment rule on directors' liability for their decisions.
4. The rights of shareholders.
5. The liability of shareholders and the duties owed by majority shareholders.

Chapter 25: Corporate Directors, Officers, and Shareholders

WHAT THIS CHAPTER IS ABOUT

This chapter outlines the rights and responsibilities of all participants—directors, officers, and shareholders—in a corporate enterprise. Also noted are the ways in which conflicts among these participants are resolved.

CHAPTER OUTLINE

I. ROLE OF DIRECTORS

The board of directors governs a corporation. Officers handle daily business.

A. ELECTION OF DIRECTORS

1. **Number of Directors**
   Set in a corporation's articles or bylaws. Corporations with fewer than fifty shareholders can eliminate the board of directors [RMBCA 8.01].

2. **How Directors Are Chosen**
   The first board (appointed by the incorporators or named in the articles) serves until the first shareholders' meeting. Subsequent directors are elected by a majority vote of the shareholders (see below).

3. **Removal of Directors**
   A director can be removed for cause by shareholder action (or the board may have the power). In most states, a director cannot be removed without cause, unless the shareholders have reserved the right.

B. DIRECTORS' QUALIFICATIONS AND COMPENSATION

A few states have minimum age and residency requirements. Compensation for directors is ordinarily specified in the articles or bylaws.

C. BOARD OF DIRECTORS' MEETINGS

1. Formal Minutes and Notice

A board conducts business by holding formal meetings with recorded minutes. The dates for regular meetings are usually set in the articles and bylaws or by board resolution, and no other notice is required. Special meetings require notice to all directors.

2. Quorum Requirements and Voting

Quorum requirements vary. If the firm specifies none, in most states a quorum is a majority of the number of directors authorized in the articles or bylaws. Voting is done in person, one vote per director.

D. RIGHTS OF DIRECTORS

1. Participation and Inspection

A director has a right to participate in corporate business. A director must have access to all corporate books and records to make decisions.

2. Compensation and Indemnification

Nominal sums may be paid to directors, and there is a trend to provide more. Most states permit a corporation to indemnify a director for costs and fees in defending against corporate-related lawsuits. Many firms buy insurance to cover indemnification.

E. MANAGEMENT RESPONSIBILITIES

1. Areas of Responsibility

Major policy and financial decisions; appointment, supervision, pay, and removal of officers and other managerial employees.

2. Executive Committee

Most states permit a board to elect an executive committee from among the directors to handle management between board meetings. The committee is limited to ordinary business matters.

II. ROLE OF CORPORATE OFFICERS AND EXECUTIVES

Officers and other executive employees are hired by the board. Officers act as agents of the corporation (see Chapter 21).

A. QUALIFICATIONS

At the discretion of the firm; included in the articles or bylaws. A person can hold more than one office and also be a director.

B. RIGHTS AND DUTIES

The rights of corporate officers and other high-level managers are defined by employment contracts. Officers normally can be removed by the board at any time (but the corporation could be liable for breach of contract). Officers' duties are the same as those of directors.

III. DUTIES OF DIRECTORS AND OFFICERS

Directors and officers are fiduciaries of the corporation.

A. DUTY OF CARE

Directors and officers must act in good faith, in what they consider to be the best interests of the corporation, and with the care that an ordinarily prudent person would exercise in similar circumstances.

1. **Duty to Make Informed and Reasonable Decisions**
Directors must be informed on corporate matters and act in accord with their knowledge and training. A director can rely on information furnished by competent officers, or others, without being accused of acting in bad faith or failing to exercise due care [RMBCA 8.30].

2. **Duty to Exercise Reasonable Supervision**
Directors must exercise reasonable supervision when work is delegated to others.

3. **Duty to Attend Board Meetings**
Directors must attend board meetings; if not, he or she should register a dissent to actions taken (to avoid liability for mismanagement).

B. DUTY OF LOYALTY

Directors and officers cannot use corporate funds or confidential information for personal advantage. Specifically, they cannot—

1. Compete with the corporation.
2. Usurp a corporate opportunity.
3. Have an interest that conflicts with the interest of the corporation.
4. Engage in insider trading (see Chapter 27).
5. Authorize a corporate transaction that is detrimental to minority shareholders, or (6) sell control over the corporation.

C. CONFLICTS OF INTEREST

Directors and officers must disclose fully any conflict of interest that might occur in a deal involving the corporation. A contract may be upheld if it was fair and reasonable to the firm when it was made, there was full disclosure of the interest of the officers or directors involved, and it was approved by a majority of disinterested directors or shareholders.

IV. LIABILITY OF DIRECTORS AND OFFICERS

A. THE BUSINESS JUDGMENT RULE

Honest mistakes of judgment and poor business decisions do not make directors and officers liable to the firm for poor results, if the decision complies with management's fiduciary duties, has a reasonable basis, and is within managerial authority and the power of the corporation.

B. LIABILITY FOR TORTS AND CRIMES

Directors and officers are personally liable for their torts and crimes, and may be liable for those of subordinates (under the "responsible corporate officer" doctrine or the "pervasiveness of control" theory). The corporation is liable for such acts when committed within the scope of employment.

V. ROLE OF SHAREHOLDERS

A. SHAREHOLDERS' POWERS

Shareholders own the corporation, approve fundamental corporate changes, and elect and remove directors.

B. SHAREHOLDERS' MEETINGS

Regular meetings must occur annually; special meetings can be called to handle urgent matters.

1. **Notice of Meeting Must be in Writing in Advance**
   Notice of a special meeting must state the purpose.

2. **Proxies**
   Rather than attend a meeting, shareholders normally authorize third parties to vote their shares. A proxy may be revocable and may have a time limit. When a firm sends proxy materials to its shareholders, it must allow them to vote on pending policy proposals.

C. SHAREHOLDER VOTING

1. **Quorum Requirements**
   At the meeting, a quorum must be present. A majority vote of the shares present is required to pass resolutions. Fundamental changes require a higher percentage.

2. **Voting Techniques**
   Each common shareholder has one vote per share. The articles can exclude or limit voting rights.

   a. **Cumulative Voting**
      The number of members of the board to be elected is multiplied by the total number of voting shares. This is the number of votes a shareholder has and can be cast for one or more nominees.

   b. **Shareholder Voting Agreements**
      A group of shareholders can agree to vote their shares together. A shareholder can vote by proxy. Any person can solicit proxies.

   c. **Voting Trust**
      Exists when legal title (recorded ownership on the corporate books) is transferred to a trustee who is responsible for voting the shares. The shareholder retains all other ownership rights.

D. RIGHTS OF SHAREHOLDERS

1. **Stock Certificates**
   Notice of shareholder meetings, dividends, and corporate reports are distributed to owners listed in the corporate books, not on the basis of possession of stock certificates (which most states do not require).

2. **Preemptive Rights**
   Usually apply only to additional, newly issued stock sold for cash and must be exercised within a specified time (usually thirty days). When new shares are issued, each shareholder is given **stock warrants**.

3. **Dividends**
   Dividends can be paid in cash, property, or stock. Once declared, a cash dividend is a corporate debt. Dividends are payable only from (1) retained earnings, (2) current net profits, or (3) any surplus.

   a. **Illegal Dividends**
      A dividend paid when a corporation is insolvent is illegal and must be repaid. A dividend paid from an unauthorized account or causing a corporation to become insolvent may have to be repaid. In any case, the directors can be held personally liable.

b. If the Directors Fail to Declare a Dividend
Shareholders can ask a court to compel a declaration of a dividend, but to succeed, the directors' conduct must be an abuse of discretion.

4. Inspection Rights
Shareholders (or their attorney, accountant, or agent) can inspect and copy corporate books and records for a proper purpose, if the request is made in advance [RMBCA 16.02]. This right can be denied to prevent harassment or to protect confidential corporate information.

5. Transfer of Shares
Any restrictions on transferability must be noted on the face of a stock certificate. Restrictions must be reasonable—for example, a right of first refusal remains with the corporation or the shareholders for only a specified time or a reasonable time.

6. Corporate Dissolution
Shareholders can petition a court to dissolve a firm if [RMBCA 14.30]—

a. The directors are deadlocked, shareholders are unable to break the deadlock, and there is or could be irreparable injury to the firm.

b. The acts of the directors or those in control of the corporation are illegal, oppressive, or fraudulent.

c. Corporate assets are being misapplied or wasted.

d. The shareholders are deadlocked in voting power and have failed, for a specified period (usually two annual meetings), to elect successors to directors.

7. Shareholder's Derivative Suit
If directors fail to sue in the corporate name to redress a wrong suffered by the firm, shareholders can do so (after complaining to the board). Any recovery normally goes into the corporate treasury.

VI. LIABILITY OF SHAREHOLDERS

In most cases, if a corporation fails, shareholders lose only their investment. Exceptions include (see also Chapter 24)—

A. STOCK-SUBSCRIPTIONS

Once a subscription agreement is accepted, any refusal to pay is a breach, resulting in personal liability.

B. WATERED STOCK

In most cases, a shareholder who receives watered stock (stock sold by a corporation for less than par value) must pay the difference to the corporation. In some states, such shareholders may be liable to creditors of the corporation for unpaid corporate debts.

VII. DUTIES OF MAJORITY SHAREHOLDERS

A single shareholder (or a few acting together) who owns enough shares to control the corporation owes a fiduciary duty to the minority shareholders and creditors when they sell their shares.

TRUE-FALSE QUESTIONS

___ **1.** Both directors and officers may be immunized from liability for poor business decisions under the business judgment rule.

___ **2.** Because their positions involve similar decision making and control, officers have the same duties as directors.

___ **3.** The rights of shareholders are established solely in the articles of incorporation.

___ **4.** Dividends can be paid in cash or property.

___ **5.** Any damages recovered in a shareholder's derivative suit are normally paid to the shareholder or shareholders who brought the suit.

___ **6.** As a general rule, shareholders are not personally responsible for the debts of the corporation.

___ **7.** Officers, but not directors, owe a duty of loyalty to the corporation.

___ **8.** The business judgment rule makes a director liable for losses to the firm that result from the director's authorized, good faith business decisions.

___ **9.** Shareholders may vote to elect directors and they may vote to remove directors.

___ **10.** Par-value shares have a specific face value.

FILL-IN QUESTIONS

A stock certificate may be lost or destroyed, ______________________ (and ownership is/but ownership is not) destroyed with it. A new certificate ______________ (can/cannot) be issued to replace one that has been lost or destroyed. Notice of meetings, dividends, and operational and financial reports are all distributed according to the individual ____ (in possession of the certificate/recorded as the owner in the corporation's books).

MULTIPLE-CHOICE QUESTIONS

___ **1.** Space, Inc., offers to buy Time Corporation. Time's board accepts the offer without investigating the value of Time and without determining whether a higher price could be obtained. Time's shareholders sue the directors. If the directors are held liable, it will be because they

a. breached their fiduciary duty to act in the shareholders' best interests.
b. are expected to act in accord with their own knowledge and training.
c. cannot rely on information furnished by officers or employees, professionals such as attorneys and accountants, or an executive committee of the board.
d. did not dissent from the board decisions and are therefore liable for mismanagement.

___ **2.** Jim is a director of Facts & Figures, Inc. As a director, Jim has a right to

a. participate in board meetings.
b. inspect all corporate books and records.
c. both a and b.
d. none of the above.

___ **3.** Honi Corporation's board announces that to accumulate funds for expansion, it will stop paying dividends for five years. Honi's minority shareholders sue to compel a dividend. If the shareholders win, it will be because

a. the board abused its discretion.
b. it is illegal not to declare a dividend.
c. dividends are like a debt—they must be paid.
d. there is sufficient surplus or earnings available to pay a dividend.

___ **4.** Jill is a shareholder of United Manufacturing Company. As a shareholder, Jill's rights include all of the following EXCEPT a right to

a. one vote per share, subject to any limitation in the articles.
b. access to corporate books and records, subject to the firm's right to protect itself from potential abuse.
c. transfer shares, subject to any valid restriction.
d. take title to and sell corporate property when directors are mishandling corporate assets, subject to any limitation in the articles.

___ **5.** The management of R&B Properties, Inc., is at odds with the shareholders over some recent decisions. The shareholders file several suits against the directors and officers. Which of the following is NOT a shareholder's derivative suit?

a. A suit alleging that officers misused corporate assets
b. A suit alleging that directors misused corporate assets
c. A suit alleging that the board's plan to merge with another corporation is designed to dilute the shareholders' voting power
d. A suit alleging that directors authorized an improper premium paid to a majority shareholder

___ **6.** Oxford Corporation uses cumulative voting in its elections of directors. Bill owns 3,000 Oxford shares. At an annual meeting at which three directors are to be elected, how many votes may Bill cast for any one candidate?

a. 1,000
b. 3,000
c. 9,000
d. 27,000

___ **7.** Poit Corporation's chief financial officer resigns. The board forms a committee to find a replacement. The committee finds and recommends three individuals. After an investigation, the board hires Ed. Ed turns out to be dishonest. Poit's shareholders sue the board. The board's best defense is

a. the business judgment rule.
b. its appointment of an executive committee to conduct the search.
c. the shareholders' power to remove directors.
d. board immunity from derivative suits.

___ 8. Wallace is a director and shareholder of the Stevens Corporation and of Tennessee Hills, Inc. If a resolution comes before the Stevens board to make an offer to contract with Tennessee, Wallace

a. must resign the directorship with Stevens.
b. must resign the directorship with Tennessee.
c. must disclose the potential conflict of interest.
d. need not disclose the potential conflict of interest.

___ 9. Julio and Gloria are officers of the World Export Corporation. As corporate officers, their rights, with respect to the corporation, are set out in

a. state corporation statutes.
b. World Export's certificate of authority.
c. their employment contracts with World Export.
d. international agreements with non-resident shareholders.

___ 10. Mike is a director of Calcom, Inc. Mike buys stock in Textron, a Calcom competitor. As to Mike's relationship to Calcom, this is a breach of

a. Mike's duty of care.
b. the business judgment rule.
c. Mike's duty of loyalty.
d. none of the above.

SHORT ESSAY QUESTIONS

1. How do the duty of care and the duty of loyalty govern the conduct of directors and officers in a corporation?

2. What are the rights of the shareholders of a corporation?

ISSUE SPOTTERS

1. Glen is a director and shareholder of the Diamond Corporation and of Ruby Rock, Inc. If a resolution comes before the Ruby board to compete with Diamond, what is Glen's responsibility?

2. Joe is a director and officer of Wild River Corporation. Joe makes a decision about the marketing of Wild River products that results in a dramatic decrease in profits for Wild River and its shareholders. The shareholders accuse Joe of breaching his fiduciary duty to the corporation. What is Joe's best defense?

3. Medtech Corporation's board of directors—among whom are Tom and Kate, officers of the firm—is deadlocked over whether to market a new product. Consequently, corporate investment is frozen. Ed, a minority shareholder, suspects that Tom and Kate are taking advantage of the deadlock to use corporate assets—offices, equipment, supplies, staff time—to initiate a competing enterprise. Is Ed powerless to intervene?

4. JKL Development Corporation has an opportunity to buy stock in Delong Properties, Inc. The directors decide that, instead of JKL buying the stock, the directors will buy it. After they buy the stock, Franco, a JKL shareholder, learns of the circumstances and wants to sue the directors on JKL's behalf. Can he do so?

5. Pam is Mayer Corporation's majority shareholder. Pam owns enough stock in Mayer that if she were to sell it, the sale would be a transfer of control of the firm. Does Pam owe any duty to Mayer or the minority shareholders in selling her shares?

QUICKEN CD-ROM BUSINESS LAW PARTNER APPLICATIONS

Open **Quicken Business Law Partner**. Click on the *New Documents* icon. Choose the *Corporate Proxy, Corporate Worksheet, Minutes, Notice of Meeting, Unanimous Consent,* and *Waiver of Notice* documents. Respond to the *Interview* questions with actual facts or hypothetical ones. For example, imagine that Delgado is a shareholder and Guerra is a director of Lima, Inc. As you complete the *Interview,* answer the following questions.

____ **1.** To organize and print business records regarding Delgado and other shareholders, Guerra and other directors, or Lima officers, employees, or other related individuals, the appropriate form to use is

a. *Corporate Proxy.*
b. *Minutes.*
c. *Corporate Worksheet.*
d. any of the above.

____ **2.** For Delgado to permit another person to represent and vote for Delgado at a shareholders' meeting, the appropriate form to use is

a. *Corporate Proxy.*
b. *Minutes.*
c. *Corporate Worksheet.*
d. any of the above.

____ **3.** To record official actions taken during a meeting of the board of directors, Guerra, or another appropriate director, should direct the use of

a. *Corporate Proxy.*
b. *Minutes.*
c. *Corporate Worksheet.*
d. any of the above.

____ **4.** To notify Delgado or Guerra, and other shareholders or directors, of the time, date, and place of an upcoming meeting, the appropriate form to use is

a. *Corporate Proxy.*
b. *Minutes.*
c. *Corporate Worksheet.*
d. any of the above.

____ **5.** If Delgado or Guerra, or other shareholders or directors, wish to waive their right to be notified of an upcoming meeting, they should use

a. *Corporate Proxy.*
b. *Minutes.*
c. *Corporate Worksheet.*
d. any of the above.

 **Learning Objectives**

The learning objectives in this chapter include:

1. Procedures involved in a merger or a consolidation.
2. What appraisal rights are and how they function.
3. The effects of a corporation's purchase of all or substantially all of another corporation's assets.
4. The effects of a corporation's purchase of a substantial number of voting shares of another corporation's stock.
5. The phases of corporate termination.

Chapter 26: Corporate Merger, Consolidation, and Termination

WHAT THIS CHAPTER IS ABOUT

This chapter covers corporate mergers, consolidations, purchase of another corporation's assets, and purchase of a controlling interest in another corporation. The chapter also touches on the reasons for, and methods used in, terminating a corporation.

CHAPTER OUTLINE

I. MERGER AND CONSOLIDATION

Whether a combination is a merger or a consolidation, the rights and liabilities of shareholders, the corporation, and its creditors are the same.

A. MERGER

1. What a Merger Is

The combination of two or more corporations, often by one absorbing the other. After a merger, only one of the corporations exists.

2. The Results of a Merger

The surviving corporation has all of the rights, assets, liabilities, and debts of itself and the other corporation. Its articles of incorporation are deemed amended to include changes stated in the articles of merger.

B. CONSOLIDATION

In a **consolidation**, two or more corporations combine so that each corporation ceases to exist and a new one emerges. The results of a consolidation are essentially the same as the results of a merger.

C. PROCEDURE FOR MERGER OR CONSOLIDATION

1. **The Basic Steps**
(1) Each board approves the merger or consolidation plan; (2) each firm's shareholders vote on the plan at a shareholders' meeting; (3) the plan is filed, usually with the secretary of state; and (4) the state issues a certificate of merger or consolidation.

2. **Short-form Merger**
A substantially owned subsidiary corporation can merge into its parent corporation without shareholder approval, if the parent owns at least 90 percent of the subsidiary's outstanding stock.

D. SHAREHOLDER APPROVAL
Actions taken on extraordinary matters (sale, lease, or exchange of all or substantially all corporate assets; amendment to the articles of incorporation; merger; consolidation; dissolution) must be authorized by the board of directors and the shareholders.

E. APPRAISAL RIGHTS
If provided by statute, a shareholder can dissent from a merger, consolidation, sale of substantially all the corporate assets not in the ordinary course of business, and (in some states) amendments to the articles.

1. **Procedure**
The shareholder must file written notice of dissent before the shareholders vote on the proposed transaction. If the transaction is approved, the shareholder must make a written demand for payment.

2. **Fair Value**
The value on the day before the date on which the vote is taken [RMBCA 13.01]. The corporation must make a written offer to buy the shareholder's stock. If fair value cannot be agreed to, a court will set it.

II. PURCHASE OF ASSETS

A. IS SHAREHOLDER APPROVAL REQUIRED?
A corporation that buys all or substantially all of the assets of another corporation does not need shareholder approval. The corporation whose assets are acquired must obtain approval of its board and shareholders.

B. ASSUMPTION OF LIABILITY
An acquiring corporation is not responsible for the seller's liabilities, unless there is (1) an implied or express assumption, (2) a sale amounting to a merger or consolidation, (3) a buyer retaining the seller's personnel and continuing the business, or (4) a sale executed in fraud to avoid liability.

III. PURCHASE OF STOCK
A purchase of a substantial number of the voting shares of a corporation's stock enables an acquiring corporation to control a target corporation. The acquiring corporation deals directly with shareholders to buy shares.

A. TENDER OFFERS
A tender offer is a public offer. The offer can turn on the receipt of a specified number of shares by a specified date.

1. **The Price Offered for the Target's Stock**
Generally higher than the stock's market price before the tender offer. May involve an exchange of stock or cash for stock in the target.

2. **Federal and State Securities Laws**
Federal laws control the terms, duration, and circumstances in which most tender offers are made. Most states also impose regulations.

B. TARGET RESPONSES

1. **Good Faith Decision**
The directors of the target firm must make a good faith decision as to whether the shareholders' acceptance or rejection of the offer would be most beneficial. The directors must fully disclose all material facts.

2. **To Resist a Takeover**
Among other tactics, a target may make a self-tender. A target may also sell its most desirable assets or take other defensive measures.

IV. TERMINATION

A. DISSOLUTION
Dissolution may be brought about by—

1. **Act of the Legislature in the State of Incorporation**

2. **Expiration of the Time in the Certificate of Incorporation**

3. **Voluntary Approval of the Shareholders and the Board**

4. **Unanimous Approval of the Shareholders**

5. **Court Decree**

   a. In an action brought by the secretary of state or the state attorney general, a corporation may be dissolved for [RMBCA 14.20]—

      1) Failing to comply with corporate formalities or other administrative requirements.

      2) Procuring a charter through fraud or misrepresentation.

      3) Abusing corporate powers (*ultra vires* acts).

      4) Violating the state criminal code after a demand to discontinue the violation has been made by the secretary of state.

      5) Failing to commence business operations.

      6) Abandoning operations before starting up.

   b. In an action by shareholders, a court may dissolve a corporation when a board is deadlocked or for mismanagement [RMBCA 14.30].

B. LIQUIDATION
Corporate assets are converted into cash and distributed among creditors and shareholders according to specific rules.

1. **Board Supervision**
If dissolution is by voluntary action, the members of the board act as trustees of the assets, and wind up the affairs of the corporation for the benefit of corporate creditors and shareholders.

2. **Court Supervision**
If dissolution is involuntary, the board does not wish to act as trustee, or shareholders or creditors can show why the board should not act as trustee, a court will appoint a receiver to wind up the corporate affairs.

TRUE-FALSE QUESTIONS

___ 1. If a parent corporation owns are least 90 percent of the outstanding shares of its subsidiary corporation, the subsidiary can be merged into its parent without the approval of the shareholders of either corporation.

___ 2. Appraisal rights are available only when a statute specifically provides for them.

___ 3. Shareholders must normally approve actions to be taken in extraordinary business matters.

___ 4. Shareholders must normally approve the purchase of all or substantially all of another corporation's assets.

___ 5. Federal laws strictly control the terms, duration, and circumstances under which most tender offers are made.

___ 6. During the liquidation of a corporation, corporate assets are converted to cash and distributed to creditors and shareholders.

___ 7. Shareholders who disapprove of a merger or a consolidation may be entitled to be paid the fair value of their shares.

___ 8. A corporation that purchases the assets of another corporation always assumes the selling corporation's liabilities as part of the deal.

___ 9. The board of directors can amend the articles of incorporation without shareholder approval.

___ 10. Appraisal rights are not ordinarily available in sales of substantially all of a corporation's assets.

FILL-IN QUESTIONS

If provided by statute, a shareholder can dissent from any ________________ (extraordinary/ordinary) fundamental changes in a corporation. To do so, the ________________ (corporation/shareholder) must file a written notice of dissent ________________ (after/before) the shareholders vote on the proposed change. If the change is approved, the shareholder must make a written demand for payment. The fair value of shares is usually their value on the day ________________ (after/before) the date on which ________________ (the change is made/the vote is taken).

MULTIPLE-CHOICE QUESTIONS

___ 1. Which of the following is a result of a merger?

a. One firm acquires all the assets previously held by two firms without a formal transfer.
b. One firm becomes subject to the provisions of two sets of articles.
c. Both a and b
d. None of the above

___ **2.** Norm, Tracy, and Grant are the shareholders of Canyon Outfitters, Inc. Over time, Canyon sells off all its assets, except for one store. When Grant, the Canyon president, contracts to sell the last store for what he believes is a fair price, Norm and Tracy object. If they sue, they will

a. win, because their approval is required to sell the store.
b. win, because the store is Canyon's last asset and thus cannot be sold.
c. lose, because their approval is not required to sell the store.
d. lose, because Grant contracted for what he believed was a fair price.

___ **3.** Mary and Adam are the directors and majority shareholders of U.S. Imports, Inc., and Overseas Corporation. U.S. Imports owes $5,000 to Maple Transport, Inc. To avoid the debt, Mary and Adam vote to sell all U.S. Imports' assets to Overseas. If Maple sues Overseas on the debt, Maple will

a. win, because an acquiring corporation automatically assumes a selling corporation's liabilities.
b. win, because the sale was fraudulently executed to avoid liability.
c. lose, because Overseas refused to assume U.S. Imports' debt.
d. lose, because U.S. Imports has ceased to exist.

___ **4.** Which of the following is NOT part of a merger or a consolidation?

a. The board of directors of each corporation approves the combination.
b. The shareholders of each corporation approve the combination.
c. The officers of each corporation approve the combination.
d. The articles of merger or consolidation are filed with the appropriate state official.

___ **5.** In which of the following situations might the attorney general of the state of incorporation seek a court decree to dissolve a corporation?

a. A corporation does not pay annual franchise fees.
b. A corporation does not or file an annual report.
c. Both a and b
d. None of the above

___ **6.** Pepper Corporation and Salt Products, Inc., decide to combine. Afterwards, Pepper will cease to exist—only Salt will function, as the surviving corporation. The combination of Pepper and Salt is

a. a consolidation.
b. a merger.
c. both a and b.
d. none of the above.

___ **7.** Which of the following will NOT cause the dissolution of a corporation?

a. An act of the legislature in the state of incorporation
b. The expiration of the time provided in the certificate of incorporation
c. A failure to obtain shareholder approval to acquire another corporation
d. The voluntary approval of the shareholders and the board of directors

___ **8.** Which of the following is a result of a consolidation?

a. One firm has all the rights and powers previously held by two firms.
b. One firm is liable for all the debts previously owed by two firms.
c. Both a and b
d. None of the above

___ **9.** Daven Corporation and Burl Company decide to combine. Afterwards, Daven and Burl will cease to exist—a new organization, DB, Inc., will function in their place. The combination of Daven and Burl is

a. a consolidation.
b. a merger.
c. both a and b.
d. none of the above.

___ **10.** A state's attorney general may seek a court decree to dissolve a corporation when there has been

a. an abuse of corporate power (*ultra vires* acts).
b. a failure to commence business operations.
c. an attempt to take over another corporation through stock acquisition.
d. both a and b.

SHORT ESSAY QUESTIONS

1. Define these takeover defense terms: greenmail; Pac-man; poison pill; scorched-earth tactic; shark repellant; and white knight.

2. What are the steps in the process by which a corporation is dissolved and liquidated?

ISSUE SPOTTERS

1. Kinata Corporation combines with MC, Inc. MC ceases to exist—Kinata is the surviving firm. Warner Corporation and Special Animation Company combine. Afterwards, Warner and Special Animation cease to exist. Fine Points, Inc., a new firm, functions in their place. Which of these is a merger and which is a consolidation?

2. Delacroix Corporation asks its shareholders to vote on a proposed merger with Hugo, Inc. Deb, a Delacroix shareholder, votes against it, but is outvoted by Delacroix's other shareholders. Deb is unwilling to become a Hugo shareholder. Is there anything she can do to avoid being forced to go along with the transaction?

3. Champ Sports Corporation buys the assets of Athletic Authority Company (AAC). Champ continues AAC's business and retains the same personnel. AAC is a firm on paper only, with many unpaid debts. Is Champ liable for AAC's debts?

4. Beloit Corporation makes a public offer to buy Fort, Inc., stock. The price of the offer is higher than the market price of the stock, but Fort's board believes that it should be resisted. What can Fort do to retain control over itself?

5. Dee and Jim form Home Remodeling, Inc. After three years, they decide to cease business and go their separate ways. Can they simply dissolve Home at will? Could Dee or Jim seek dissolution of Home alone (as a partner can dissolve a partnership)?

Learning Objectives

The learning objectives in this chapter include:

1. What is meant by the term *securities.*
2. The purpose and provisions of the Securities Act of 1933.
3. The purpose and provisions of the Securities Exchange Act of 1934.
4. Federal laws that specifically regulate investment companies.
5. State securities laws.

Chapter 27: Investor Protection

WHAT THIS CHAPTER IS ABOUT

The general purpose of securities laws is to provide sufficient, accurate information to investors to enable them to make informed buying and selling decisions about securities. This chapter provides an outline of federal securities laws.

CHAPTER OUTLINE

I. SECURITIES ACT OF 1933

Requires that all essential information concerning the issuance (sales) of new securities be disclosed to investors.

A. WHAT IS A SECURITY?

1. Courts' Interpretation of the Securities Act

A security exists in any transaction in which a person (1) invests (2) in a common enterprise (3) reasonably expecting profits (4) derived *primarily* or *substantially* from others' managerial or entrepreneurial efforts.

2. A Security Is an Investment

Examples: stocks, bonds, investment contracts in condominiums, franchises, limited partnerships, and oil or gas or other mineral rights.

B. REGISTRATION STATEMENT

Before offering securities for sale, issuing corporations must (1) file a registration statement with the Securities and Exchange Commission (SEC) and (2) provide investors with a prospectus that describes the security being sold, the issuing corporation, and the investment or risk.

1. **Contents of a Registration Statement**

   a. Description of the significant provisions of the security and how the registrant intends to use the proceeds of the sale.
   b. Description of the registrant's properties and business.
   c. Description of the management of the registrant; its security holdings; its remuneration and other benefits, including pensions and stock options; and any interests of directors or officers in any material transactions with the corporation.
   d. Financial statement certified by an independent public accountant.
   e. Description of pending lawsuits.

2. **Twenty-Day Waiting Period after Registration**
   Securities cannot be sold for twenty days (oral offers can be made).

3. **Advertising**
   During the waiting period, very limited written advertising is allowed. After the period, no written advertising is allowed, except a tombstone ad, which simply tells how to obtain a prospectus.

4. **Violations and Penalties**
   Liability exists if a registration statement or prospectus contains material false statements or material omissions. Potentially liable parties include anyone who signed the statement. Penalties include damages, fines, and imprisonment.

C. EXEMPT SECURITIES
Securities that can be sold (and resold) without being registered include—

1. **Small Offerings under Regulation A**
   An issuer's offer of up to $5 million in securities in any twelve-month period (including up to $1.5 million in nonissuer resales). The issuer must file with the SEC a notice of the issue and an offering circular (also provided to investors before the sale). A company can **test the waters** (determine potential interest) before preparing the circular.

2. **Other Exempt Securities**

   a. All bank securities sold prior to July 27, 1933.
   b. Commercial paper if maturity does not exceed nine months.
   c. Securities of charitable organizations.
   d. Securities resulting from a reorganization issued in exchange for the issuer's existing securities and certificates issued by trustees, receivers, or debtors in possession in bankruptcy (see Chapter 21).
   e. Securities issued exclusively in exchange for the issuer's existing securities, provided no commission is paid (such as stock splits).
   f. Securities issued to finance the acquisition of railroad equipment.
   g. Any insurance, endowment, or annuity contract issued by a state-regulated insurance company.
   h. Government-issued securities.
   i. Securities issued by banks, savings and loan associations, farmers' cooperatives, and similar institutions.

D. EXEMPT TRANSACTIONS
Securities that can be sold without being registered include those sold in transactions that consist of—

1. **Limited Offers (Regulation D)**
Offers that involve a small amount of money or are not made publicly.

    a. **Small Offerings**
    Noninvestment company offerings up to $1 million in a twelve-month period [Rule 504].

    b. **Blank-Check Company Offerings**
    Offerings up to $500,000 in any one year by companies with no specific business plans are exempt if (1) no general solicitation or advertising is used, (2) the SEC is notified of the sales, and (3) precaution is taken against nonexempt, unregistered resales [Rule 504a].

    c. **Small Offerings**
    Private, noninvestment company offerings up to $5 million in a twelve-month period if (1) no general solicitation or advertising is used; (2) the SEC is notified of the sales; (3) precaution is taken against nonexempt, unregistered resales; and (4) there are no more than thirty-five unaccredited investors. If the sale involves any unaccredited investors, all investors must be given material information about the company, its business, the securities [Rule 505].

    d. **Private Offerings**
    Essentially the same requirements as Rule 505, except (1) there is no limit on the amount of the offering and (2) the issuer must believe that each unaccredited investor has sufficient knowledge or experience to evaluate the investment [Rule 506].

2. **Intrastate Issues**
Offerings in the state in which the issuer is organized and doing business are exempt [Rule 147] if, for nine months after the sale, no resale is made to a nonresident.

3. **Offers to Accredited Investors Only**
An offer up to $5 million is exempt if (1) no general solicitation or advertising is used; (2) the SEC is notified of the sales; (3) precaution is taken against nonexempt, unregistered resales; and (4) there are no unaccredited investors [Section 4(6)].

4. **Resales—"Safe Harbors"**
Most securities can be resold without registration. Resales of blank-check company offerings [Rule 504a], small offerings [Rule 505], private offerings [Rule 506], and offers to accredited investors only [Section 4(6)] are exempt from registration if—

    a. **The Securities Have Been Owned for Three Years or More**
    If seller is not an **affiliate** (in control with the issuer) [Rule 144].

    b. **The Securities Have Been Owned for at Least Two Years**
    There must be adequate public information about the issuer, the securities must be sold in limited amounts in unsolicited brokers' transactions, and the SEC must be notified of the resale [Rule 144].

    c. **The Securities Are Sold Only to an Institutional Investor**
    The securities, on issue, must not have been of the same class as securities listed on a national securities exchange or a U.S. automated interdealer quotation system, and the seller on resale must take steps to tell the buyer they are exempt [Rule 144A].

II. SECURITIES EXCHANGE ACT OF 1934

Regulates the markets in which securities are traded by requiring disclosure by Section 12 companies (corporations with securities on the exchanges and firms with assets in excess of $5 million and five hundred or more shareholders).

A. INSIDER TRADING—SECTION 10(b) AND SEC RULE 10b-5

Section 10(b) proscribes the use of "any manipulative or deceptive device or contrivance in contravention of such rules and regulations as the [SEC] may prescribe." Rule 10b-5 prohibits the commission of fraud in connection with the purchase or sale of any security (registered or unregistered).

1. What Triggers Liability

Any material omission or misrepresentation of material facts in connection with the purchase or sale of any security.

2. Who Can Be Liable

Those who take advantage of inside information when they know that it is unavailable to the person with whom they are dealing.

a. Insiders

Officers, directors, majority shareholders, and persons having access to or receiving information of a nonpublic nature on which trading is based (accountants, attorneys).

b. Outsiders

1) Tipper/Tippee Theory

One who acquires inside information as a result of an insider's breach of fiduciary duty to the firm whose shares are traded can be liable, if he or she knows or should know of the breach.

2) Misappropriation Theory

One who wrongfully obtains inside information and trades on it to his or her gain can be liable, if a duty to the lawful possessor of information was violated and harm to another results.

B. INSIDER REPORTING AND TRADING—SECTION 16(b)

Officers, directors, and shareholders owning 10 percent of the securities registered under Section 12 are required to file reports with the SEC concerning their ownership and trading of the securities.

1. Corporation Is Entitled to All Profits

A firm can recapture *all* profits realized by an insider on *any* purchase and sale or sale and purchase of its stock in any six-month period.

2. Applicability of Section 16(b)

Applies to stock, warrants, options, securities convertible into stock.

C. INSIDER-TRADING SANCTIONS

1. Insider Trading Sanctions Act of 1984

The SEC can bring suit in federal court against anyone violating or aiding in a violation of the 1934 act or SEC rules. Penalties may include triple the profits gained or the loss avoided by the guilty party.

2. Insider Trading and Securities Fraud Enforcement Act of 1988

a. **Provisions**
Enlarged the class of persons subject to civil liability for insider-trading violations, increased criminal penalties, and gave the SEC authority to (1) reward persons providing information and (2) make rules to prevent insider trading.

b. **Penalties**
Maximum jail term is ten years; fines up to $1 million for individuals and to $2.5 million for partnerships and corporations.

D. **PROXY STATEMENTS—SECTION 14(A)**
Regulates the solicitation of proxies from shareholders of Section 12 companies. Whoever solicits a proxy must disclose, in the proxy statement, all of the pertinent facts.

III. THE EXPANDING POWERS OF THE SEC

Congress enacted the Securities Enforcement Remedies and Penny Stock Reform Act of 1990 to expand the types of cases that SEC administrative law judges can hear; allow courts to bar persons convicted of fraud from serving as directors or officers; and allow sanctions against those who violate foreign securities laws.

IV. REGULATION OF INVESTMENT COMPANIES

Investment companies and mutual funds are regulated by the Investment Company Act of 1940, the Investment Company Act Amendments of 1970, the Securities Act Amendments of 1975, and later amendments.

A. **WHAT AN INVESTMENT COMPANY IS**
Any entity that (1) is engaged primarily "in the business of investing, reinvesting, or trading in securities" or (2) is engaged in such business and has more than 40 percent of the company's assets in investment securities. (Does not include banks, finance companies, and others).

B. **WHAT AN INVESTMENT COMPANY MUST DO**
Register with the SEC by filing a notification of registration and, each year, file reports with the SEC. All securities must be in the custody of a bank or stock-exchange member.

C. **WHAT AN INVESTMENT COMPANY CANNOT DO**
No dividends may be paid from any source other than accumulated, undistributed net income. There are restrictions on investment activities.

V. STATE SECURITIES LAWS

All states regulate the offer and sale of securities within individual state borders. Exemptions from federal law are not exemptions from state laws, which have their own exemptions.

TRUE-FALSE QUESTIONS

___ 1. Generally, if a security does not qualify for an exemption, it must be registered before it is offered to the public.

___ 2. A nonexempt security must be accompanied by a prospectus to investors.

___ 3. Securities issued by banks are normally exempt from the SEC registration requirements.

___ **4.** Securities resulting from a corporate reorganization issued for exchange with the issuer's existing security holders are exempt from the SEC registration requirements.

___ **5.** The Securities Act of 1933 is concerned primarily with the *resale* of securities, and the Securities Exchange Act of 1934 is concerned primarily with disclosure on the *issuance* of securities.

___ **6.** Rules requiring full and accurate disclosure of all pertinent facts apply to proxy statements under the Securities Exchange Act of 1934.

___ **7.** All states regulate the offer and sale of securities within their borders.

___ **8.** Penalties for insider trading may include triple the profits gained or the loss avoided by the guilty party.

___ **9.** SEC Rule 10b-5 prohibits the commission of fraud in connection with the purchase or sale of registered securities only.

___ **10.** No security can be resold without registration.

FILL-IN QUESTIONS

The SEC can award "bounty" payments to persons providing information leading to the ________________________ (conviction/prosecution) of insider-trading violations. Civil penalties include ______________ (double/triple) the profits gained or the loss avoided. Criminal penalties include maximum jail terms of ____________ (five/ ten) years. Individuals and corporations ____________ (may/may not) also be subject to million dollar fines.

MULTIPLE-CHOICE QUESTIONS

___ **1.** Which of the following is NOT an element of the definition of a security?

a. An investment
b. A common enterprise
c. A reasonable expectation of profits derived from the entrepreneurial efforts of others
d. An expectation of profits derived entirely from the efforts of the investor

___ **2.** Gene is an officer for Max Software, Inc. In April, Gene learns that market tests indicate Max's new product will sell well. He buys 1,000 shares of Max stock. In May, the product is released, and sales exceed expectations. In July, as part of a corporate reorganization, Gene is laid off. In August, he sells his stock at a profit. If Max sues Gene under Section 16(b), Max will

a. win, because Gene was a Max officer who bought and sold Max stock within a six-month period.
b. win, because Gene used inside information in connection with the purchase and sale of Max stock.
c. lose, because Gene was not a Max officer when he realized the stock profit.
d. lose, because Gene did not use inside information in connection with the purchase and sale of Max stock.

___ **3.** Superior, Inc., is a private, noninvestment company. In one year, Superior advertises a $300,000 offering. This offering is

a. exempt from registration because of the low amount of the issue.
b. exempt from registration because the offering was advertised.
c. exempt from registration because the issuer is a private company.
d. not exempt from registration.

___ **4.** Huron, Inc., makes a $5.5 million private offering to twenty accredited investors and less than thirty unaccredited investors. Huron advertises the offering and believes that the unaccredited investors are sophisticated enough to evaluate the investment. Huron gives material information about itself, its business, and the securities to all investors. This offering is

a. exempt from registration because of the low amount of the issue.
b. exempt from registration because the offering was advertised.
c. exempt from registration because the issuer believed that the unaccredited investors were sophisticated enough to evaluate the investment.
d. not exempt from registration.

___ **5.** Ontario, Inc., in one year, advertises two $2.25 million offerings. Buying the stock are twelve accredited investors. This offering is

a. exempt from registration because of the low amount of the issue.
b. exempt from registration because the offering was advertised.
c. exempt from registration because only accredited investors bought stock.
d. not exempt from registration.

___ **6.** A registration statement must include

a. a description of the security and its relationship to the registrant's other securities.
b. how the registrant intends to use the proceeds from the sale of the issue.
c. both a and b.
d. none of the above.

___ **7.** A registration statement must include

a. a description of the registrant's properties and management.
b. a description of pending lawsuits.
c. both a and b.
d. none of the above.

___ **8.** Ed is an officer of Cafe Corporation (CC). Ed learns that CC has developed a new process for its products. Ed believes that when the process is announced, CC stock's price will increase. Ed tells Lyn, Ed's attorney, who tells Dick, Lyn's accountant. Lyn and Dick are aware that Ed has breached a fiduciary duty to CC in disclosing this information. Ed, Lyn, and Dick each buy CC stock through a national exchange without telling the sellers of the new process. When the process is announced, the price increases, and Ed, Lyn, and Dick sell their stock. Who may be liable under Rule 10b-5?

a. All of them
b. Ed and Lyn only
c. Ed only
d. None of them

____ **9.** Erie, Inc., is a noninvestment company. In one year, Erie advertises two $1.75 million offerings. Buying the issues are sixty accredited investors and twenty unaccredited investors. Erie gives information about itself, its business, and the securities to unaccredited investors only. This offering is

a. exempt from registration because of the low amount of the issue.
b. exempt from registration because the offering was advertised.
c. exempt from registration because the unaccredited investors were informed.
d. not exempt from registration.

____ **10.** Great Lakes Company is a private, noninvestment company. Last year, as part of a $250,000 advertised offering, Great Lakes sold stock to John, a private investor. John would now like to sell the shares. This resale is

a. exempt from registration because of the low amount of the original issue.
b. exempt from registration because the offering was advertised.
c. exempt from registration because all resales are exempt.
d. not exempt from registration.

SHORT ESSAY QUESTIONS

1. What do federal securities laws require of a company that sells nonexempt securities to the public? Be sure to state what a registration statement must include and what a company can do before, during, and after the required waiting period.

2. How is insider trading regulated by Section 10(b), SEC Rule 10b-5, and Section 16(b)?

ISSUE SPOTTERS

1. What agency investigates securities fraud and regulates the activities of investment brokers? What agency supervises the activities of mutual funds? What agency recommends the prosecution of those who violate securities laws?

2. When a corporation wishes to issue certain securities, it must provide sufficient information for an unsophisticated investor to evaluate the financial risk involved. Specifically, the law imposes liability for making a false statement or omission that is "material." What sort of information would an investor consider material?

3. Mel is a vice president of Flax, Inc. Mel knows that a Flax engineer has just discovered a new lode of platinum, an element essential to Flax operations. Mel believes that when the news is made public, the price of Flax's stock will increase. Can Mel take advantage of this information to buy and sell Flax stock?

4. The Securities Act of 1933, the Securities Exchange Act of 1934, and other securities regulation is federal law. Mott Assembly Corporation incorporated in Ohio, does business exclusively in Ohio, and offers its securities for sale only in Ohio. Are there state securities laws to regulate the sale of securities within individual state borders?

5. What is the most important action a firm takes before selling its shares to the public?

 **Learning Objectives**

The learning objectives in this chapter include:

1. The difference between personal property and real property.
2. Types of property ownership and the ways in which property can be acquired.
3. Rights to mislaid, lost, or abandoned property.
4. The elements of a bailment.
5. The rights and duties of a bailee and a bailor.

Chapter 28: Personal Property and Bailments

WHAT THIS CHAPTER IS ABOUT

This chapter covers the nature of personal property, forms of property ownership, the acquisition of personal property, and bailments. Note that personal property can be tangible (such as a car) or intangible (such as stocks, bonds, patents, or copyrights).

CHAPTER OUTLINE

I. PROPERTY OWNERSHIP

Ownership can be viewed as the rights to possess property and to dispose of it.

A. FEE SIMPLE

A person who holds all of the rights is an owner in fee simple (see Chapter 29); on death, the owner's interest descends to his or her heirs.

B. CONCURRENT OWNERSHIP

Persons who share ownership rights simultaneously are concurrent owners.

1. **Tenancy in Common**
   Each of two or more persons owns an undivided interest (each has rights in the whole—if each had rights in specific items, the interests would be divided). On death, a tenant's interest passes to his or her heirs.

2. **Joint Tenancy**
   Each of two or more persons owns an undivided interest in the property; a deceased joint tenant's interest passes to the surviving joint tenant or tenants. Can be terminated at any time before a joint tenant's death by gift or by sale.

3. **Tenancy by the Entirety**
Created by a transfer of real property to a husband and wife; neither spouse can transfer separately his or her interest during his or her life.

4. **Community Property**
Each spouse owns an undivided half interest in property acquired by either spouse during their marriage. Recognized in only some states.

II. ACQUIRING OWNERSHIP OF PERSONAL PROPERTY

A. POSSESSION
An example of acquiring ownership by possession is the capture of wild animals. (Exceptions: (1) wild animals captured by a trespasser are the property of the landowner, and (2) wild animals captured or killed in violation of statutes are the property of the state.)

B. PRODUCTION
Those who produce personal property have title to it. (Exception: employees do not own what they produce for their employers.)

C. GIFTS
A **gift** is a voluntary transfer of property ownership not supported by consideration.

1. **Requirements for an Effective Gift**
There are three requirements for an effective gift—

a. **Donative Intent**
Determined from the language of the donor and the surrounding circumstances (relationship between the parties and the size of the gift in relation to the donor's other assets).

b. **Delivery**

1) **Constructive Delivery**
If a physical object cannot be delivered, an act that the law holds to be equivalent to an act of real delivery is sufficient (a key to a safe-deposit box for the contents of the box, for example).

2) **Delivery by a Third Person**
If the person is the donor's agent, the gift is effective when the agent delivers the property to the donee. If the person is the donee's agent, the gift is effective when the donor delivers the property to the agent.

3) **Giving Up Control**
Effective delivery requires giving up control over the property.

c. **Acceptance**
Courts assume a gift is accepted unless shown otherwise.

2. **Gifts *Inter Vivos* and Gifts *Causa Mortis***
Gifts *inter vivos* are made during one's lifetime. Gifts *causa mortis* are made in contemplation of imminent death, do not become effective until the donor dies, and are automatically revoked if the donor does not die.

D. ACCESSION

Occurs when someone adds value to a item of personal property by labor or materials. Ownership can be at issue if—

1. **Accession Occurs without Permission of the Owner**
   Courts tend to favor the owner over the one who improved the property (and deny the improver any compensation for the value added).

2. **Accession Greatly Increases the Value or Changes the Identity**
   If the accession is in good faith, then the greater the increase, the more likely that ownership will pass to the improver, who must compensate the original owner for the value of the property before the accession.

E. CONFUSION

Commingling goods so that one person's cannot be distinguished from another's. Frequently involves fungible goods. If goods are confused due to a wrongful act, the innocent party acquires all. If confusion is by agreement, mistake, or a third party's act, the owners share as tenants in common.

III. MISLAID, LOST, AND ABANDONED PROPERTY

A. MISLAID PROPERTY

Property that has been voluntarily placed somewhere by the owner and then inadvertently forgotten. When the property is found, the owner of the place where it was mislaid (not the finder) becomes the caretaker.

B. LOST PROPERTY

Property that is involuntarily left. A finder can claim title against the whole world, except the true owner. Many states require the finder to make a reasonably diligent search to locate the true owner. Estray statutes allow finders, after passage of a specified time, to acquire title to the property if it remains unclaimed.

C. ABANDONED PROPERTY

Property that has been discarded by the true owner, who has no intention of claiming title to it. A finder acquires title good against the whole world, including the original owner. A trespasser does not acquire title, however; the owner of the real property on which it was found does.

IV. BAILMENTS

A **bailment** is formed by the delivery of personal property, without transfer of title, by a bailor to a bailee, usually under an agreement for a particular purpose, after which the property is returned or otherwise disposed of.

A. ELEMENTS OF A BAILMENT

1. **Personal Property**
   Only personal property is bailable.

2. **Delivery of Possession (Without Title)**
   Bailee must (1) be given exclusive possession and control of the property and (2) knowingly accept it. Delivery may be physical or constructive.

3. **Bailment Agreement**
   The agreement must provide for the return of the property to the bailor or a third person, or for its disposal by the bailee.

B. ORDINARY BAILMENTS

The three types of ordinary bailments are: (1) Bailment for the sole benefit of the bailor, (2) bailment for the sole benefit of the bailee, and (3) bailment for their mutual benefit.

1. Rights of the Bailee

a. Right to Control and Possess the Property

This right permits a bailee to recover damages from any third persons for damage or loss to the property.

b. Right to Use the Property

The extent to which a bailee can use property depends on the bailment agreement.

c. Right of to Be Compensated

A bailee has a right to be compensated as agreed and to be reimbursed for costs and services in the keeping of the property. To enforce the right, a bailee can put a possessory lien on the property.

d. Right to Limit Liability

Bailees can limit their liability as long as—

1) Limitations Are Called to the Attention of the Bailor

Fine print on the back of a ticket stub is not sufficient.

2) Limitations Are Not Against Public Policy

If a bailee attempts to exclude liability for his or her own negligence, the clause is unenforceable.

2. Duties of the Bailee

a. Duty of Care

A bailment for the sole benefit of the bailor requires a slight degree of care; a bailment for the sole benefit of the bailee requires great care. A mutual-benefit bailment requires reasonable care. Failure to use the right amount of care results in tort liability.

b. Duty to Return Bailed Property

When a bailment ends, the bailee must relinquish the property. Failure to do so is a breach of contract (unless the property is destroyed, lost, or stolen through no fault of the bailee, or given to a third party with a superior claim) and could be conversion.

c. Presumption of Negligence

If the bailee has the property and damage occurs that normally results only from someone's negligence, the bailee's negligence is presumed. The bailee must prove that he or she was not at fault.

3. Rights of the Bailor

The bailor's rights are essentially the same as the duties of the bailee.

4. Duties of the Bailor

A bailor has a duty to provide the bailee with goods that are free from defects that could injure the bailee. This has two aspects—

a. In a mutual-benefit bailment, the bailor must notify the bailee of all *known* defects and any *hidden* defects that the bailor knew of or could have discovered with reasonable diligence and inspection.

b. In a bailment for the sole benefit of the bailee, the bailor must notify the bailee of any *known* defects.

c. Liability extends to anyone who might be expected to come in contact with the goods. A bailor may also incur liability under UCC Article 2A's implied warranties.

C. SPECIAL TYPES OF BAILMENTS

1. Common Carriers

Common carriers are publicly licensed to provide transportation services to the general public.

a. Strict Liability

Common carriers are absolutely liable, regardless of negligence, for all loss or damage to goods in their possession, except if it is caused by an act of God, an act of a public enemy, an order of a public authority, an act of the shipper, or the nature of the goods.

b. Limits to Liability

Common carriers can limit their liability to an amount stated on the shipment contract.

2. Warehouse Companies

Warehouse companies are liable for loss or damage to property resulting from negligence. A warehouse company can limit the dollar amount of liability, but the bailor must be given the option of paying an increased storage rate for an increase in the liability limit.

3. Innkeepers

Those who provide lodging to the public for compensation as a regular business are strictly liable for injuries to guests.

a. Hotel Safes

In many states, innkeepers can avoid strict liability for loss of guests' valuables by providing a safe. Statutes often limit the liability of innkeepers for articles that are not kept in the safe.

b. Parking Facilities

If an innkeeper provides parking facilities, and the guest's car is entrusted to the innkeeper, the innkeeper will be liable under the rules that pertain to parking lot bailments (ordinary bailments).

TRUE-FALSE QUESTIONS

___ 1. Generally, those who produce personal property have title to it.

___ 2. If goods are confused due to a wrongful act and the innocent party cannot prove what percentage is his or hers, the wrongdoer gets title to the whole.

___ 3. To constitute a gift, a voluntary transfer of property must be supported by consideration.

___ **4.** If an accession is performed in good faith, the improver keeps the property as improved, whether or not there has been any change in the value.

___ **5.** One who finds abandoned property acquires good title to the property against the whole world, except the true owner.

___ **6.** Any delivery of personal property from one person to another creates a bailment.

___ **7.** Regardless of the type of bailment, a bailee is not responsible for the loss of bailed property in his or her care.

___ **8.** A bailee has only one responsibility: to surrender the property at the end of the bailment.

___ **9.** In ordinary bailments, under some circumstances, bailees can limit their liability.

___ **10.** Warehouse companies have the same duty of care as ordinary bailees.

FILL-IN QUESTIONS

A gift made during the donor's lifetime is a gift ______________ (*causa mortis/inter vivos*). A gift ______________ (*causa mortis/inter vivos*) is made in contemplation of imminent death. Gifts ______________ (*causa mortis/inter vivos*) do not become absolute until the donor dies from the contemplated illness or disease. A gift ______________ (*causa mortis/inter vivos*) is revocable at any time up to the death of the donor and is automatically revoked if the donor recovers. A gift ______________ (*causa mortis/inter vivos*) is revocable at any time before the donor's death.

MULTIPLE-CHOICE QUESTIONS

___ **1.** Meg wants to give Lori a pair of diamond earrings that Meg has in her safe-deposit box at the First National Bank. Meg gives Lori the key to the box and tells her to go to the bank and take the earrings from the box. Lori does so. Two days later, Meg dies. Who do the earrings belong to?

a. Lori
b. Meg's heirs
c. The First National Bank
d. The state government

___ **2.** John is employed in remodeling homes bought and sold by Best Sale Realty. In one of the homes, John finds an item of jewelry and takes it to Hall Gems, Inc., to be appraised. The appraiser removes some of the jewels. Who has the best title to the jewels that were removed?

a. John
b. Hall Gems, Inc.
c. Best Sale Realty
d. John's employer

___ 3. Jane, Mark, and Guy are farmers who store their grain in three silos. Jane contributes half of the grain, Mark a third, and Guy a sixth. A tornado hits two of the silos and scatters the grain. If each farmer can prove how much he or she deposited in the silos, how much of what is left belongs to each?

a. Jane owns half, Mark a third, and Guy a sixth
b. Because only a third is left, Mark owns it all
c. Because Jane and Mark lost the most, they split what is left equally
d. Jane, Mark, and Guy share what is left equally

___ 4. Lee is the father of twins, Barb and Bob. Lee wants to give each $10,000 in stock. Lee and Barb agree that Barb's accountant can credit the stock to the twins' accounts. Lee tells the accountant, who credits the accounts. Lee dies before any stock certificates change hands. Who owns the stock?

a. Barb, but not Bob
b. Bob, but not Barb
c. Barb and Bob
d. Lee's estate

___ 5. Marcy goes to Don's Salon for a haircut. Behind a plant on a table in the waiting area, Marcy finds a wallet containing $5,000. Who is entitled to possession of the wallet?

a. Marcy because the money was lost
b. Don because the money was mislaid
c. The state under an estray statute
d. The police under the local finders' law

___ 6. Linda parks her car in Ben's parking lot. At the request of the attendant, she leaves the keys in the car. Linda is given a receipt that says, in fine print on the back, "We assume no responsibility for your vehicle." She does not read the receipt. While she is gone, her car is stolen. Ben is

a. liable for the theft.
b. not liable for the theft.
c. jointly liable with Linda for the theft.
d. liable for the theft only if Ben's attendant was the thief.

___ 7. Kay checks her coat at a restaurant. Hidden in the sleeve is her purse. By accepting the coat, the restaurant is a bailee of

a. the coat only.
b. the purse only.
c. both the coat and the purse.
d. none of the above.

___ 8. Fred leases a boat to Pam. Fred is not aware that the throttle sticks, but he could have discovered this on a reasonable inspection. Pam is injured when the throttle sticks and the boat runs aground. Fred is

a. strictly liable.
b. liable because the defect could've been discovered by reasonable inspection.
c. not liable, because his duty was to tell Pam of known defects only.
d. not liable, because Pam voluntarily leased the boat.

____ **9.** Adams Corporation ships three loads of goods via Baker Transport Company. Which, if any, of the following losses is Baker liable for?

a. The first load is lost because Adams failed to package the goods properly.
b. The second load is lost because the goods are perishable and are shipped too late to survive the transport.
c. The third load is lost in an accident that is the fault of Baker's driver.
d. None of the above

____ **10.** Bill stores goods in Carla's warehouse for a six-month term. At the end of the term, Carla refuses to return the goods. This is

a. a breach of contract.
b. accession.
c. abandonment of property.
d. none of the above.

SHORT ESSAY QUESTIONS

1. State the principal features of the four forms of concurrent property ownership: tenancies in common, joint tenancies, tenancies by the entirety, and community property.

2. What are the rights and duties of a bailee in a typical bailment situation?

ISSUE SPOTTERS

1. Property ownership can be seen as a bundle of rights. A person who holds all of the rights is an owner in fee simple. What rights are these?

2. Dave and Paul share ownership rights in a multimedia computer set-up. When they acquired the computer, they agreed in writing that if one dies, the other inherits his interest. Are Dave and Paul tenants in common or joint tenants?

3. Kane Corporation sends important documents to Trager, Inc., via Speedy Messenger Service. While the documents are in Speedy's care, Al causes an accident to Speedy's delivery vehicle that results in the loss of the documents. Does Speedy have a right to recover from Al for the loss of the documents?

4. Bob leaves his clothes with Corner Dry Cleaners to be cleaned. When the clothes are returned, some are missing and others are greasy and smell bad. Is Corner liable?

5. Cambridge Corporation ships a loads of goods via the Southern Cartage Company. The load is lost in a hurricane in Florida. Who suffers the loss?

★ **Learning Objectives**

The learning objectives in this chapter include:

1. Types of possessory ownership interests in real property.
2. Types of nonpossessory interests in real property.
3. How ownership in real property can be transferred.
4. What a leasehold estate is and how a landlord-tenant relationship is created.
5. Rights of landlords and tenants concerning the leased property.

Chapter 29: Real Property

WHAT THIS CHAPTER IS ABOUT

This chapter covers ownership rights in real property, including the nature of those rights and their transfer. The chapter also outlines the right of the government to take private land for public use, zoning laws, and other restrictions on ownership.

CHAPTER OUTLINE

I. THE NATURE OF REAL PROPERTY

Real property consists of land and the buildings, plants, and trees on it.

A. LAND

Includes the soil on the surface of the earth, natural products or artificial structures attached to it, the water on or under it, and the air space above.

B. AIR AND SUBSURFACE RIGHTS

Limitations on air rights or subsurface rights normally have to be indicated on the deed transferring title at the time of purchase.

1. Air Rights

Flights over private land do not normally violate the owners' rights.

2. Subsurface Rights

Ownership of the surface can be separated from ownership of the subsurface. In excavating, if a subsurface owner causes the land to subside, he or she may be liable to the owner of the surface.

C. PLANT LIFE AND VEGETATION

A sale of land with growing crops on it includes the crops, unless otherwise agreed. When crops are sold by themselves, they are personal property.

D. FIXTURES

Personal property so closely associated with certain real property that it is viewed as part of it (such as plumbing in a building). Fixtures are included in a sale of land if the contract does not provide otherwise.

II. OWNERSHIP OF REAL PROPERTY

A. OWNERSHIP IN FEE SIMPLE

1. Fee Simple Absolute

A fee simple owner has the most rights possible—he or she can give the property away, sell it, transfer it by will, use it for almost any purpose, and possess it to the exclusion of all the world—potentially forever.

2. Fee Simple Defeasible

Conditional ownership ("to A, as long as the property is used for a school"). If condition is not met, the land reverts to the original owner.

B. LIFE ESTATES

Lasts for the life of a specified individual ("to A for his life"). A life tenant can use the land (but not commit waste), mortgage the life estate, and create liens, easements, and leases (but no longer than the life estate).

C. FUTURE INTERESTS

Residuary interest that an owner retains to retake possession if condition of the fee simple defeasible is not met or when the life estate ends.

1. Reversions and Remainders

If the owner retains ownership of a future interest, it is a reversionary interest. If the owner transfers rights in a future interest to another, it is a remainder ("to A for life, then to B").

2. Executory Interest

An interest that does not take effect immediately on the expiration of another interest ("to A for life and one year after A's death to B").

D. NONPOSSESSORY INTERESTS

1. Easements and Profits

Easement: the right of a person to make limited use of another person's land without taking anything from the property. **Profit**: the right to go onto another's land and take away a part or product of the land.

a. Effect of a Sale of Property

The benefit of an easement or profit goes with the land. The burden goes with the land only if the new owner recognizes it, or knew or should have known of it.

b. Creation of an Easement or Profit

By deed, will, contract, implication, necessity, or prescription.

c. Termination of an Easement or Profit

Terminates when deeded back to the owner of the land that is burdened, its owner becomes the owner of the property burdened, or it is abandoned with the intent to relinquish the right to it.

2. License

The revocable right of a person to come onto another person's land.

III. TRANSFER OF OWNERSHIP

A. DEEDS

Possession and title to land can be passed by deed without consideration.

1. Requirements

(1) Names of the grantor and grantee, (2) words evidencing an intent to convey, (3) legally sufficient description of the land, (4) grantor's (and usually the spouse's) signature, and (5) delivery.

2. Warranty Deed

Provides the most protection against defects of title—covenants that grantor has title to, and power to convey, the property; that the property is not subject to any outstanding interests that diminish its value; and that the buyer will not be disturbed in his or her possession.

3. Quitclaim Deed

Warrants less than any other deed. Conveys to the grantee only whatever interest the grantor had.

4. Recording Statutes

Recording statutes require transfers to be recorded in public records (generally in the county in which the property is located) to give notice to the public that a certain person is the owner. Many states require the grantor's signature and two witnesses' signatures.

B. WILL OR INHERITANCE

Transfers by will or inheritance are outlined in Chapter 30.

C. ADVERSE POSSESSION

A person who possesses another's property acquires title good against the original owner if the possession is (1) actual and exclusive; (2) open, visible, and notorious; (3) continuous and peaceable for a required period of time; and (4) hostile, as against the whole world.

D. EMINENT DOMAIN

The government can take private property for public use. To obtain title, a condemnation proceeding is brought. The Fifth Amendment requires that just compensation be paid for a taking; thus, in a separate proceeding a court determines the land's fair value (usually market value) to pay the owner.

IV. LEASEHOLD ESTATES

Created when an owner or landlord conveys a right to possess and use property to a tenant. The tenant's interest is a leasehold estate.

A. TENANCY FOR YEARS

Created by an express contract by which property is leased for a specific period (a month, a year, a period of years). At the end of the period, the lease ends (without notice). If the tenant dies during the lease, the lease interest passes to the tenant's heirs.

B. PERIODIC TENANCY

Created by a lease that specifies only that rent is to be paid at certain intervals. Automatically renews unless terminated. Terminates, at common law, on one period's notice.

C. TENANCY AT WILL

A tenancy for as long as the landlord and tenant agree. Exists when a tenant for years retains possession after termination with the landlord's consent before payment of the next rent (when it becomes a periodic tenancy). Terminates on the death of either party or tenant's commission of waste.

D. TENANCY AT SUFFERANCE

Possession of land without right (without the owner's permission).

V. LANDLORD-TENANT RELATIONSHIPS

A. CREATING THE LANDLORD-TENANT RELATIONSHIP

1. Form of the Lease

To ensure the validity of a lease, it should be in writing and—

a. Express an intent to establish the relationship.

b. Provide for transfer of the property's possession to the tenant at the beginning of the term.

c. Provide for the landlord to retake possession at the end of the term.

d. Describe the property (include the address).

e. Indicate the length of term and the amount and due dates of rent.

2. Legal Requirements

A landlord cannot discriminate against tenants on the basis of race, color, religion, national origin, or sex. A tenant cannot promise to do something against these (or other) laws.

B. RIGHTS AND DUTIES

1. Possession

a. Landlord's Duty to Deliver Possession

A landlord must give a tenant possession of the property at the beginning of the term.

b. Tenant's Right to Retain Possession

The tenant retains possession exclusively until the lease expires.

c. Covenant of Quiet Enjoyment

The landlord promises that during the lease term no one having superior title to the property will disturb the tenant's use and enjoyment of it. If so, the tenant can sue for damages for breach.

d. Eviction

If the landlord deprives the tenant of possession of the property or interferes with his or her use or enjoyment of it, an eviction occurs. **Constructive eviction** occurs when this results from a landlord's failure to perform adequately his or her duties under the lease.

2. Use and Maintenance of the Premises

a. Tenant's Use

Generally, a tenant may make any legal use of the property, as long as it is reasonably related to the purpose for which the property is ordinarily used and does not harm the landlord's interest. A tenant is not responsible for ordinary wear and tear.

b. **Landlord's Maintenance**
A landlord must comply with local building codes.

3. **Implied Warranty of Habitability**
In most states, a landlord must furnish residential premises that are habitable. This applies to substantial defects that the landlord knows or should know about and has had a reasonable time to repair.

4. **Rent**
A tenant must pay rent even if he or she moves out or refuses to move in (if the move is unjustifiable). If the landlord violates the implied warranty of habitability, a tenant may withhold rent, pay for repair and deduct the cost, cancel the lease, or sue for damages.

C. TRANSFERRING RIGHTS TO LEASED PROPERTY

1. **Transferring the Landlord's Interest**
A landlord can sell, give away, or otherwise transfer his or her real property. If complete title is transferred, the tenant becomes the tenant of the new owner, who must also abide by the lease.

2. **Transferring the Tenant's Interest**
Before a tenant can assign or sublet his or her interest, the landlord's consent may be required (it cannot be unreasonably withheld). If the assignee or sublessee later defaults, the tenant must pay the rent.

TRUE-FALSE QUESTIONS

___ 1. A fee simple absolute is potentially infinite in duration and can be disposed of by deed or by will.

___ 2. The owner of a life estate has the same rights as a fee simple owner.

___ 3. An easement allows a person to use land and take something from it, but a profit allows a person only to use land.

___ 4. Deeds convey different interests and offer different degrees of protection against defects of title.

___ 5. Under the Fifth Amendment, private property may be taken for public use without just compensation under the government's power of eminent domain.

___ 6. A covenant of quiet enjoyment guarantees that a buyer will not be disturbed in his or her possession of land by the seller or any third person.

___ 7. Government has the power to take private property for private uses only.

___ 8. The covenant of quiet enjoyment forms the essence of the landlord-tenant relationship. If it is breached, the tenant can sue the landlord for damages.

___ 9. Generally, a tenant must pay rent even if he or she refuses to occupy the property or moves out, if the refusal or the move is unjustifiable.

___ 10. Even if a lease states the time that it will end, a landlord must give a tenant notice that the lease is going to expire as the time approaches.

FILL-IN QUESTIONS

1. An owner in fee simple absolute who conveys the estate to another in fee simple defeasible retains ______________________________ (a reversionary/an executory) interest. If the conditions of the conveyance are not met, the ______________________________ (next designated heir/original owner) takes ownership of the estate.

2. An owner in fee simple who conveys the estate to another as a life estate retains a ______________________________ (remainder/reversion). When a life estate is conveyed and the grantor has not disposed of the interest in the land remaining after the grantee's life, the grantor retains a ______________________________ (remainder/reversion) that will become possessory on the grantee's death.

3. When an owner transfers a future interest, the interest in the property held by the buyer or receiver is known as either ______________________________ (a reversionary/an executory) interest or a ______________________________ (remainder/reversion).

MULTIPLE-CHOICE QUESTIONS

____ 1. Lou owns two hundred acres next to Brook's lumber mill. Lou sells to Brook the privilege of removing timber from his land to refine into lumber. The privilege of removing the timber is

a. an easement.
b. a profit.
c. a license.
d. none of the above.

____ 2. Toni conveys her estate "to Al so long as no liquor is consumed on the premises." No liquor is consumed on the premises during Al's life, and the estate passes to Al's heir, Julie. Julie conveys the estate to Manny. Manny opens a bar on the property. The estate

a. reverts to Julie.
b. reverts to some heir of Al's besides Julie.
c. reverts to Toni or Toni's heirs.
d. none of the above.

____ 3. Evan owns an apartment building in fee simple. Evan can

a. give the building away.
b. sell the building for a price or transfer it by a will.
c. both a and b.
d. none of the above.

____ 4. Gina conveys her warehouse to Sam under a warranty deed. Later, Rosa appears, holding a better title to the warehouse than Sam's. Rosa proceeds to evict Sam. Sam can recover from Gina

a. the purchase price of the property.
b. damages from being evicted.
c. both a and b.
d. none of the above.

___ **5.** Lana owns a cabin on Long Lake. Bob takes possession of the cabin without Lana's permission and puts up a sign that reads "No Trespassing by Order of Bob, the Owner." The statutory period for adverse possession is ten years. Bob is in the cabin for eleven years. Lana sues to remove Bob. She will

a. win, because she sued Bob after the statutory period for adverse possession.
b. win, because Bob did not have permission to take possession of the cabin.
c. lose, because the no-trespassing sign misrepresented ownership of the cabin.
d. lose, because Bob acquired the cabin by adverse possession.

___ **6.** Dan owns a half acre of land that fronts on Blue Lake. Rod owns the property behind Dan's land. No road runs to Dan's land, but Rod's driveway runs between a road and Dan's property, so Dan uses Rod's driveway. The right-of-way that Dan has across Rod's property is

a. an easement.
b. a profit.
c. a license.
d. none of the above.

___ **7.** Dave owns an office building. Dave sells the building to P&I Corporation. To be valid, the deed that conveys the property from Dave to P&I must include a description of the property and

a. only Dave's name and P&I's name.
b. only words evidencing Dave's intent to convey.
c. only Dave's signature (witnessed and acknowledged).
d. words evidencing Dave's intent to convey, Dave's name, P&I's name, and Dave's signature (witnessed and acknowledged).

___ **8.** Ray operates the Family Restaurant in space that he leases in the Village Mall. The Village Mall is owned by VM Associates. VM Associates sells the mall to BB Properties. For the rest of the lease term, Ray owes rent to

a. VM Associates.
b. BB Properties.
c. the Family Restaurant.
d. none of the above.

___ **9.** Susan signs a lease for an apartment, agreeing to make rental payments before the fifth of each month. The lease does not specify a termination date. This tenancy is

a. a periodic tenancy.
b. a tenancy for years.
c. a tenancy at will.
d. a tenancy at sufferance.

___ **10.** Jim leases an apartment from Maria. With Maria's consent, Jim assigns the lease to Nell for the last two months of the term, after which Nell exercises an option under the original lease to renew for three months. One month later, Nell moves out. Regarding the rent for the rest of the term

a. no one is liable.
b. Jim can be held liable.
c. only Nell is liable.
d. Maria is liable.

SHORT ESSAY QUESTIONS

1. Describe the power of eminent domain and the process by which private property is condemned for a public purpose.

2. What does the implied warranty of habitability require, and when does it apply?

ISSUE SPOTTERS

1. Rob owns a commercial building in fee simple. Rob transfers temporary possession of the building to the Alliance Corporation. Can Alliance transfer possession for even less time to the Web Company?

2. Roxane leases office space in Alvin's building for a one-year term. If Roxane dies during the period of the lease, what happens to the leased property?

3. Charles sells his house to Diane under a warranty deed. Later, Carol appears, holding a better title to the house than Diane. Carol wants Diane off the property. What can Diane do?

4. John leases a store in Dean's shopping mall. Dean sells the mall to Travis Properties, Inc. Does John owe rent for the remainder of the lease term to Dean, or is John now Travis's tenant? If Travis collects rent from John, is Travis bound by the terms of the original lease?

5. Tyler owns an orchard behind Ruth's house and property. The only access to the orchard is Ruth's driveway, which Tyler uses to get to his land. Tyler sells the orchard to Sheila. Can Sheila now use the right-of-way across Ruth's property?

QUICKEN CD-ROM BUSINESS LAW PARTNER APPLICATIONS

Open **Quicken Business Law Partner**. Click on the *New Documents* icon. Select the *Real Estate Lease—Commercial, Rental Application,* and *Renter's Inspection Worksheet*. Respond to the *Interview* questions with actual facts or hypothetical ones. For example, imagine that Adams owns a warehouse and an apartment building. Eagle Equipment, Inc., wants to lease the warehouse. Paul wants to rent an apartment. As you complete the *Interview*, answer the following questions.

___ **1.** Adams (the landlord) would use the *Rental Application* to document

a. criteria for accepting Eagle, Paul, or anyone else as a tenant.
b. reasons for rejecting Eagle, Paul, or anyone else as a tenant.
c. information for future use in collecting damages, if necessary.
d. all of the above.

___ **2.** Adams (the landlord) could use the *Rental Application* to ask a prospective tenant's

a. source of income.
b. bank references.
c. both a and b.
d. none of the above.

___ **3.** Adams (the landlord) would use the *Renter's Inspection Worksheet* to document the condition of rental property

a. before a tenant's occupancy of rental premises.
b. after a tenant's occupancy of rental premises.
c. at the end of a lease.
d. all of the above.

___ **4.** Adams (the landlord) would use the Holdover clause in the *Real Estate Lease—Commercial* to provide that if Eagle (the tenant) does not vacate the warehouse at the end of the lease term, the holdover constitutes

a. automatic renewal of the lease.
b. a month-to-month tenancy.
c. a tenancy by the entirety.
d. a joint tenancy.

___ **5.** According to the *Real Estate Lease—Commercial* form, the party responsible for obtaining insurance on the premises is

a. Adams only.
b. Eagle only.
c. Adams, Eagle, or both.
d. none of the above.

QUICKEN BUSINESS LAW PARTNER ENHANCEMENT: EXPLORING THE PERSONAL LAW HANDBOOK

Personal Law Handbook, within Topic 1, Renting a Home, gives you a useful review of important residential landlord-tenant issues.

 **Learning Objectives**

The learning objectives in this chapter include:

1. When an insurable interest arises in regard to life and property insurance.
2. The difference between an insurance broker and an insurance agent.
3. Clauses that are typically included in insurance contracts.
4. The requirements of a valid will.
5. How property is transferred when a person dies without a valid will.

Chapter 30: Insurance, Wills, and Trusts

WHAT THIS CHAPTER IS ABOUT

Insurance is a contract in which an insurance company promises to pay the insured or a beneficiary if the insured is injured or the insured's property is damaged as a result of a specified contingency. This chapter covers law relating to insurance. This chapter also covers some of the law governing wills and trusts.

CHAPTER OUTLINE

I. INSURANCE

A. RISK MANAGEMENT

Risk management consists of plans to protect personal and financial interests should some event undermine their security. The most common method is to transfer risk from a business or individual to an insurance company.

B. CLASSIFICATIONS OF INSURANCE

Insurance is classified according to the nature of the risk involved.

C. INSURANCE TERMINOLOGY

An insurance company is an **underwriter** or an **insurer**; the party covered by insurance is the **insured**; an insurance contract is a **policy**; consideration paid to an insurer is a **premium**; policies are obtained through an **agent** or **broker**.

D. INSURABLE INTEREST

To obtain insurance, one must have a sufficient interest in what is insured.

1. **Property Insurance**
One has an insurable interest in property if one would suffer a pecuniary loss from its destruction. This interest must exist *when the loss occurs.*

2. **Life Insurance**
One must have a reasonable expectation of benefit from the continued life of another. The benefit may be related to money or may be founded on a relationship (by blood or affinity).

   a. **Key-Person Insurance**
   A business (partnership, corporation) can insure the life of an employee who is important to that organization (partner, officer).

   b. **When the Insurable Interest Must Exist**
   An interest in someone's life must exist *when the policy is obtained.*

E. THE INSURANCE CONTRACT

1. **Application**
The application is part of the contract. Misstatements can void a policy, especially if the insurer shows that it would not have issued the policy if it had known the facts.

2. **Effective Date**
A policy is effective when (1) a binder is written, (2) the policy is issued, or (3) a certain time elapses.

   a. **When a Policy Is Obtained from a Broker**
   A broker is the agent of the applicant. Until the broker obtains a policy, the applicant is normally not insured.

   b. **When a Policy Is Obtained from an Agent**
   An agent is the agent of the insurer. One who obtains a policy from an agent can be protected from the moment the application is made (under a binder), or the parties may agree to delay coverage until a policy is issued or some condition is met (such as a physical exam).

3. **Provisions and Clauses**
Some important clauses include—

   a. **Incontestability Clause**
   After a policy has been in force for a certain time (two or three years), the insurer cannot cancel the policy or avoid a claim on the basis of statements made in the application.

   b. **Coinsurance Clause**
   If an owner insures property up to a specified percentage (usually 80 percent) of its value, he or she will recover any loss up to the face amount of the policy. If the insurance is for less than this percentage, the owner is responsible for a proportionate share.

4. **Cancellation**
A policy may be canceled for nonpayment of premiums, fraud or misrepresentation, conviction for a crime that increases the hazard insured against, or gross negligence that increases the hazard insured against. An insurer may be required to give advance written notice.

5. **Defenses against Payment**
Fraud, misrepresentation, violation of warranties, and improper actions that are against public policy or that are otherwise illegal.

II. WILLS

A **will** is a declaration of how a person wants property disposed of after death; it is a formal instrument that must follow certain requirements to be effective.

A. TERMINOLOGY OF WILLS

A **testator** is a person who makes a will; a **probate court** oversees the administration of a will by an **executor** (appointed by the testator in the will) or by an **administrator** (appointed by the court).

B. TYPES OF GIFTS

A gift of real estate by will is a **devise**; the recipient is a **devisee**. A gift of personal property is a **bequest** or **legacy**; a recipient is a **legatee**. Gifts can be specific, general, or residuary. If there are not enough assets to pay all general bequests, an **abatement** reduces the gifts.

C. PROBATE PROCEDURES

Probate: establish the validity of a will and administer the estate. Statutes providing for the distribution of estates vary from state to state. The Uniform Probate Code (UPC) includes rules and procedures for resolving conflicts in settling estates and relaxes some of the will requirements.

1. **Informal Probate**
In some states, cars, bank accounts, etc., can pass by filling out forms, or property can be transferred by affidavit. Most states allow heirs to distribute assets themselves after a will is admitted to probate.

2. **Formal Probate**
For large estates, a probate court supervises distribution.

3. **Property Transfers outside the Probate Process**
Will substitutes include *inter vivos* trusts (see below), life insurance policies with named beneficiaries, and joint tenancies.

D. REQUIREMENTS FOR A VALID WILL

1. **Testamentary Capacity**
When a will is made, the testator must be of legal age (in most states, at least eighteen years old) and sound mind (intend the document to be a will, comprehend the property being distributed, and remember family members and others for whom a person normally has affection).

2. **Writing Requirements**
Generally, a will must be in writing. In a few states, an oral (**nuncupative**) will is valid to pass personal property below a certain value if made in the expectation of imminent death.

3. **Signature Requirements**
The testator must sign with the intent to validate the will; the signature need not be at the end.

4. **Witness Requirements**
The number of witnesses (two or three) and other rules vary from state to state. A witness does not have to read the will.

5. **Publication Requirements**
In a few states, the testator must declare orally to the witnesses that the document they are about to sign is his or her will.

E. UNDUE INFLUENCE
If the testator's plan of distribution was the result of improper pressure by another person, the will is invalid.

F. REVOCATION OF WILLS
A will is revocable, in whole or in part, by its maker any time during the maker's lifetime by physical act (intentionally obliterating or destroying a will, or directing someone else to do so); by a document (a codicil, a new will); or by operation of law (marriage, divorce, annulment, birth of child).

G. INTESTACY LAWS
State statutes regulate how property is distributed when a person dies without a valid will.

1. **Surviving Spouse and Children**
First, the debts of the decedent are paid out of the estate, and then other assets pass to the surviving spouse and children.

a. **Legitimate Heirs**
The spouse receives a share; the children receive the rest (stepchildren are not kin). If no children or grandchildren survive, the spouse receives all of it.

b. **Illegitimate Children**
In some states, intestate succession between a father and an illegitimate child can occur only if the child is legitimized by ceremony or was acknowledged by the father.

2. **Other Heirs**

a. **Lineal Descendants**
If there is no surviving spouse or child, then grandchildren, brothers and sisters, and (in some states) parents share in the property of the estate.

b. **Collateral Heirs**
If there are no lineal descendants, then nieces, nephews, aunts, and uncles share. If none survive, property goes to the next of kin of collateral heirs (relatives by marriage are not considered kin).

3. **Methods of Distribution**
Per stirpes: a class or group of distributees take the share that their deceased parent would have been entitled to if that parent lived. ***Per capita***: each person takes an equal share of the estate.

III. TRUSTS
Arrangements by which a grantor (settlor) transfers legal title to the trust property to a trustee, who administers the property as directed by the grantor for the benefit of the beneficiaries.

A. ESSENTIAL ELEMENTS OF A TRUST

1. A designated beneficiary.
2. A designated trustee.
3. A fund sufficiently identified to enable title to pass to the trustee.
4. Actual delivery to the trustee with the intention of passing title.

B. EXPRESS TRUSTS

1. ***Inter Vivos* Trust**
Created by trust deed to exist during the settlor's lifetime.

2. **Testamentary Trust**
Created by will to come into existence on the settlor's death (if the will is invalid, the trust is invalid). If not named in the will, a trustee is appointed by a court. Trustee's actions are subject to judicial approval.

C. IMPLIED TRUSTS

1. **Resulting Trust**
Arises when the conduct of the parties raise an inference that the party holding legal title to the property does so for the benefit of another.

2. **Constructive Trust**
An equitable remedy that enables plaintiffs to recover property from defendants who would otherwise be unjustly enriched. A court declares the legal owner of the property to be a trustee for those entitled to the benefit of the property.

D. SPECIAL TYPES OF TRUSTS

1. **Charitable Trust**
Designed to benefit a segment of the public or the public in general, usually for charitable, educational, religious, or scientific purposes.

2. **Spendthrift Trust**
Prevents a beneficiary's transfer of his or her right to future payments of income or capital by placing restraints on the transfer of funds.

3. **Totten Trust**
Created when one person deposits money in his or her own name as trustee. Revocable at will until the depositor dies or completes the gift.

TRUE-FALSE QUESTIONS

___ 1. Risk management involves the transfer of certain risks from an individual or a business to an insurance company.

___ 2. Insurance is classified by the nature of the person or interest protected.

___ 3. An insurance broker is an agent of an insurance company.

___ 4. An insurance applicant is usually protected from the time an application is made, if a premium has been paid, possibly subject to certain conditions.

___ 5. A person can insure anything in which he or she has an insurable interest.

___ 6. A will is revocable only after the testator's death.

___ 7. The testator generally must sign a will.

___ 8. If a person dies without a will, all of his or her property automatically passes to the state in which that person lived most of his or her life.

___ 9. An *inter vivos* trust is a trust created by a grantor during his or her lifetime.

___ 10. A testamentary trust is created by will to begin on the settlor's death.

FILL-IN QUESTIONS

When a person dies, a personal representative settles the decedent's affairs. A personal representative named in a will is an ________________ (administrator/executor). A personal representative appointed by a court for a decedent who dies without a will, who fails to name a personal representative in a will, who names a personal representative lacking the capacity to serve, or who writes a will that the court refuses to admit to probate is an ________________ (administrator/executor).

MULTIPLE-CHOICE QUESTIONS

___ 1. Satellite Communications, Inc., takes out an insurance policy on its plant. For which of the following reasons could the insurer cancel the policy?

a. Satellite's president appears as a witness in a case against the company.
b. Satellite begins using grossly careless manufacturing practices.
c. Two of Satellite's drivers have their driver's licenses suspended.
d. All of the above

___ 2. Sue applies for an A&I Insurance Company fire insurance policy for her warehouse. To obtain a lower premium, she misrepresents the age of the property. The policy is granted. After the warehouse is destroyed by fire, A&I learns the true facts. A&I can

a. refuse to pay on the ground of fraud in the application.
b. refuse to pay on the ground that the warehouse has been destroyed by fire.
c. not refuse to pay, because an application is not part of an insurance contract.
d. not refuse to pay, because the warehouse has been destroyed by fire.

___ 3. Jim is an executive with E-Tech Corporation. Because his death would cause a financial loss to E-Tech, the firm insures his life. Later, Jim resigns to work for MayCom, Inc., one of E-Tech's competitors. Six months later, Jim dies. Regarding payment for the loss, E-Tech can

a. collect, because its insurable interest existed when the policy was obtained.
b. not collect, because its insurable interest did not exist when a loss occurred.
c. not collect, because it suffered no financial loss from the death of Jim, who resigned to work for one of its competitors.
d. none of the above.

___ **4.** Tom takes out a mortgage with the First National Bank to buy a house. Tom obtains a fire insurance policy, partially payable to the bank. After Tom makes the last mortgage payment, the house is destroyed by fire. Regarding payment for the loss, the bank can

a. collect, because its insurable interest existed when the policy was obtained.
b. collect, because its mortgage required Tom to take out the policy.
c. not collect, because its insurable interest did not exist when a loss occurred.
d. not collect, because its mortgage required Tom to take out the policy.

___ **5.** Technon Corporation manufactures computers. To insure its products to cover injuries to consumers if the products prove defective, Technon should buy

a. group insurance.
b. liability insurance.
c. major medical insurance.
d. term life insurance.

___ **6.** Joe's will provides for specific items of property to be given to certain individuals, including employees of Joe's business. The will also provides for certain sums of money to be given to Joe's daughters, Gail and Laura. Because Joe's assets are insufficient to pay in full all of the bequests

a. all of the property must be sold and the proceeds distributed to the heirs.
b. the employees, who are not in a blood relationship with Joe, get nothing.
c. Gail and Laura get nothing.
d. the gifts to Gail and Laura will be reduced proportionately.

___ **7.** Donna dies without a will, but with many relatives—a spouse, children, adopted children, sisters, brothers, uncles, aunts, cousins, nephews, and nieces. Who gets what is determined by the state's

a. intestacy law.
b. statute of frauds.
c. trustee, who is appointed by Donna's executor.
d. personal representative, who is appointed by a probate court.

___ **8.** Paul executes a will that leaves all his property to Dave. Two years later, Paul executes a will that leaves all his property to Nora. The second will does not expressly revoke the first will. Paul dies. Who gets his property?

a. Dave, because he was given the property in the first will
b. Dave, because the second will did not expressly revoke the first will
c. Nora, because the first will was revoked by the second will
d. Nora, because two years separated the execution of the wills

___ **9.** Tony dies intestate, survived by Lisa, his mother; Grace, his wife; Abby and Selena, their two daughters; and Brock, the son of Cliff, their son, who predeceased his father. Under intestacy laws,

a. Grace receives one-third of Tony's estate, and Abby, Selena, and Brock receive equal portions of the rest.
b. Abby and Selena receive half of Tony's estate, and Grace receives the rest.
c. Lisa and Grace receive equal portions of Tony's estate.
d. Grace receives all of Tony's estate.

___ **10.** Kate wants Bev and Nina, her daughters, to get the benefit of Kate's farm when she dies. She believes that her daughters cannot manage the farm effectively, because they live in other states. She can provide for them to get the farm's income, under another party's management, by setting up

a. a constructive trust.
b. a resulting trust.
c. a testamentary trust.
d. an interstate trust.

SHORT ESSAY QUESTIONS

1. Define the concept of insurable interest and state its effect on insurance payments.

2. List the ways in which a will may be revoked.

ISSUE SPOTTERS

1. Why is an insurance premium small relative to the amount of coverage that an insurance company offers?

2. Sheila makes out a will, leaving her property in equal thirds to Mark and Ellen, her children, and Carla, her niece. Two years later, Sheila is adjudged mentally incompetent, and that same year, she dies. Can Mark and Ellen have Sheila's will revoked, on grounds that she did not have the capacity to make a will?

3. Neal applies to Farm Insurance Company for a life insurance policy. On the application, Neal understates his age. Neal obtains the policy, but for a lower premium than he would have had to pay had he disclosed his actual age. The policy includes an incontestability clause. Six years later, Neal dies. Can the insurer refuse payment?

4. Al is divorced and owns a house. Al has no reasonable expectation of benefit from the life of Bea, his ex-spouse, but applies for insurance on her life anyway. Al obtains a fire insurance policy on the house, then sells the house. Ten years later, Bea dies and the house is destroyed by fire. Can Al obtain payment for these events?

5. Lee's will provides for a distribution of Lee's property. First, the assets need to be collected and inventoried, however. They may also need to be appraised. Creditors' claims must be sorted out. Federal and state income taxes must be paid. Finally, the assets must be distributed. Who does these things?

Learning Objectives

The learning objectives in this chapter include:

1. Areas in which professionals may be liable at common law.
2. Liability that may be imposed on accountants under the securities laws.
3. Accountants' potential criminal liability.
4. Professionals' privileges concerning working papers.
5. The protection of professionals and their clients for their communications.

Chapter 31: Professional Liability

WHAT THIS CHAPTER IS ABOUT

This chapter outlines the potential common law liability of professionals, the potential liability of accountants under securities laws and the Internal Revenue Code, and the duty of professionals to keep their clients' communications confidential.

CHAPTER OUTLINE

I. COMMON LAW LIABILITY TO CLIENTS

A. LIABILITY FOR BREACH OF CONTRACT

For a professional's breach of contract, a client can recover damages, including expenses incurred to secure another professional to provide the services and other reasonable and foreseeable losses.

B. LIABILITY FOR NEGLIGENCE

Professionals must exercise the standard of care, knowledge, and judgment generally accepted by members of their professional group.

1. **Principles and Standards for Accountants**
   Accountants must comply with generally accepted accounting principles (GAAP) and generally accepted auditing standards (GAAS) (though compliance does not guarantee relief from liability). Violation of either is *prima facie* evidence of negligence. Note: There may be a higher state law standard.

2. **Duty to Act in Good Faith**
   If an accountant conforms to GAAP and acts in good faith, he or she will not be liable to a client for incorrect judgment.

3. **Suspicious Financial Transactions**
An accountant who uncovers suspicious financial transactions and fails to investigate the matter fully or to inform his or her client of the discovery can be held liable to the client for the resulting loss.

4. **Defenses to Negligence**

a. The accountant was not negligent.

b. If the accountant was negligent, the negligence was not the proximate cause of the client's loss.

c. The client was also negligent.

5. **Accountants' Qualified Opinions and Disclaimers**
An accountant is not liable for damages resulting from whatever is qualified or disclaimed.

C. LIABILITY FOR FRAUD

1. **Actual Fraud**
A professional may be liable if he or she intentionally misstates a material fact to mislead his or her client and the client justifiably relies on the misstated fact to his or her injury.

2. **Constructive Fraud**
A professional may be liable for constructive fraud whether or not he or she acted with fraudulent intent (for example, an accountant who is grossly negligent; gross negligence includes the intentional failure to perform a duty in reckless disregard of the consequences).

II. AUDITORS' LIABILITY TO THIRD PARTIES

Most courts hold that auditors can be held liable to third parties for negligence.

A. THE *ULTRAMARES* RULE

1. **The Privity Requirement**
An accountant does not owe a duty to a third person with whom he or she has no direct contractual relationship (privity) or no relationship "so close as to approach that of privity."

2. **The "Near Privity" Rule**
In a few states, if a third party has a sufficiently close relationship or nexus with an accountant, the *Ultramares* privity requirement may be satisfied without establishing an accountant-client relationship.

B. THE *RESTATEMENT* RULE

Most courts hold accountants liable for negligence to persons whom the accountant "intends to supply the information or knows that the recipient intends to supply it" and persons whom the accountant "intends the information to influence or knows that the recipient so intends" [*Restatement (Second) of Torts*, Section 552].

C. LIABILITY TO REASONABLY FORESEEABLE USERS

A few courts hold accountants liable to any users whose reliance on an accountant's statements or reports was reasonably foreseeable.

III. LIABILITY OF ACCOUNTANTS UNDER SECURITIES LAWS

A. LIABILITY UNDER THE SECURITIES ACT OF 1933

1. Misstatements or Omissions in Registration Statements

An accountant may be liable for misstatements and omissions of material facts in registration statements (which they often prepare for filing with the Securities and Exchange Commission (SEC) before an offering of securities—see Chapter 27) [Section 11].

a. To Whom an Accountant May Be Liable

Anyone who acquires a security covered by the statement. A plaintiff must show that he or she suffered a loss on the security. There is no requirement of privity or proof of reliance.

b. Due Diligence Defense

An accountant may avoid liability by showing that, in preparing the financial statements, he or she had—

1) Reasonable Grounds to Believe That the Statements Were True
After a reasonable investigation, the accountant believed that the statements were true and omitted no material facts.

2) Followed GAAP and GAAS
Failure to follow GAAP and GAAS is proof of a lack of due diligence.

3) Verified Information Furnished by Officers and Directors
This defense requires that accountants verify information furnished by the offering firm's officers and directors.

c. Other Defenses to Liability

1) There were no misstatements or omissions.

2) The misstatements or omissions were not of material facts.

3) The misstatements or omissions had no causal connection to the purchaser's loss.

4) The purchaser invested in the securities knowing of the misstatements or omissions.

2. Misstatements or Omissions in Other Communications in an Offer

Anyone offering or selling a security may be liable for fraud for communicating to an investor a misstatement or omission [Section 12(2)].

3. Penalties and Sanctions for Violations

The U.S. Department of Justice brings criminal actions against willful violators. Penalties: fines up to $10,000; imprisonment up to five years. The SEC can seek an injunction and other relief (such as an order to refund profits).

B. LIABILITY UNDER THE SECURITIES EXCHANGE ACT OF 1934

1. False or Misleading Statements in Certain SEC Documents

An accountant may be liable for making or causing to be made in an application, report, document, or registration statement filed with the SEC a statement that at the time and in light of the circumstances was false or misleading with respect to any material fact [Section 18].

a. **To Whom an Accountant May Be Liable**
Only sellers and purchasers who can prove (1) the statement affected the price of the security and (2) they relied on the statement and were unaware of its inaccuracy.

b. **Defenses**

1) **Proof of Good Faith**
Proof that the accountant did not know the statement was false or misleading. This can be refuted by showing the accountant's (1) intent to deceive or (2) reckless conduct and gross negligence.

2) **Buyer or Seller Knew the Statement Was False or Misleading**

3) **Statute of Limitations Tolled**
An action must be brought within one year after the discovery of facts constituting the cause and within three years after the cause accrues.

2. **Misstatements or Omissions under Section 10(b) and Rule 10b-5**
Covers written and oral statements.

a. **Section 10(b)**
Makes it unlawful for any person to use, in connection with the purchase or sale of any security, any manipulative or deceptive device or contrivance in contravention of SEC rules and regulations.

b. **Rule 10b-5**
Makes it unlawful for any person, by use of any means or instrumentality of interstate commerce, to—

1) Employ any device, scheme, or artifice to defraud.

2) Make any untrue statement of a material fact or to omit to state a material fact necessary to make the statements made, in light of the circumstances, not misleading.

3) Engage in any act, practice, or course of business that operates or would operate as a fraud or deceit on any person, in connection with the purchase or sale of any security.

c. **To Whom An Accountant May Be Liable**
Only to sellers or purchasers. Privity is not required. To recover, a plaintiff must prove (1) *scienter*, (2) a fraudulent action or deception, (3) reliance, (4) materiality, and (5) causation.

C. THE PRIVATE SECURITIES LITIGATION REFORM ACT OF 1995

An auditor must use adequate procedures in an audit to detect any illegal acts. If something is detected, the auditor must disclose it to the board, audit committee, or SEC, depending on the circumstances. A party is liable only for the proportion of damages for which he or she is responsible.

IV. POTENTIAL CRIMINAL LIABILITY OF ACCOUNTANTS

A. THE SECURITIES ACTS

An accountant may be subject to imprisonment of up to five years and a fine of up to $10,000 under the 1933 act and up to $100,000 under the 1934 act.

B. THE INTERNAL REVENUE CODE

1. **Aiding or Assisting in the Preparation of a False Tax Return**
A felony punishable by a fine of $100,000 ($500,000 in the case of a corporation) and imprisonment for up to three years [Section 7206(2)].

2. **Understatement of a Client's Tax Liability**
Liability is limited to one penalty per taxpayer per tax year.

a. **Negligent or Willful Understatement**
A tax preparer is subject to a penalty of $250 per return for negligent understatement and $1,000 for willful understatement or reckless or intentional disregard of rules or regulations [Section 6694].

b. **Aiding and Abetting an Individual's Understatement**
$1,000 per document ($10,000 in corporate cases) [Section 6701].

3. **Other Liability Related to Tax Returns**
A tax preparer may be subject to penalties for failing to furnish the taxpayer with a copy of the return, failing to sign the return, or failing to furnish the appropriate tax identification numbers [Section 6695].

C. STATE LAW
Most states impose criminal penalties for knowingly certifying false or fraudulent reports; falsifying, altering, or destroying books of account; and obtaining property or credit through the use of false financial statements.

V. WORKING PAPERS

In a number of states, working papers are the accountant's property. The client has a right of access to them, and they cannot be transferred to another accountant or otherwise disclosed without the client's permission (or a court order). Unauthorized disclosure is a ground for a malpractice suit.

VI. CONFIDENTIALITY AND PRIVILEGE

The confidentiality of attorney-client communications is protected by law. The client holds the privilege, and only the client may waive it. In response to an order by a federal court and by most state courts, an accountant must provide the information sought; there is no privilege.

VII. LIMITING PROFESSIONALS' LIABILITY

Professionals may limit their liability for misconduct of other professionals with whom they work by organizing as a professional corporation or a limited liability partnership (see Chapter 23).

TRUE-FALSE QUESTIONS

___ 1. Professionals must exercise the standard of care, knowledge, and judgment generally observed by their peers.

___ 2. A violation of GAAP and GAAS is *prima facie* evidence of negligence.

___ 3. Compliance with GAAP and GAAS will relieve an accountant of liability.

___ 4. In all states, an accountant is liable to anyone who relies on the accountant's negligently prepared reports.

___ 5. Accountants are not subject to criminal penalties under the Securities Act of 1933 or the Securities Exchange Act of 1934.

___ 6. A tax preparer may be subject to penalties under the Internal Revenue Code for assisting in filing a false tax return.

___ 7. There is no penalty under the Internal Revenue Code for failing to give the taxpayer a copy of the return.

___ 8. State-provided rights to confidentiality of accountant-client communications are not recognized in federal cases.

___ 9. Under the Private Securities Litigation Reform Act of 1995, a party is liable only for the proportion of damages for which he or she is responsible.

___ 10. For an accountant to be liable to a seller or purchaser for misstatements or omissions under SEC Rule 10b-5, there must be privity.

FILL-IN QUESTIONS

Accountants must comply with generally accepted accounting principles (GAAP) and generally accepted auditing standards (GAAS). An accountant who conforms to GAAP and acts in good faith ___________ (may/will not) be liable to a client for incorrect judgment. An accountant who uncovers suspicious financial transactions but fails to investigate fully or to inform the client ___________ (may/will not) be liable. If a client suffers a loss due to fraud that an accountant negligently fails to discover, the accountant ___________ (may/will not) be liable.

MULTIPLE-CHOICE QUESTIONS

___ 1. Betty, an accountant, accumulates working papers in performing an audit for her client, Multimedia Corporation. Under which of the following circumstances is Betty entitled to release those papers?

a. Only with Multimedia's permission
b. Only on the request of another accountant
c. Under any circumstances
d. Under no circumstances

___ 2. Turbo, Inc., asks Ed, an accountant, to prepare financial statements for its "internal, corporate use only." Despite what Turbo tells Ed, the firm uses the statements to obtain a loan from the First National Bank. The loan is not repaid. The bank sues Ed for negligence. In most states, the bank would

a. win, because Ed should have known the bank would rely on the statements.
b. win, because Ed has committed malpractice.
c. lose, because Ed was not in privity with the bank.
d. lose, because Ed was unaware the bank would rely on the statements.

___ 3. In most states, under which of the following circumstances can an accountant be compelled to disclose a client's communication?

a. Only with the client's permission
b. Only on a court order
c. Under any circumstances
d. Under no circumstances

___ **4.** Jay, an accountant, audits financial statements for Tarkon Corporation and issues an unqualified opinion on them. Delia buys 100 shares of Tarkon stock and later suffers losses due to misrepresentations in the statements. Delia sues Jay under the Securities Exchange Act of 1934. Delia will

a. win, if the misstatements were material.
b. win, if Jay prepared the statements with knowledge of the misstatements.
c. lose, if Jay and Delia were not in privity.
d. lose, because Delia relied on the statements.

___ **5.** In auditing Artic, Inc.'s books, Mary is assisted by Ann, an Artic employee. Mary does not discover Ann's theft of Artic funds because Ann hides records that would reveal it. When Ann absconds with the funds, Artic sues Mary. Artic will

a. win, because Mary did not discover the theft.
b. win, because Mary did not inform Artic of the theft.
c. lose, because Mary could not reasonably have been expected to discover the theft.
d. lose, because Mary is not liable for the results once she has performed.

___ **6.** Alman, Inc., includes financial statements prepared by Sam, an accountant, in a registration statement filed with the SEC as part of a public stock offer. Bob buys 100 shares and later suffers losses due to misstatements of fact in the statements prepared by Sam. Bob sues Sam under the Securities Act of 1933. Bob will

a. win, if the misstatements were material.
b. win, if Sam prepared the statements with knowledge of the misstatements.
c. lose, if Sam and Bob were not in privity.
d. lose, because Bob relied on the statements.

___ **7.** Don, an accountant, breaches his contract with Harrigan's, a local restaurant chain. Any damages that Harrigan's may recover include

a. the cost to secure the contracted-for services elsewhere.
b. penalties imposed for failing to meet deadlines.
c. both a and b.
d. none of the above.

___ **8.** Polly is injured in an automobile accident, but the insurance company refuses to pay her claim. She hires Doug, an attorney, to handle her case. Doug fails to file Polly's suit against the insurance company before the time for filing the suit runs out. Polly sues Doug. She will

a. win, because the insurance company refused to pay her claim.
b. win, because Doug committed malpractice.
c. lose, because Doug could not reasonably have been expected to file on time.
d. lose, because clients are ultimately responsible for such deadlines.

___ **9.** To avoid fraudulent financial reporting, a company could do all of the following EXCEPT

a. review all financial statements carefully before they are issued to the public.
b. employ outsiders to help recognize potentially fraudulent reporting.
c. overstate earnings to cover any potentially fraudulent financial reports.
d. review internal controls that are intended to thwart fraud.

___ **10.** Jane is an accountant whom Gail, a former client, charges with negligence. Jane's defenses include

a. that she was not negligent.
b. that if she was negligent, this was not the proximate cause of Gail's losses.
c. both a and b.
d. none of the above.

SHORT ESSAY QUESTIONS

1. Contrast an accountant's past and present potential common law liability to third persons.

2. Under a court order, what information must an accountant disclose about a client?

ISSUE SPOTTERS

1. What is a professional liable for, at common law, if he or she *un*intentionally misstates a material fact that misleads a client?

2. Rita, an accountant, prepares a financial statement for Toby & Company, a client, knowing that Toby will use the statement to obtain a loan from the First National Bank. If Rita makes negligent omissions in the statement that results in a loss to the bank, could the bank successfully sue Rita?

3. Ron, an accountant, prepares a financial statement as part of a registration statement that MMF, Inc., files with the Securities and Exchange Commission before making a public offering of securities. In the statement is a misstatement of material fact not attributable to Ron's fraud or negligence. Gina relies on the misstatement, buys some of the securities, and suffers a loss. Can Ron be held liable to Gina?

4. Can an accountant who prepares a tax return for a client be held liable for any false statements in the return? Can a person who is not an accountant and who prepares a tax return for someone else be held liable for any false statements in the return?

5. Professionals are restrained by the ethical tenets of their professions from disclosing communications with their clients. In some instances, professional-client communications are privileged under state and federal law. What professional is most restricted from disclosing a client's communication?

QUICKEN CD-ROM
BUSINESS LAW PARTNER APPLICATIONS

Open **Quicken Business Law Partner**. Click on the *New Documents* icon. Select the *Consulting Agreement*. Respond to the *Interview* questions with actual facts or hypothetical ones. For example, imagine that Kay is an accountant whom Escorp, Inc., a software firm, wants to hire as a consultant. As you complete the *Interview*, answer the following questions.

___ **1.** This form includes

a. a covenant not to compete.
b. a clause regarding confidentiality.
c. both a and b.
d. none of the above.

___ **2.** According to the Payment clause in this form, Kay (the consultant) must be paid

a. once.
b. monthly.
c. weekly.
d. none of the above.

___ **3.** According to the Disclosure clause in this form, if Kay has any conflict of interest regarding Escorp (the client) and another client, Kay

a. must disclose the conflict to Escorp.
b. may disclose the conflict to Escorp but is not required to do so.
c. must not disclose the conflict to Escorp.
d. must not disclose the conflict to Escorp or to the other client.

___ **4.** According to this form, Escorp must provide Kay with

a. office space.
b. office supplies.
c. staff and secretarial services.
d. none of the above.

___ **5.** In this form, the parties can specify who will determine the manner in which Kay performs and the hours she works. If Escorp takes control of Kay's methods and hours, she would most likely be considered Escorp's

a. agent.
b. employee.
c. independent contractor.
d. none of the above.

Notes

Notes

Notes

Notes

Notes

Notes

Notes

Notes

Notes

Notes

Notes

Notes

Notes

Notes

Notes

Notes

Notes

Notes

Notes

Notes